Supply Chain Management
Beiträge zu Beschaffung und Logistik

Herausgegeben von
M. Eßig, München, Deutschland
W. Stölzle, St. Gallen, Schweiz

Industrielle Wertschöpfung wird immer komplexer. Der steigende Wettbewerbsdruck zwingt zu differenzierten Angeboten, gleichzeitig nimmt der Kostendruck zu. Unternehmen können diesen gestiegenen Anforderungen nur gerecht werden, wenn sie neben der Optimierung eigener Produktion besonderen Wert auf die Gestaltung effektiver und effizienter Netzwerke legen. Supply Chain Management befasst sich mit unternehmensübergreifenden Wertschöpfungsaktivitäten von der Rohstoffgewinnung bis zur Endkundendistribution. Die Schriftenreihe sieht sich dabei besonders den lange vernachlässigten betriebswirtschaftlichen Teildisziplinen Beschaffung und Logistik verpflichtet, die als Treiber des Supply Chain Management gelten.

Herausgegeben von

Prof. Dr. Michael Eßig
Universität der Bundeswehr München

Prof. Dr. Wolfgang Stölzle
Universität St. Gallen

Konstantin Gebert

Performance Control in Buyer-Supplier Relationships

The Design and Use of Formal Management Control Systems

Springer Gabler

Konstantin Gebert
Lst. f. Logistikmgt.
Universität St. Gallen
St. Gallen, Switzerland

Dissertation Universität St.Gallen, 2012

ISBN 978-3-658-01892-4 ISBN 978-3-658-01893-1 (eBook)
DOI 10.1007/978-3-658-01893-1

The Deutsche Nationalbibliothek lists this publication in the Deutsche Nationalbibliografie; detailed bibliographic data are available in the Internet at http://dnb.d-nb.de.

Library of Congress Control Number: 2013943123

Springer Gabler

Printed on acid-free paper

Springer Gabler is a brand of Springer DE.
Springer DE is part of Springer Science+Business Media.
www.springer-gabler.de

Geleitwort

Der wirtschaftliche Erfolg eines Industrieunternehmens wird heutzutage oftmals zu grossen Teilen von der Leistungsfähigkeit der beteiligten Supply Chain-Partner beeinflusst. Diese Abhängigkeit macht eine unternehmensübergreifende Betrachtung von Geschäftsbeziehungen unabdingbar und verlangt nach einem Wandel vom traditionellen, isolierten Kunden- bzw. Lieferantenmanagement hin zu einer gemeinsam koordinierten Steuerung der Leistungsparameter von Geschäftsbeziehungen. Dies gilt bereits für so genannte dyadische Beziehungen zwischen Zulieferern und Abnehmern.

Die von Herrn Gebert verfasste Dissertationsschrift greift diesen Leitgedanken auf und befasst sich mit den Determinanten der unternehmensübergreifenden Performancesteuerung in industriellen Zulieferer-Abnehmer-Beziehungen. Dabei werden die für solche Geschäftsbeziehungen relevanten Leistungsparameter identifiziert, in Vergleich gesetzt und ihre jeweilige Wirkung auf den Erfolg der unternehmensübergreifenden Logistikprozesse auf quantitativem Wege analysiert. Entscheidend dabei ist die parallele Ermittlung von branchen- und produktspezifischen Rahmenbedingungen, um so systematisch strukturelle Optimierungspotenziale und Leistungstreiber in Zulieferer-Abnehmer-Beziehungen identifizieren zu können.

Die auf diesem Wege gewonnenen Erkenntnisse können Praktikern helfen, grundsätzliche Zusammenhänge und Wechselwirkungen an der Schnittstelle zwischen Unternehmen besser zu verstehen. Zudem zeigt die Arbeit nachweislich die Bedeutung unternehmensübergreifender Steuerungsprozesse für den Erfolg von industriellen Geschäftsbeziehungen auf.

Die damit verbundene, signifikante Praxisrelevanz der vorliegenden Arbeit manifestiert sich unter anderem in der Verleihung des BME-Wissenschaftspreises 2012[1]. Vor diesem Hintergrund ist der vorliegenden Arbeit von Konstantin Gebert eine weite Verbreitung in Wissenschaft und Praxis zu wünschen.

Prof. Dr. Wolfgang Stölzle

[1] Die hierfür eingereichte Zusammenfassung der vorliegenden Dissertation wurde veröffentlicht unter: Gebert, Konstantin: Performance Control in Buyer-Supplier Relationships: The Design and Use of Formal Management Control Systems. In: Supply Management Research. Aktuelle Forschungsergebnisse 2012. Wiesbaden: Gabler, 2012, S. 29-53.

Vorwort

Die vorliegende Dissertation entstand im Rahmen meiner Forschungstätigkeit am Lehrstuhl für Logistikmanagement der Universität St.Gallen (LOG-HSG). Die Arbeit befasst sich mit den Determinanten der unternehmensübergreifenden Performancesteuerung in industriellen Zulieferer-Abnehmer-Beziehungen. Die Motivation, sich diesem Thema zu widmen, erwuchs aus der Idee, grundsätzliche Zusammenhänge und Wechselwirkungen an der Schnittstelle zwischen industriellen Unternehmen besser zu verstehen und dabei auf quantitativem Wege die Bedeutung unternehmensübergreifender Steuerungsprozesse für den Erfolg von Geschäftsbeziehungen aufzuzeigen.

An dieser Stelle möchte ich die Möglichkeit nutzen, all jenen zu danken, die mich im Dissertationsprozess begleitet, gefördert und unterstützt haben.

An erster Stelle möchte ich meinem akademischen Lehrer Prof. Dr. Wolfgang Stölzle danken, der den Dissertationsprozess persönlich begleitet sowie die Arbeit mit wertvollen Impulsen inhaltlich bereichert hat. Ebenfalls gilt mein herzlicher Dank Prof. Dr. Andreas Herrmann für die Übernahme des Korreferats.

Grossen Dank richte ich auch an Dr. Erik Hofmann für seinen Zeiteinsatz und die kritische Diskussion der Forschungsthematik. Besonders hervorheben möchte ich in diesem Zusammenhang auch die Unterstützung durch Anne Suphan und Christian Purucker, welche mich mit grossem und unermüdlichem Einsatz in die methodischen Tiefen multivariater statistischer Verfahren eingeführt haben. Ohne Euch wäre mir die Erstellung der Arbeit in dieser Form nicht möglich gewesen.

Darüber hinaus möchte ich meinen Kollegen vom LOG-HSG für die freundschaftliche Arbeitsatmosphäre, die vielen anregenden inhaltlichen Diskussionen sowie die zahlreichen privaten Aktivitäten danken, die gleichermassen zu meinem Wohlbefinden in St. Gallen beigetragen haben. Dabei möchte ich vor allem meine beiden Kollegen und Freunde Patrick Beck und Daniel Maucher namentlich hervorheben. Ihnen wie auch den anderen Kollegen danke ich für ihr offenes Ohr und den beruflichen und privaten Austausch.

Schliesslich möchte ich meinen Eltern Edeltraud und Gunter Gebert für die zeitlebens entgegengebrachte, bedingungslose Unterstützung danken. Der familiäre Rückhalt ermöglichte mir den Grundstein für das Gelingen dieser Arbeit.

Der grösste Dank gilt meiner Lebensgefährtin Ariane, die mich zu jeder Zeit mit viel Geduld und Verständnis begleitet hat. Dabei trug sie besonderes in arbeitsintensiven Phasen durch moralischen und liebevollen Zuspruch erheblich zum erfolgreichen Abschluss dieser Arbeit bei. Ihr ist daher meine Dissertation gewidmet.

Konstantin Gebert

Table of contents

PART I
Need for research & theoretical framework

PART II

Theory building & empirical analysis

PART III
Critical appraisal & future research

List of figures

List of tables

List of abbreviations

BSR	Buyer-supplier relationship
KPI	Key performance indicator
MCS	Management control system
RQ	Research question
SCM	Supply chain management

Abstract

Efficiency and effectiveness of transactional processes and activities are central to value generation in today's globalized business environments. Thus, a company's ability to best exploit performance potentials within buyer-supplier relationships has become a critical success factor in securing competition and improving a company's overall performance.

One powerful attempt to meet this challenge can be found in the application of cross-company management accounting approaches in order to execute performance control. However, implementation of suitable mechanisms and execution of control activities across company boundaries – commonly executed by both partners – is often insufficient because actual improvement potentials are not identified correctly.

This thesis addresses these challenges by providing a control process-oriented guideline, helping managers to systematically identify and analyze the weak points of their cross-company control activities. Furthermore, a conceptual model is developed to better understand conditions under which managerial control is effective by embedding the main control processes in an inter-organizational context.

Based on data from two equally structured surveys, one for the buy side and one for the supply side, the idea and potential of unbiased cooperative performance control is assessed on a quantitative basis. Embedded in a contingency-based research framework, several statistical methods are combined, to empirically test the assumed causalities. On the one hand, variance analysis is used to systemize and quantify the impact of contingent external factors on performance to give implications for performance evaluation processes. On the other hand, structural equation modeling helps to assess the mediating effect of control on the relationship's performance.

Findings support existing concepts in the fields of supply chain management and management accounting. As such, they contribute to the discussion by harmonizing existing knowledge from both disciplines. The findings also open the field for further research supporting companies in the design and use of performance control systems in buyer-supplier relationships.

PART I

Need for research & theoretical framework

1. Practical relevance

The work at hand addresses the design and use of formal management control systems (MCSs) in buyer-supplier relationships (BSRs). To provide a sound basis for the following discussion, a brief background is given and the relevance of the research project from a managerial perspective is indicated (chapter 1.1). Based on the identified issues, research objectives are defined (chapter 1.2), and the structure of the thesis is outlined (chapter 1.3).

1.1. Background and relevance from a managerial perspective

In today's business environments, various functional activities have transcended companies' boundaries, such as procurement, production and transportation (Hsu, 2005: 857), and complexity of BSRs has continuously increased over last two decades (Terpend, 2008: 28). As a result, BSRs have gained importance for the conduct of business in general (O'Toole and Donaldson, 2002: 197; Ploetner and Ehret, 2006: 4). This assumption is widely supported in literature, as transactional processes at the buyer-supplier interface have been proven to be positively linked to various other performance-related aspects, such as customer satisfaction (e.g. Gunasekaran et al., 2004), the speed of new product developments (e.g. Dyer, 1996) and the involved companies' overall profitability (e.g. Joseph et al., 1995). A company's ability to manage performance[2] of BSRs can thus represent a critical success factor in securing competition (Foggin and Mentzer, 2004: 827). This is in line with Meira et al. (2010: 149) confirming that inter-firm relationships in general (including BSRs[3]) can be understood as competitive tools used to prevail in globalized business

[2] Different understandings in terms of performance of BSRs exist. In the following, the understanding of performance of BSRs will draw on O'Toole and Donaldson's (2002: 197). According to the authors, performance incorporates both non-financial and financial aspects that can be grouped in so-called performance dimensions, such as flexibility and quality of transactional activities. For an extended discussion of performance related to BSRs see chapter 3.4.

[3] The authors distinguish between different forms of inter-firm relationships such as alliances, joint-ventures and business relationships in supply chains (Meira et al., 2010: 149). The latter represent BSRs in the meaning of this doctoral thesis. In consequence, 'inter-firm relationships' can be understood as an umbrella term, including different types of cross-company business relationships.

environments. Especially in dynamic and globalized business environments, companies are continuously forced to find new ways of improving cross-company material and information flows (Perea et al., 2000: 1143).

Numerous approaches for enhancing performance of these relationships have long been acknowledged, such as systematic supplier selection and development (Carter and Elram, 2003: 29)[4] or integration of processes and resources (Klein, 2007: 615) to name a few. Recent reviews[5] of supply chain management (SCM) literature explore the wide range of performance-related issues in industrial business relationships investigated within the last two decades. One attempt to meet this challenge can be found in the application of adequate cross-company management accounting approaches to execute performance control (Mahama, 2006: 332). In line with this, Meira et al. (2010: 150) stressed the suitability and potential of management accounting approaches to support and develop inter-firm relationships. Due to their ability to clearly systemize performance control activities, in particular so-called formal control approaches[6] seem to be suitable (Fisher, 1995: 26). Adopting this opinion, the investigation in this doctoral thesis will be limited to formal MCSs, and Fisher's (1995: 26) understanding of formal MCS will basically be adopted. Transferred to a BSR-specific context, formal MCSs can thus be defined as the cybernetic feedback process of

[4] Analyzing articles of 35 years of the journal of supply chain management, the authors provide a broad overview of subjects addressed in the field of SCM.

[5] For a comprehensive overview of performance-related topics addressed in SCM literature see Giunipero's et al (2008) meta-analysis of existing reviews on SCM literature. Additional useful reviews with diverging focuses have been conducted by Sachan and Datta (2005), Terpend et al. (2008) and Ross et al. (2009).

[6] MCSs in general have been subject of research for more than 40 years (Ferreira and Otley, 2009: 264) and numerous contributions to the topic have been made (Mahama, 2006: 320). As a result, a broad range of definitions of the term MCS exists (Fisher, 1995: 25). However, at least two basic types of control can be distinguished (Giglioni and Bedeian, 1974: 293; Fisher, 1995: 27; Malmi and Brown, 2008: 288): first, there is so-called formal control which aims at measuring performance and comparing it to predetermined standards. Second, there is control of subordinates addressing the direction of personnel by aspects not directly measureable, such as firm structure, firm culture and human resources policies.

(1) defining performance indicators for relevant activities and processes at the buyer-supplier interface and setting standards which reflect the targets of the companies involved, (2) measurement of the actual performance, (3) comparison of these measurement values against the predetermined standards in order to (4) identify optimization potentials, as well as (5) selection and (6) execution of corrective action addressing the identified performance issues (afterwards, the control loop starts all over).

Figure 1 displays formal control processes and gives an overview of how these processes are connected.

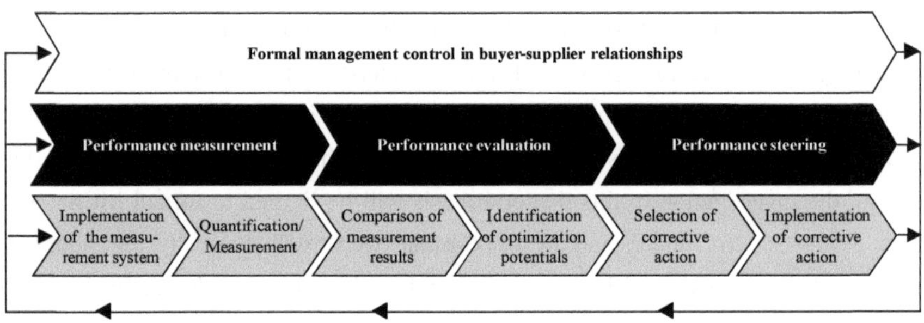

Figure 1: Formal control processes

Challenges in the design and use of formal management control systems in buyer-supplier relationships

Despite the simplicity of the six basic sub-processes, adapting formal MCSs to a BSR-specific context can cause enormous difficulties in practice as companies' boundaries are exceeded (Meira et al., 2010; 150). In contrast to common control activities which are limited to a single company, performance control in BSRs affects transactional activities between two legally independent entities (Day, 2000: 25). This legal independency can be seen as a major reason for many issues that are typical for cross-company performance control in general as Caglio and Ditillo's (2008: 891) in-depth review[7] and discussion of managerial control in inter-firm relationships shows. Taking a problem-oriented perspective, the authors identify cooperation and coordination concerns[8] as basic control problems. As BSRs represent a subset of inter-firm relationships, these concerns have to be considered relevant to BSRs as well. The assumption that efficiency and effectiveness of coordinative and cooperative processes between buyers and suppliers are crucial to the overall success of both companies, has also been confirmed by several recent empirical examinations (e.g. Cousins et al., 2008; Hult et al., 2007; Swink et al., 2007; Vickery et al., 2003). In detail, the two problem types can be described as follows:

(i) Cooperation problems: Cooperation often goes along with long-term agreements (Arshinder and Deshmukh, 2007: 422; Nyaga at al., 2010: 103) and requires the willingness of all involved parties to work together and to invest in the relationship (Wu et al., 2006: 494; Morris and Carter, 2005: 34). Moreover, the strategic goals of both partners have to be aligned to each other (Morgan, 2007: 259; Morris and Carter, 2005: 34). However, despite being a substantiate prerequisite for control, cooperation often is limited as the partners want to protect themselves against the others' opportunistic behavior. Both sides of the relationship cannot be sure "that partners are operating in the interests of the cooperative venture [...] as autonomous partners may have incentives to cheat and free-ride in order to attain their own specific goals at the expense of the objectives of the collective undertaking " (Caglio and Ditillo, 2008: 891).

[7] In their review, Caglio and Ditillo (2008: 891) also draw connections between control issues and theories that have been applied to address them. Among them, theories such as transaction cost economics, agency theory and contingency-theory can be found. Discussion of theories and their suitability to serve as theoretical basis in this doctoral thesis takes place in chapter 4.2.

[8] Caglio and Ditillo's (2008: 891) also discuss a third type of control problems, so-called appropriation concerns that occur when the resources exchanged are misappropriated and when the value of the joint output is not fairly distributed between partners. As the focus of the thesis is on the actual implementation and use of formal MCSs, appropriation issues are considered of subordinate importance and will hence not be considered in the following.

(ii) Coordination problems: Besides the basic willingness to cooperate and to commit to the relationship, the authors conclude that formal control asks for systematic coordination mechanisms to align objectives of both partners and joint actions across company boundaries (Caglio and Ditillo, 2008: 891). Lambert and Cooper (2000: 65) emphasize the need to move away from a company-specific view on the BSRs to a more integrated perspective on the relationship, commonly taken by both partners of the BSR. This addresses implementation and continuous development of mechanisms, as well as execution of routine control activities. As a result, additional resources from both sides are required to enable effective control-related coordination activities as cross-company management of information and material flows requires "active participation in joint activities, information sharing and synthesis of expertise" (Eng, 2006: p. 763). Accordingly, various coordination-related concerns can occur, such as lack of resources, insufficient information or inefficient communication. All of these issues have in common that they negatively affect coordination mechanisms, representing the actual control activities. Consequently, guaranteeing the quality of measurement and evaluation processes is decisive. Furthermore, knowledge about how to address the identified performance issues in an effective manner can be considered a major challenge when implementing MCSs in BSRs.

These two types of control problems determine the effectiveness of formal MCSs in BSRs and are strongly connected to each other. Coordination, executed to control, requires cooperation between both partners of the relationship. These interdependencies are illustrated in figure 2.

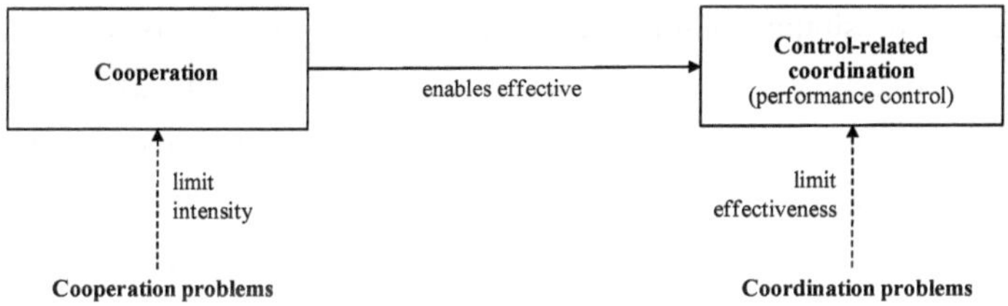

Figure 2: The basic problem types of performance control in BSRs.

Besides Caglio and Ditillo (2008), several studies can be found, which confirm that these two basic problem types still represent current issues in research on performance control in BSRs. Especially in recent years, an increasing number of articles has been published, empirically confirming the direct influence of cooperation (e.g. Hsu et al., 2008; Hult et al., 2007; Kaynak and Hartley, 2008) and coordination (e.g. Cousins et al., 2008, Ordanini and Rubera, 2008; Ramaswani and Srivastava, 2009; Swink et al., 2007) on performance-related topics.

The assumption that the requirements of formal management control – when executed across company borders –still present today's companies with enormous challenges, is also supported by a case study which was conducted by the author. To further specify the challenges that can occur in formal MCSs in BSRs, findings of the case study are described in the following section.

Formal management control in buyer-supplier relationships– Implications from a case study in the semiconductor industry

The case thoroughly analyzes a restructuring project between a buying and its supplying company which was initiated to improve delivery reliability at the buyer-supplier interface. In addition, it also aimed at optimizing efficiency and effectiveness of transactions connected to activities and processes. The project was conducted in cooperation with both firms, which allowed for an unbiased observation of the business relationship from both sides of the dyad. It is an explanatory study that analyzed the situation after the restructuring project which took place in spring 2010.

Therefore, no possibility of influencing the research setting existed. The database consisted of project data and documentation and the information was completed by in depth semi-structured interviews with one of the responsible project managers. The research study can be classified as an empirical case because the data was originally generated and 'observation' and 'interviews' served as research techniques. Within the logistics research framework of Mentzer and Kahn (1995: 233), the study equals the first level of research during which research ideas are generated through observation of a real-life phenomena.

The selected dyad is an interface between a raw material supplier for technical goods and a firm from the semiconductor industry. The business unit of the supplying company has approximately 200 employees and a turnover of more than 100 mio. Euro in European markets. The company demanding the commodity has more than 50.000 employees (in the group) at 15 main production sites and sales of more than 8 billion Euro. It specializes in high-tech products requiring extremely high quality commodities. The products are in the form of liquids, which are stored and transported in vessels, tankcontainers (large filling quantity) or barrels (small filling quantity). The supplier who is responsible for delivery and product quality owns the containers and all packaging material. These products' market situation is oligopolistic for both sides. Demand is highly volatile and depends on the buyer's economic situation in the electronic industry. Within this industry, business relations are usually long-term and strategic. Because the involved goods are of such high value, supply shortages and production stops are very costly, making delivery reliability important.

The project was initiated, after supply shortages were prevented only through special and expensive supplying initiatives in 2009. In addition, it was also suspected that major inefficiencies existed in logistics processes. To identify the root causes, an intensive analysis of cross-company processes between the two companies was conducted. Areas of analysis were distribution and transportation, inventory and consignment stock management, as well as supply chain visibility in general. The process followed the basic steps of formal MCSs:

(1) selection of indicators to measure efficiency and effectiveness of transactional activities, (2) data collection from both companies' financial and controlling departments, data refinement and analysis, (3) evaluation of the indicators measured and (4) identification of improvement potential, as well as (5) selection and (6) implementation of corrective actions, based on estimation of cost saving potentials.

During these steps, several control-related problems occurred as the following explanations show. Data on capacity utilization and delivery reliability, fulfillment of inventory targets in terms of stock outs, as well as production-related data was collected and analyzed. This data was gathered from different systems of both partners and refined. Next, it was tried to identify weak points. This required determining reference values to seek out optimization potential. During this process, it was difficult classifying values into 'high' or 'low' performance variables. Even though both companies basically used the same key figures, these values varied strongly. This is mainly because products and their logistic requirements differ widely within different business relationships. Several reference values from earlier periods existed, which enabled the evaluation of performance indicators' relative development. An assessment of actual efficiency and effectiveness was, however, based mainly on subjective estimations of involved employees. Therefore, it was hardly possible to conduct a thorough comparison and exact quantification of performance gaps. Determining exact ranges of tolerance that trigger corrective measures was also a weak point. Due to lack of comparable reference values and resulting benchmarks, only general process improvements were initiated, such as: implementation of clear inventory management principles that utilize analytical inventory targets to increase delivery reliability. Furthermore, improving the forecasting ability was attempted through increased communication and networking, which increases the occupancy rate of transport. However, it was also hardly possible to estimate all corrective actions' impact on different performance areas between company interfaces. This applies equally to measures to improve forecasting – whose applicability is assumed – although a precise quantification of effects on performance is not possible beforehand.

In summary, several weak points within the control activities have been identified that indicate two basic issues: On the one hand, the level of cooperation, i.e. in terms of information sharing and IT integration, led to a restricted applicability of control mechanisms as a whole. On the other hand, coordination problems occurred, further limiting the effectiveness of the actual control processes.

- Even though both companies basically used the same key indicators, measurement values varied strongly, indicating that performance values were either calculated differently or that the available data was not harmonized. Moreover, indicators were only treated independently from each other as there was no common understanding of the relationship's 'overall performance', combining and weighting the selected indicators.
- A systematic identification of optimization potentials was not possible, as the comparability of the reference values could not be guaranteed. Also no exact ranges could be defined for when to trigger corrective action.
- The overall impact of corrective actions on the selected indicators could not be quantified due to lack of knowledge about how to systematically address the identified issues.

Relevance of formal performance control in buyer-supplier relationships

After having discussed recent problems of formal performance control in BSRs from a managerial perspective, it can be assumed that research on the design and use of formal MCSs in BSRs can help to increase knowledge about how to systematically measure, evaluate and improve performance of BSRs. Moreover, findings give implications under which conditions the use of formal MCSs is recommendable and most effective. Especially conceptual approaches, adaptable to their specific business environment, might allow practitioners to improve cross-company control activities by overcoming control-related coordination problems and by better understanding the role of cooperation (which is limited by cooperation problems) in designing effective routine control mechanisms.

1.2. Research objectives and practical contribution of the research project

The main objective consists in providing guidance for the effective design and use of formal MCSs in BSRs. Findings are ought to create a better understanding of the special challenges that occur when implementing such control systems in practice. Also, it is intended to put forward the scientific discussion by harmonizing and structuring knowledge from different research areas, and by developing conceptual approaches to systematically implementing and improving formal control activities in BSRs. To achieve these goals, it is required to understand the requirements for successful performance control and to systematically address the relevant coordination problems. Drawing on findings from the case study and from existing contributions to the field, this affects the following sub-objectives:

Coordination-related sub-objectives

Coordination problems are directly linked to the actual control processes of measuring, evaluating and improving the BSR's performance. This covers several aspects. First, efficiency and effectiveness of cross-company activities in BSRs has to be made measurable and, most importantly, the defined measurement systems must reflect the goals of the involved companies in an adequate manner (buyer vs. supplier perspective[9]). Thus, it is required to create a clear definition of 'performance' in the context of BSRs, as the understanding of the term may vary depending on the view on the BSR and the strategic goals of the companies involved. This primarily addresses the selection and weighting of suitable performance indicators (labeled as *'performance variables'*). Second, measurement results must be made comparable because optimization potential can only be identified through comparison with appropriate reference values. This requires the identification and classification of relevant contingent performance determining factors (labeled as *'performance contingencies'*), as correctness of the performance evaluation processes strongly depends on the quality of the reference values. Third, relevant performance-

---

[9] For discussion of perspectives in BSRs see chapter 3.3.

influencing capabilities (labeled as *'performance capabilities'*) have to be correctly identified, as the effectiveness of corrective action results from the extent to which these capabilities are directly or indirectly addressed. Distinction between 'capabilities' and 'contingencies' can also be found in literature (e.g. Sousa and Voss, 2008; Klein et al., 2007). The latter represent the given conditions and are determined by context, meaning they cannot be manipulated (Fisher, 1998: 48). Compared to contingency variables, capabilities represent the performance potential, which can be influenced in a direct or indirect way by the involved companies.

> *This research project is intended to address these coordination-related issues by identifying and systemizing the decisive indicator variables, contingencies and capabilities for a BSR's performance. Findings are integrated in a sophisticated approach to systematically designing effective formal MCSs in BSRs. Furthermore, quantitative analysis of causal relationships between performance and contingent performance-determinants aims for sharpening the understanding of the contextual conditions under which performance values are comparable. The selection process of countermeasures shall be supported as well.*

Cooperation-related sub-objectives

Cooperation problems result from the way buyer and supplier interact with each other, i.e. if the partners lack willingness to work together and to invest in the relationship. This can be the case, if not enough human or technical resources for effective cross-company performance control provided. To enable successful control-related coordination in BSRs (in form of formal MCSs), it must be know under which conditions control can be executed in an adequate manner. In other words, the cooperative conditions under which cross-company control activities are most effective have to be systematically identified by research in order to derive implications for the design and use of formal MCSs in practice. This requires the identification of variables that enable control-related coordination activities. They represent the BSR's ability to exercise control (labeled as *'control capabilities'*[10]).

Consequently, the work at hand aims to empirically assess effectiveness of formal performance control in BSRs by identifying control capabilities and analyzing causalities between them, as well as determining the effect of control activities on performance of BSRs.

> *Thus, the focus of this study lies on better understanding the influence of cooperation (e.g. the level of IT integration and information sharing between the two partners) on control activities' effectiveness. It is not in the scope of this study to discuss the actual cooperation problems (e.g. information asymmetry) and the reasons for these problems (e.g. opportunistic behavior) which determine the level of cooperation.*[11]
>
> *In order to guarantee relevance and applicability of this approach, special emphasis will also be put on critically assessing the idea and potential of unbiased cooperative performance control in BSRs by investigating the role of perspective (buyer vs. supplier) for the design and use of MCSs.*

1.3. Thesis outline

The research activities, conducted to achieve the stated objectives by answering the research questions, will be described in several steps, represented by *eight chapters*. These chapters have been grouped in *three major parts* which can be understood as higher-level categories, giving the work at hand its basic structure. In detail, the remainder of the doctoral thesis is outlined as follows (figure 3):

In a first step, the theoretical relevance of the research project is evaluated by identifying relevant research fields (chapter 2.1) and by conducting a literature review to assess state of the art in research on formal MCSs in BSRs (chapter 2.2). Based on

[10] In contrast to performance capabilities, which refer to the actual performance of the BSR, control capabilities refer to the two companies' ability to commonly execute performance control activities.

[11] For a more differentiated discussion on cooperation, cooperation problems and control capabilities in the context of theories/theoretical explanation patterns see chapter 4.2.

the identified gaps, research questions are derived and implications for scientific contribution are drawn (chapter 2.3).

Next, the research framework of the dissertation is developed and the research subjects are defined (chapter 3) in three basic steps. First, general conceptual aspects of formal MCSs in BSRs are high-lighted in order to provide a sophisticated theoretical basis for the following discussion. In detail, this affects BSR-specific issues such as the identification of constituent attributes of BSRs (chapter 3.1), BSRs in the context of supply chains (chapter 3.2) and the role of perspective in BSRs (chapter 3.3). Additionally, different forms of performance related to BSRs are distinguished to create a common understanding (chapter 3.4). Second, based on these considerations, the conceptual framework of the research project is built and further implications for the subsequent research activities are given (chapter 3.5). Third, research subjects are outlined and embedded in the research framework (chapter 3.6).

Characterization of the research design and positioning of the research project is done next (chapter 4). Accordingly, the tripartite structure can be found in the following sub-chapters as well. Affecting three different levels of research, the theoretical fundamentals to characterize research activities are described first (chapter 4.1). Then, the different research phases are characterized in terms of underlying theories (theoretical level – chapter 4.2), methods applied and empirical basis (methodological level – chapter 4.3), and the meta-methodological level (chapter 4.4). At the end of the section, a summary of those characteristics is provided and positioning of research within scientific theory is done (chapter 4.5). Pointing out the relevance of the issues addressed by the following research activities, and creating a sound theoretical basis for these, content of chapters 1 to 4 can be summarized as the *need for research and theoretical framework (part I)*.

Due to the cumulative nature of the thesis, theory building and empirical analysis has been split in three phases, each resulting in a separate scientific contribution. These can be found in chapters 5, 6, and 7. Chapter 5 was also submitted and accepted in an earlier version for the 8th International Management Control Research Conference, 8-10 September, 2010, University of Greenwich, London. Accordingly, these three chapters can be summarized as the second part of the thesis, named *theory building and empirical analysis (part II)*.

Finally, the basic research results of part II are summarized and comprehensively discussed (chapter 8). Key findings of three phases of empirical analysis are presented (chapter 8.1), and managerial as well as scientific implications are derived (chapter 8.2 and 8.3). Also, limitations are discussed (chapter 8.4) and recommendations for future research are given (chapter 8.5). The thesis closes with chapter 8, providing a *critical appraisal and implications for future research (part III)*.

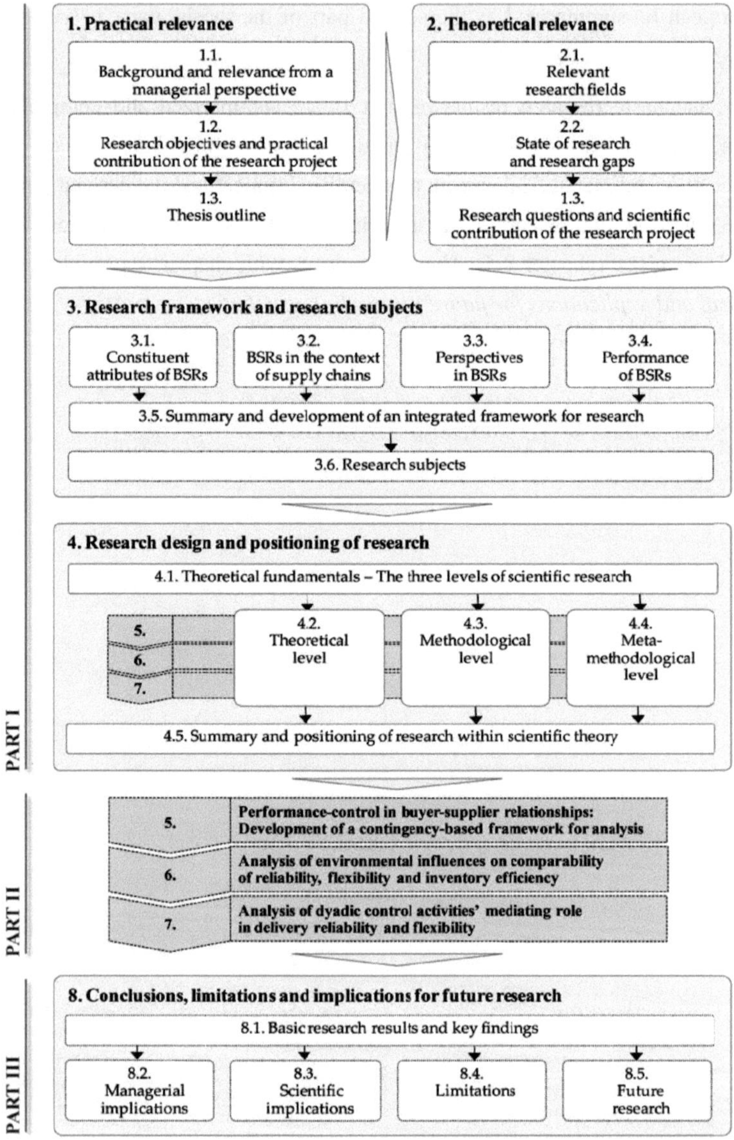

Figure 3: Outline of the thesis

2. Theoretical relevance

Having identified the research objectives, required to meet the challenges of the design and use of formal MCS in BSRs in practice, relevance of the research project must now be assessed from a theoretical point of view. This can be done in four steps. First, the theoretical starting position needs to be clarified by identifying relevant research streams (chapter 2.1) and research gaps within these areas (chapter 2.2). Then, research questions can be developed and implications for the theoretical relevance can be derived (chapter 2.3).

2.1. Relevant research fields

To get a holistic overview of relevant literature streams contributing to the topic, research fields need to be considered simultaneously addressing performance control-related issues and inter-firm relationships. This includes various scientific disciplines, such as *marketing* (e.g. Day, 2000; Hunt, 1983), *management accounting* (e.g. Dekker, 2004; Free, 2008) and *SCM*[12] (e.g. Humphreys et al., 2003; Klein et al., 2007). As the theoretical considerations in the previous chapters revealed, especially the latter two are of importance and will be central to the following discussion

Relevant research fields within the discipline of supply chain management

SCM consists of various sub-disciplines and can be classified in almost unlimited ways. Several recent, very thorough reviews on SCM literature give an impression of various possible subject categories (e.g. Burgess et al., 2006; Giunipero et al., 2008; Kouvelis et al., 2006; Sachan and Datta, 2005). Burgess et al. (2006: 710), for instance, define SCM disciplines as territories of activity and identify eight relevant areas, including logistics, purchasing, strategy, information and operations management. When it comes to assessing the relevance of SCM research for this thesis, two aspects are of particular importance: a direct connection to performance control (1st research criterion) must be given and the contribution must either directly

[12] For a differentiated discussion on BSRs in the context of SCM see 3.2.

be related or adaptable to BSRs (2nd research criterion). Thus, simultaneously addressing these two aspects can be considered the decisive search criteria.

There are only a few research fields directly addressing the issue of performance control (1st research criterion). Basically aiming to support the strategic configuration of corporate networks and the governance of inter-organizational processes (Westhaus, 2007: 46), supply chain control can be considered as one of them. Covering a very broad field of activities, related articles are only suitable to this research project to a limited extent as more control-specific input is required. Another discipline of interest can be found in the field of supply chain performance management. Focusing on the improvement of efficiency and effectiveness of inter-organizational processes, control-related activities such as design and maintenance of integrated measurement systems are discussed in an inter-organizational context (e.g. Karrer, 2006: 211; Stölzle, 2002: 15). However, supply chain performance management also encompasses aspects such as strategy implementation and alignment which are out of scope in this doctoral thesis. In consequence, only contributions directly addressing performance control-related issues in BSRs will be taken into account, independently from the specific sub-discipline of SCM (i.e. supply chain control or supply chain performance management) they refer to.

The need for taking a cross-sectional perspective also applies when assessing SCM research from a BSR perspective (2nd research criterion). Reviews (e.g. Giunipero et al., 2008; Sachan and Datta, 2005) show that BSRs cannot be clearly assigned to specific SCM sub-disciplines as well, as they play an essential role in almost all of them. All classification schemes and conceptual frameworks consist primarily of categories addressing relational issues at the interface between affiliated companies. These issues are either discussed in a direct way (e.g. supplier development and relationship management), or indirectly through categories, influenced by both parties involved and based on contractual cooperation (e.g. strategy and information sharing). In consequence, the same simplifications that apply to the 1st criterion, also apply to the 2nd one, as BSRs can be 'cut free' from the SCM-specific context for this research project.

However, in order to also cover relevant contributions to the field from other literature streams which are, strictly spoken, not part of SCM as they are addressing BSRs only from one side of the dyad, the focus will be extended as follows: on the supply side, in particular the domains of demand planning and customer relationship management are expected to contribute to the discussion. On the buy side, areas that focus on supply planning-related topics such as supply management and purchasing will be included as they meet the scope of this thesis. As such, they will be subsumed under the term 'SCM' and performance-related studies encompassing BSR-related topics from these areas will also be considered in the discussion on SCM in chapter 2.2.

Relevant research fields within the discipline of management accounting

In terms of relevant management accounting, the research stream of management control can be considered as crucial to the topic of performance control in BSRs. However, basic limitations can be made here as well by narrowing down the scope to the sub-discipline of management control in inter-firm settings. Besides supply chain relationships, these kind of inter-organizational relationships also cover outsourcing activities and horizontal integration (Caglio and Ditillo, 2008: 866), which do not need to be considered. Moreover, restrictions have to be made regarding the nature of the control mechanisms under investigation as only formal MCSs are of relevance.

Summary

It can be concluded that there is not a single literature stream, which covers performance control in BSRs in a comprehensive manner, as relevant contributions to the field are embedded in various *SCM* disciplines. As a result, a cross-sectional viewpoint must be taken and both disciplines have to be searched with a narrow focus on the relevance for the underlying research scope. In terms of management accounting literature, the focus can be clearly narrowed down to the stream of *management control in inter-firm-relationships.* Findings of both areas then need to be combined and research gaps have to be pointed out. The following chapter will give an overview of the current state of research in these fields.

2.2. State of research and research gaps

A main feature of the research approach to analyzing and improving formal performance control activities in BSRs lies in systematically connecting relationship-specific capabilities and contingencies to control processes of formal MCS, by embedding the main control processes in an inter-organizational context. Thus, the following review[13] of *SCM literature* focuses on how these capabilities and contingencies were analyzed and in which way they were linked to performance. This also includes the role of perspective on the buyer-supplier dyad. Moreover, *management control literature* is reviewed through a BSR-lens and existing frameworks for analyzing dyadic control systems will be assessed in terms of their suitability for the use in BSRs.

Dyadic performance control in buyer-supplier relationships – State of the art in supply chain management literature

In supply chain performance literature,[14] various scientific contributions exist, analyzing causal interdependencies between interface-related aspects and performance outcomes. Eng (2006) for instance, inquires about interdependencies of information-sharing, mutual trust and other organizational norms with cross-functional coordination, supply chain responsiveness and firm-performance. Lambert and Pohlen (2001) take a similar route by analyzing effects of supplier relationship management on economic value added, whereas Fynes et al. (2005) concentrate on causal relationships between cross-company communication, trust, adaption and cooperation and firm-specific performance dimensions such as quality and cost. Stressing the role of cross-company capabilities, Kim (2006) investigates the effect of interaction between corporate competition capability and supply chain operational capability on firm-performance. Hsu et al. (2008), in turn, look at the influence of information

[13] A more deep analysis of recent contribution from SCM and management accounting literature can be found in paper A (annex A). The paper also includes a structured review of performance related articles in supply chain management literature.

[14] As mentioned in chapter 2.1, this also covers research areas that are relevant to performance management in an inter-organizational context even though they cannot be assigned to the discipline supply chain performance management from a strict point of view.

sharing capability on BSRs and firm-performance. In addition, numerous additional contributions on related topics exist (e.g. Curcovic et al., 2000; Daugherty et al., 2003; Defee and Stank, 2005; Ordanini and Rubera, 2008; Stevenson and Spring, 2009). Analyzing these contributions showed that there is a broad consensus about the basic interdependencies between relationship capabilities and their limiting impact on the companies' performance. The performance-determining role of contingencies can be considered valid as well, and the decisive role of managing performance at the buyer-supplier interface to improve overall performance and competitiveness of the two interacting companies has been widely accepted. However, causal relationships between capabilities, contingencies and performance have not been systemized in an adequate manner as a comprehensive meta-analysis of relevant influence factors still seems to be missing. In order to enable significant implications for the effectiveness of MCSs in BSRs, such an investigation has to provide a holistic overview by consolidating the specific contingencies and capabilities resulting from the specific research setting of the respective contributions. These findings are in line with Terpend's et al. (2008) extensive content analysis of contributions to BSRs from 1986 to 2005. Stating that publications addressing performance improvements highly increased, the authors concluded that researcher are ought to consider more contextual variables moderating the relationships. In their opinion, especially "the effects of many buyer, supplier and market characteristics, as well as product characteristics have yet to be explored" (Terpend et al., 2008: 43). Future research, for instance, should try to find out under which market conditions information sharing and trust is beneficial to the involved companies, or how practitioners can detect under which contextual conditions coordination activities are effective (Terpend et al., 2008: 43).

In terms of the perspective adopted in the respective publications, recent meta-studies on SCM literature show, that basically all possible views on dyads have been adopted. However, conducting a content analysis on 442 SCM articles from 1999 to 2003, Sachan and Datta's (2005: 667) found out that only 18% analyzed BSR-specific issues from a dyadic perspective. Going into more detail regarding the dyadic relationships, Ross et al. (2009: 38) also emphasize the lack of analyzing the buyer-supplier interface from an unbiased point of view, also stating that most scientific studies on BSRs in manufacturing and logistics literature have either adopted a buyer or supplier firm view. Terpend et al. (2008: 41) also stressed the increasing importance of investigations of buyer-supplier mutual efforts as these have drastically increased within the second decade. But the authors also conclude that this development will have to continue to overcome the limitations of single perspective-based publications.

In summary, it can be said that the assumed interdependencies between relationship capabilities and their limiting impact on the companies' performance as well as the performance-determining role of contingencies are widely supported in the scientific community. In line with this, an urgent need for appropriate control mechanisms and techniques meeting the specific requirements of BSRs has been expressed in SCM. Reviewing this literature led to the assumption that three particular aspects are considered as underdeveloped from an inter-company perspective. First, evidence that interface processes and activities impact both buyer's and supplier's firm-performance has not been adequately credited. With only few exceptions, analysis of BSRs in supply chains has focused on performance of either the buying or the supplying company. This differs with an opinion widely held in the SCM community, purporting that inter-company competitiveness is today's most important challenge. In reality, the need to analyze interface-performance in supply chains from an unbiased point of view is a current issue. Second, a systematic identification and classification of capabilities and contingencies is still missing and analysis of causal relationships between these factors and performance still seems to be under-developed. Third, no contribution was found that explicitly examined the actual influence and usefulness of formal control activities, to systematically enhance performance of transactional processes in BSRs.

Dyadic performance control in buyer-supplier relationships – State of the art in management control literature

The second literature stream of essential importance is the one of management control research. In order to get a holistic overview of recent contributions to the field, recent reviews of field literature have been analyzed. Focusing on performance control in inter-firm settings as a superset of supply chain relationships, two relevant meta-studies were identified. The first one was conducted by Meira et al. (2010), who analyzed MCSs in inter-organizational relationships depending on the nature of the relationship, namely 'supply chain relations', 'outsourcing' and 'others' including joint ventures and further unspecified relationships. The second one, carried out by Caglio and Distillio (2008), was selected as formal management control mechanisms were directly addressed. Combining the two review led to additional useful contributions (e.g. Coletti et al., 2005; Dekker, 2004; Free, 2008; Mahama, 2006)

Analyzing these contributions and the two meta-studies in terms of performance control in BSRs through a supply chain lens showed that the same issues still seemed to be underdeveloped in management control research. Although several of the papers address trust-related issues, Caglio and Ditillo (2008: 876) conclude that the impact of variables such as uncertainty and trust on inter-firm control mechanisms have been only partially investigated. They also state that almost all of the papers are limited to the analysis of only one variable at a time without considering the interaction amongst them. Additionally, the authors recognized a heavy predominance of a purchasing perspective on the dyads and therefore stress the need for analysis from an unbiased point of view. Some of these gaps have already been identified within the examined papers. Mahama (2006: 317), for instance, states that the link between MCSs and cooperation in general remains underdeveloped, and Free (2008: 629) identifies a strong need for further investigations of the relationships between accounting, trust and trustworthiness.

Beside contributions to performance control in specific inter-firm settings, no framework specifically designed to analyze control systems in such an inter-organizational environment could be found, even though there are conceptual frameworks for the analysis of MCSs in general existing, such as Simons' (1995) levers of control framework and Ferreira and Otley's (2009) framework for analyzing performance. However, especially the latter seems potentially suitable to be elaborated to the specific needs of formal MCSs in BSRs, systematically connecting formal control processes (performance measurement, performance assessment and implementation of corrective action) to BSR-specific performance capabilities and contingencies.

Regarding management control literature, it can be concluded that the potential role of formal MCSs in inter-firm relationships has been recognized and various scientific contributions to the debate of management control directly addressing BSRs in supply chains have been made. But despite all this discussion, the configuration of formal MCSs in supply chains seems to have been neglected in prior research. A systematic and comprehensive analysis of relevant influence factors on performance, for instance, still is missing as interdependencies between these performance-determining factors and control processes in BSR-specific MCSs have been only marginally explored. Also a framework for analyzing such systems could not be identified because existing approaches did not fully consider specific BSRs characteristics.

Based on the review of these selected contributions to control mechanisms in inter-firm relationships it can thus be concluded that de facto no research exists, helping to implement new and to systematically assess formal MCSs in supply chain BSRs. In consequence, the lack of systematic research tools for analysis has to be considered a major research gap.

2.3. Research questions and scientific contribution of the research project

After having discussed recent contributions to the topic of formal performance control in supply chain BSRs, it can be summarized that there is still a lack of knowledge about how to systematically overcome the challenges today's companies face in managing performance of their BSRs. Furthermore, empirical evidence needs to be strengthened. This could be reached by analyzing the expected interdependencies on a quantitative basis. As an example, statistical analysis of causal relationships between performance and its determinants, such as contingencies and control mechanisms, can help to assess the effectiveness of control activities depending on the inter-organizational context. Accordingly, the impact on the design and use of MCSs in BSRs, resulting from a different view on the dyad, needs to be investigated further as well. Also, there appears to be a lack of knowledge about the mediating role of dyadic control activities for performance in BSRs. This demand leads to the following primary research question:

RQ: How can effective formal performance control in BSRs be enabled and control-related coordination problems systematically overcome?

In order to sufficiently address the specific research objectives identified in chapter 1.2, further distinctions need to be made and a set of secondary, more detailed questions has to be developed.

As described, successful control mechanisms have to fulfill specific requirements of cross-company considerations for each of the three sub-processes to overcome coordination problems. Efficiency and effectiveness of cross-company activities has to be made measurable and measurement results comparable, because quality of the reference values determines the suitability of the performance evaluation processes. Also, performance drivers at the BSR-interface have to be correctly identified, as effectiveness of corrective action results from the extent to which these drivers are addressed. Accordingly, the following secondary questions need to be answered:

- RQ_a *How can key elements of performance control in BSRs (capabilities, contingencies and performance indicators) be classified and how do they interact with formal control processes?*
- RQ_b *What are the relevant performance variables in terms of formal performance control in BSRs?*
- RQ_c *What are the relevant performance contingencies in terms of formal performance control in BSRs and how do they influence comparability of measurement values?*
- RQ_d *What are the relevant performance capabilities in terms of formal performance control in BSRs and how do they influence the effectiveness of corrective actions taken?*

To enable successful formal performance control in BSRs (in form of formal MCSs), appropriate conditions to execute control-related coordination must be given. This requires control capabilities, which are, in turn, determined by the level of cooperation between the two companies. Thus, it must be know under which conditions control can be executed effectively and the following questions must be answered:

RQ_e What are the relevant control capabilities in terms of formal performance control in BSRs and how do they influence the effectiveness of control activities?

Implications for the scientific contribution of this doctoral thesis

From a scientific perspective, answering these questions addresses two aspects of current research: formal MCSs in inter-firm relationships, which are basically part of management accounting research, and performance management in BSRs, which has mainly received attention within the SCM discussion. However, it appears that there is a general shortage of studies on the use of formal MCSs in SCM, while BSR-specific examinations seem to be neglected in management accounting. As a result, contributions, comprehensively addressing formal MCSs in BSRs, are to be considered underrepresented in both areas. Combining both aspects, the work at hand can thus contribute to science by harmonizing existing knowledge from both fields and by putting forward the discussion about the design and use of formal MCSs in BSRs (figure 4).

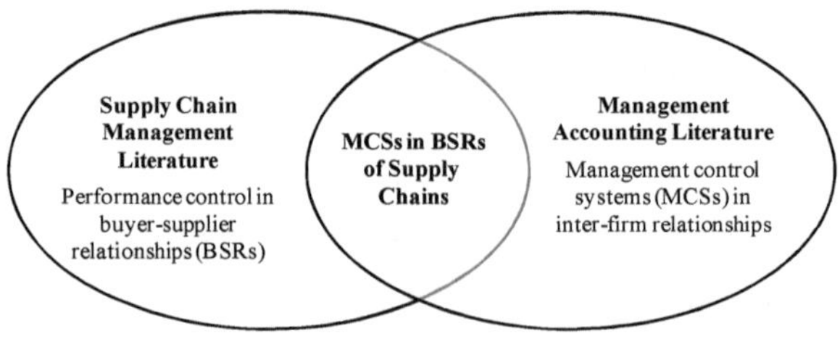

Figure 4: Integration of literature streams for harmonizing knowledge about the design and use of formal MCS in BSRs

3. Research framework and research subjects

To being able to achieve the research objectives, stated in chapter 1.2, a theoretical framework must be developed, serving as a basis for answering the research questions, defined in chapter 2.3. This requires getting from a managerial to a theoretical perspective on the identified issues of formal performance control in BSRs. The following considerations are intended to enhance the theoretical foundation of the framework by sharpening the understanding of relevant conceptual aspects of BSRs. Moreover, it is used to clearly define the scope of the doctoral thesis. Discussions cover identification of constituent attributes of BSRs (chapter 3.1), classification of BSRs in the context of supply chains (chapter 3.2) and the performance-determining role of the view on the relationship (chapter 3.3). Also, the understanding of the term 'performance of BSRs' is sharpened (chapter 3.4). Drawing on these findings, the research framework is developed and implications are given.

3.1. Constituent attributes of buyer-supplier relationships

When discussing the constituent attributes of BSRs, the basic understanding of relational exchange can be adopted from a market-based view, generally understood and accepted. Marketing exchange theories have been a subject of research since the late 1960s (e.g. Kotler and Levy, 1969; Luck, 1969). In his review of 15 years of marketing research, Hunt (1983: 9) even came to the conclusion that exchange relationships can be considered the main focus in industrial marketing discussions. In a well-founded analysis of the requirements of current business-to-business-partnerships, Ploetner and Ehret (2006: 4) confirmed the increasing impact of BSRs on competitive advantage and stressed the need for performance-based cooperation.

According to these contributions about exchange relationships, BSRs, in their most rudimentary form, can be understood as dyadic business relationships between two separate legal entities carrying out transactions of any kind. These range from transactional, characterized by anonymous and automated purchasing processes, to collaborative relationships between highly integrated supply chain partners (Day, 2000: 25; Klein et al., 2007: 1366). Figure 5 illustrates spectrum of cooperation.

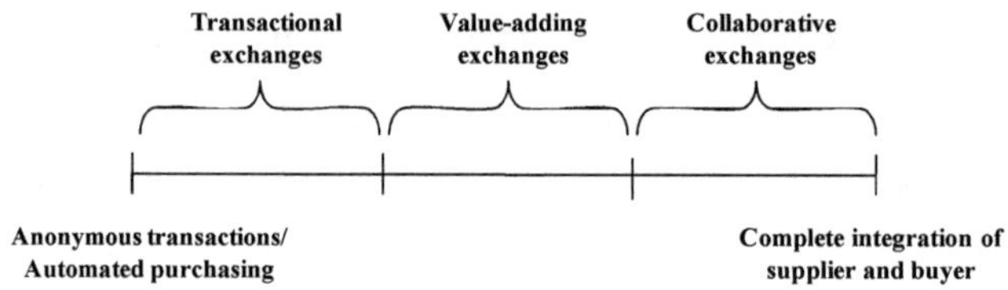

Figure 5: *The relationship spectrum of BSRs.*

One inherent feature of such relational exchange is the ongoing nature of the relationship, meaning an exchange has already occurred and is also expected to continue in the future (Dwyer et al., 1987: 11; Odekerken-Schröder et al., 2003: 178). Often, the relational exchange is also based on contracts defining precise exchange periods. After the exchange periods, both partners (buyer and supplier) can decide whether they want to continue and develop the business relations or end the cooperation (Anderson, 1995: 347). The vital importance of a contractual basis as a pre-condition for successful relationship management has been widely accepted in the industrial marketing community (e.g. Arndt, 1979; Dwyer et al., 1987; Ganesan, 1994; Krause, 1999; Macneil, 1980; Ploetner and Ehret, 2006).

As the following discussion shows, the attributes described can be considered essential to BSRs in supply chains as well, and also need to be addressed by our framework for analysis. They will be taken as a starting point to identify first basic framework requirements. Accordingly, the following working definition for BSRs will be used:

> *BSRs in supply chains can be defined as mutual inter-organizational relationships between legally independent decision-making powers consisting of buyers and suppliers. The exchange must be long-term (to enable cooperative performance control activities), and, most importantly, both partners have to be able to influence the relationship's nature and development.*

3.2. Buyer-supplier relationships in the context of supply chains

BSRs play an essential role in inter-organizational network settings. Thus, they must be brought into a supply chain context to systematically identify requirements for the framework resulting from a supply chain-based perspective performance control in BSRs. Entering the discussion on BSRs in the context of supply chains and networks, the term 'SCM' has to be sharpened first. Drawing on a number of existing definitions, Karrer (2006: 14) concludes that there is no common understanding of SCM and identifies two major reasons for variance of definitions: on the one hand, 'management' is interpreted differently (i.e. ranging from strategic relationship management to coordination of operational transactional activities); on the other hand, the understanding of 'supply chain' varies, depending on the number of companies involved. Mentzer et al. (2001: 4), for instance, consider three or more companies in a row supply chain, whereas Chopra and Meindl (2004: S.4) state that "A supply chain consists of all parties involved, directly or indirectly, in fulfilling a customer request." Many other definitions can be found[15] such, as the ones of Beamon (1999: 275), and Lambert and Cooper (2000: 69). As a result, also the understanding of SCM varies depending on definition of supply chain it refers to. Table 1 gives an overview of selected SCM definitions.

[15] An exhaustive discussion on existing interpretations of the term 'supply chain' can be found in Otto (2002: 89).

Table 1: Overview of selected SCM definitions

Author(s)	Definition
Christopher (2005: 18)	"SCM can be defined as: "The management of upstream and downstream relationships with suppliers and customers to deliver superior customer value at less cost to the supply chain as a whole."
Cooper etal. (1997: 11)	"Supply Chain Management is the integration of business processes from end user through original suppliers that provides products, services and information that add value for customers."
Mentzer et al. (2001: 18)	"Supply chain management is defined as the systemic, strategic coordination of the traditional business functions and the tactics across these business functions within a particular company and across businesses within the supply chain, for the purposes of improving the long-term performance of the individual companies and the supply chain as a whole."
Council of Supply Chain Management Professionals	"Supply chain management encompasses the planning and management of all activities involved in sourcing and procurement, conversion, and all logistics management activities. Importantly, it also includes coordination and collaboration with channel partners, which can be suppliers, intermediaries, third party service providers, and customers. In essence, supply chain management integrates supply and demand management within and across companies."
Simchi-Levi et al. (2003: 347)	"Supply Chain Management is a set of approaches utilized to efficiently integrate suppliers, manufacturers, warehouses, and stores, so that merchandise is produced and distributed at the right quantities, to the right locations, and at the right time, in order to minimize systemwide costs while satisfying service level requirements."

Despite a diverging focus, all of these considerations share an integrated view on supply side and demand side of a focal company. Consequently, at least three companies in a row are required to mark a supply chain. In case more than three companies are involved, some authors believe that the term 'supply network' would be more appropriate (e.g. Christopher, 2005: 286; Harland et al., 2001: 21) as the linear connection that a chain refers to is rarely the case in practice (Meira et al.: 151). Adopting this point of view, several levels of SCM research can be distinguished and terms will be used as shown in figure 6.

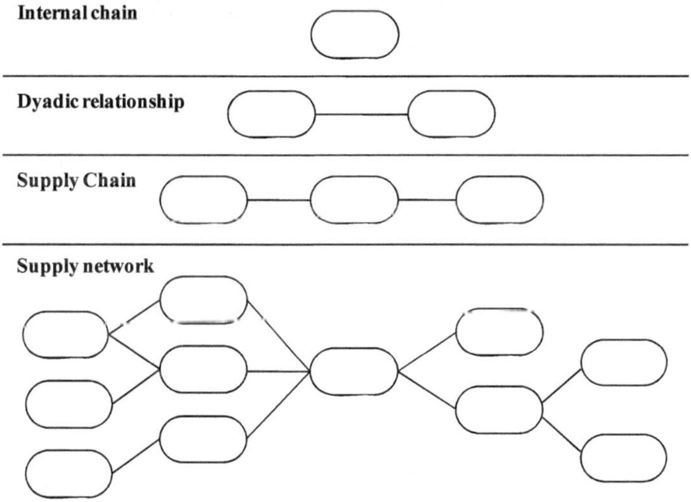

Figure 6: Levels of research in SCM.

Buyer-supplier relationships in the context of the different research levels of supply chain management

When focusing on BSRs with the different levels of research in SCM, it can be concluded that BSRs can be seen as an elementary trans-sectional component of SCM in general; one that can be analyzed independently from the specific SCM context in which they were discussed. This means that a framework for analyzing BSRs in supply chains must not necessarily differ between SCM levels, as the relevant features of BSRs – as described in chapter 3.1 – are not affected. In consequence, the focus can be placed on basic attributes of BSRs, such as recurring exchange activities, contractual issues and developmental aspects; they constitute dyadic relationships between buying and selling companies in general. As a matter of fact, neither the SCM research level nor the SCM specific context affects the basic attributes of BSRs which are independent from these considerations. Although, research activities of this thesis will essentially be based on findings from different SCM disciplines and from different SCM research levels, this circumstances allow to derive from SCM and thus no further distinction must be made in the following. The basic implication for the research framework of this thesis can be described as:

The following discussion and identification of requirements for the research framework will derive from SCM. To allow a clear and disjunctive classification, the framework must refer to a single dyad as the highest common factor of all different views. For example, a supply chain view including the focal firm's buyers and suppliers will be split into two independent dyadic relationships and discussed separately in the framework.

Consequently, a direct connection to performance control in BSRs will be seen as the decisive criterion no matter from which sub-discipline the contribution originates. For the same reasons, stated in chapter 2.1, the focus will even be extended to other BSR-related literature streams which are, strictly spoken, not part of SCM. Accordingly, customer relationship management and supplier relationship management, both addressing BSR-related issues will be considered as well. As such, they will also be subsumed under 'SCM' in the following.

Positions of buyer-supplier relationships within supply chains and supply networks and the role of logistics service providers

Companies in supply chains can take different positions. Hsu (2008: 303), for instance, differs between raw material manufacturer, component manufacturer, final product manufacturer, wholesaler and retailer. Depending on the buyer's and the supplier's position in a supply chain, numerous different combinations can occur. BSRs between component manufacturers and final product manufacturer are possible as well as BSRs between two component manufacturers. Accordingly, the relationship's features may differ enormously in terms of market- and production-characteristics (Terpend et al., 2008: 43). When it comes to performance control in such BSRs, these differences need to be considered. Accordingly, research on BSRs has to account for BSR-specific differences in an adequate manner.

Another aspect that is related to this discussion of BSR-specific differences, concerns the use of logistics service providers. As such, they are embedded in the buyer's and supplier's transactional processes. Services may range from warehousing, handling and transportation to value added services. However, the role of logistics service providers will not be credited in the following for the basic reason that this study's research focus lies on cooperation- and coordination-related aspects between buying and supplying companies. Closely linked these two aspects are the domains of supply planning (buy side) and demand planning (supply side). Both are usually not in the business of the service providers as they can be considered a core competence of the two companies. Thus, logistics service providers will not be treated separately.

3.3. Perspectives in buyer-supplier relationships

As described, BSRs can basically be understood as dyadic business relationships between two legal entities carrying out transactions of any kind, ranging from anonymous purchasing processes, to collaborative relationships between highly integrated supply chain partners (Day, 2000: 25; Klein et al., 2007: 1366). Depending on the view on the dyad, two basic perspectives on inter-firm relationships can be adopted. On the one hand, a buyer-specific view on suppliers (dyadic upstream) exists, on the other hand the corresponding supplier-specific view on customers (dyadic downstream) can occur (Giunipero et al., 2008: 73). Moreover, an integrated perspective that views the same dyad from both sides (dyadic both) can occur, mutually combining both buyer's and supplier's perspective. An overview of possible perspectives in BSRs is given in figure 7.

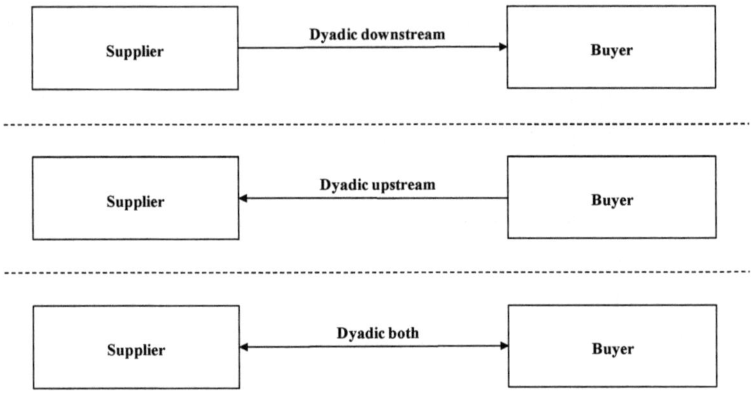

Figure 7: Perspectives in BSRs.

Due to changing views on BSRs (dyadic upstream vs. dyadic downstream) and different contexts (dyad, supply chain and network), understanding of the terms 'BSR' and especially 'performance' vary.

> *Thus, perspective-related aspects need to be clearly addressed by the research framework. Also, since both parties must be able to influence the relationship, the framework must focus on the interface between the two parties from an unbiased view (dyadic both), not taking a specific perspective of either the buyer or supplier.*

This premise can also be found in literature, where O´Toole and Donaldson (2002: 197) described BSRs as two-way relationships between buyers and suppliers. In line with this is Mahama's (2006: 317) understanding of strategic supplier relationships; he, in turn, refers to Spekman (1988) and Wood and Gray (1991).

3.4. Performance of buyer-supplier relationships

Before entering the area of performance control in BSRs, further distinction needs to be made first, as the understanding of the term 'performance' often varies in literature.

O'Toole's and Donaldson's (2002: 197) recognize this issue and contribute to structuring the field by providing a broad review of studies on relational performance. Key dimensions of performance BSRs are identified and implications for measurement and control activities are drawn. As one result, the authors distinguish between two basic types of performance: the first one directly focuses on the relationship by addressing relational activities such as delivery reliability (e.g. Swink et al., 2007; Tracey, 2004), quality of coordination between companies (e.g. Cousins et al., 2008; Hult et al., 2007) and buyer's responsiveness (e.g. Eng, 2006; Wu et al., 2006). As this kind of performance refers to the inter-organizational interface between buying and supplying companies, it is labeled as '*interface-performance*' in the following. The second one – a strictly company-specific one – reflects the indirect effect of such relational performance on both partners' intra-firm-performance. For usual, contributions examining the latter focus on analyzing the impact of efficiency and effectiveness of relational processes on firm-specific outcome such as sales volume and profitability (e.g. Germain et al., 2008; Kaynak and Hartley, 2008) and market share (e.g. Curkovic et al., 2000; Hsu et al., 2008). Accordingly, this second type of performance is labeled '*relational firm-performance*'[16] in the following. Although it is strongly connected to firm-performance, these two terms must be distinguished as relational firm-performance is a subset of firm-performance. The former represents the part of the latter that is determined by the BSR.

When characterizing interface performance, O'Toole's and Donaldson's (2002: 197) idea of performance of buyer-supplier exchanges will be applied. According to the authors, performance incorporates both non-financial and financial aspects that can be grouped in so-called performance dimensions, such as flexibility and quality of transactional activities. However, an exact definition of interface-performance cannot be given at this point, as the selection of specific performance indicators depends on various aspects, such as differing views on the dyad and strategic constraints. To give an example from the automotive industry: In a BSR for car seats which are delivered

[16] Labeling was also inspired by Heimeriks (2002: 10). Discussing the role of relationship-specific capabilities for performance in alliances, he states that relational performance – reflecting alliance's success – refers to the creation of rents for the allied companies resulting from the alliance (i.e. through complementary assets). These rents represent the firm-specific performance outcome of the alliance

just-in-time (JIT), the supplier will consider inventory levels in the finished goods warehouse when assessing efficiency of his transactional activities, as high-value products like car seats may have a great influence on his capital tied-up. The supplying car manufacturer, on the other hand, will focus on his own storage levels, not accounting for the supplier's inventory. But there are also performance-related aspects, which are perceived by both sides, such as delivery reliability and customer response times. In consequence, comprehensively assessing interface-performance from an unbiased point of view (dyadic both) requires considering buyer-specific as well as supplier-specific KPI. Figure 8 illustrates the role of perspective for the understanding of interface-performance in BSRs.

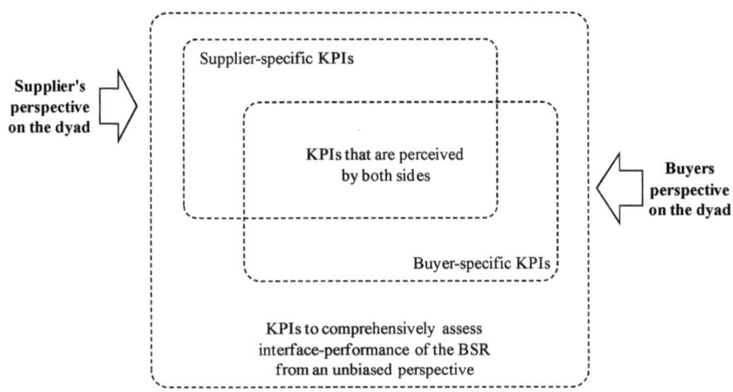

Figure 8: The role of perspective for the understanding of interface-performance

In summary, this leads to the following implications for the research framework:

Interface-performance and relational firm-performance must also be distinguished in the research framework, as performance control activities in BSRs can only address interface-performance in a direct manner. In consequence, this differentiated understanding of performance will be adopted and serve as theoretical basis in the doctoral thesis. Moreover, the influence of perspective (buyer vs. supplier) must be taken into account, as the understanding of interface-performance may vary between the two parties.

3.5. Summary and development of an integrated framework for research

In order to systematically answer the research questions, it is necessary to develop a framework that serves as a conceptual basis for the research project. It must bring together the different relevant aspects of formal MCSs in BSRs and has to show, how the units of analysis of the three phases of empirical analysis are connected to each other. This concerns findings from discussions of BSRs' conceptual aspects in the previous chapters, as well as general requirements and challenges of formal MCSs described in chapter 1 and 2. Moreover, research questions must be assignable to the elements of the framework. In summary, the following aspects must be considered adequately to guarantee usefulness and applicability of the research framework:

- The framework must include the identified key influences, affecting formal performance control in BSRs. These influences are represented by three types of coordination-related variables (performance indicators, contingencies and capabilities), and one type of cooperation-related variables (control capabilities).
- Key influences on coordination problems (variable-oriented view on MCSs in BSRs) must be connected to formal control processes (process-oriented view on MCSs in BSRs). This addresses two essential causal relationships: First, there are contingency variables that have an impact on performance. This needs to be

considered by comparing measurement results from different settings, as values for the same KPI may differ depending on the specific contextual conditions. Second, performance can only be improved by directly or indirectly addressing capability variables. Therefore, correctly and comprehensively identifying these capabilities is required before taking suitable corrective actions.

- Also, the framework must pay attention to the role of perspective on the relationship, as the understanding of interface-performance may differ between the two parties involved. In the research project, analysis must be done from an unbiased point of view, not taking a specific perspective of either the buyer or supplier.
- The nature of the BSRs – for instance in terms of integration between partners and long-term orientation – must be taken into account, because the way the companies cooperate is expected to influence the level of provided control capabilities.

The research framework, serving as basis for the research activities of the work at hand, is shown in figure 9. The research questions addressed are marked.

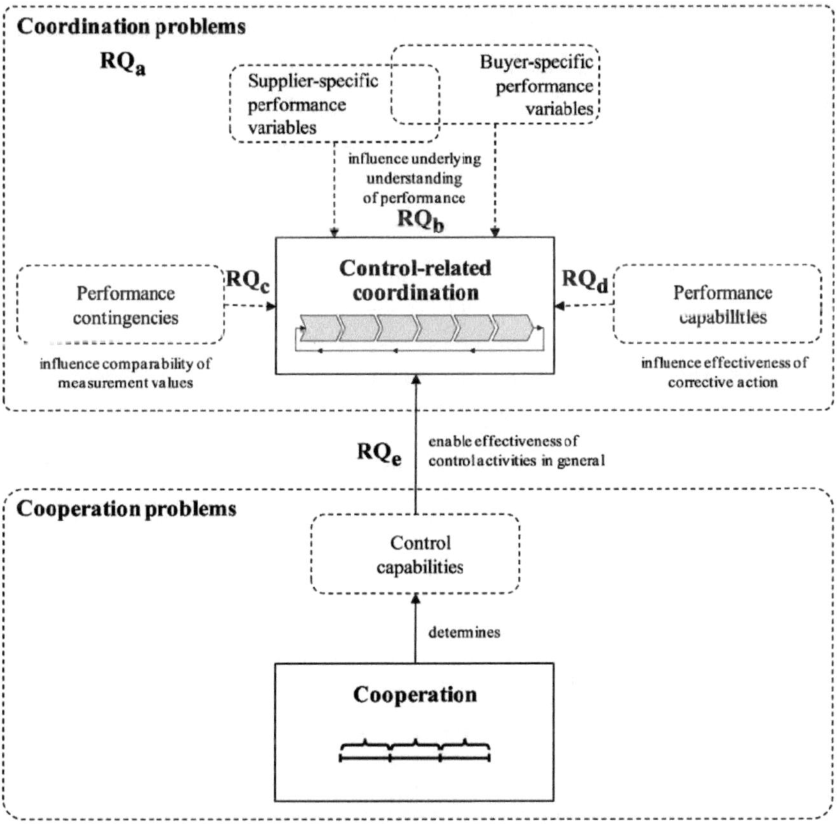

Figure 9: Research framework

3.6. Research subjects

This chapter briefly describes the research subjects of this thesis. As empirical analysis is split in three phases, research subjects are outlined separately as well. Also, the research subjects and the research questions addressed are situated within the theoretical framework.

1st phase – Development of a contingency-based framework for analysis

Phase I aims at answering RQ_a. It is intended to create a sound basis for the whole doctoral thesis by providing a sophisticated conceptual framework for analyzing the use of formal management control systems in supply chain relationships. This framework represents the conceptual part of the overall approach to analyzing and improving formal MCSs in BSRs. It consists of two basic elements: on one hand, a control process-oriented guideline is designed, helping to systematically identify and analyze the weak points of cross-company control activities. On the other hand, a conceptual model is developed that shows causal relationships between different types of performance control-related variables. The latter include indicators, contingencies and capabilities of interface-performance, as well as performance indicators for relational firm-performance. Research activities also addresses RQ_b, RQ_c and RQ_d, as they identify relevant variables and provides classification schemes for all three variable types.

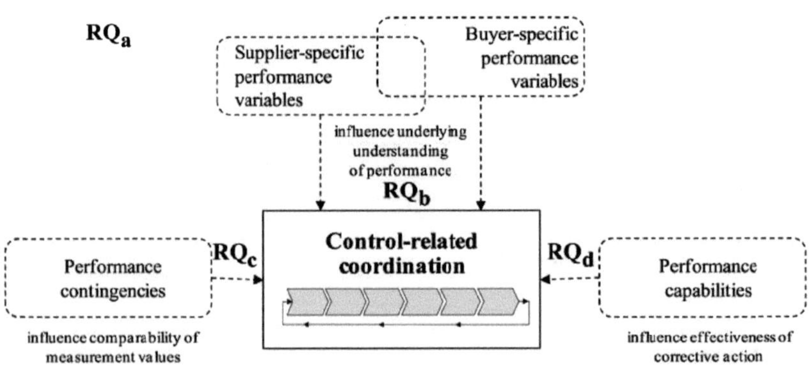

Figure 10: 1st phase of analysis in the context of the research framework

2nd phase – Analysis of environmental influences on comparability of reliability, flexibility and inventory efficiency

Phase II mainly addresses RQ_c by empirically analyzing the impact role of external performance-determining impacts on performance at the cross-company interface. In a first step, this requires identifying and systemizing relevant contingency variables, resulting from the relationship's nature and the environmental circumstances it faces. The second step consists of analyzing actual causal relationships between these contingency variables and performance at the buyer-supplier interface. As definition of interface-performance considers supplier's and buyer's perspective on the dyad, phase II activities also partly address RQ_a.

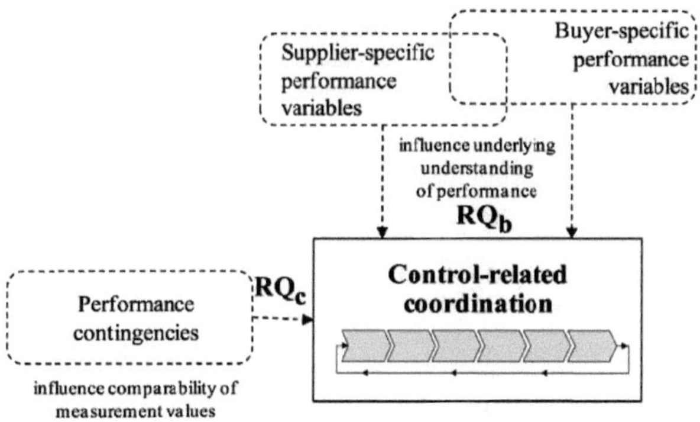

Figure 11: 2nd phase of analysis in the context of the research framework

3rd phase – Analysis of dyadic control activities' mediating role in delivery reliability and flexibility

Phase III attempts to answer RQ_e by investigating under which cooperative conditions cross-company control activities are most effective in order to derive implications for the design and use of formal MCSs in practice. Therefore, control capabilities are identified, causalities between them are analyzed, and the effect of formal control activities on interface-performance is empirically determined. In line with the second analysis phase, special emphasis is put on critically assessing the idea and potential of unbiased formal performance control in BSRs by also analyzing the role of perspective (buyer vs. supplier) for the design and use of MCSs.

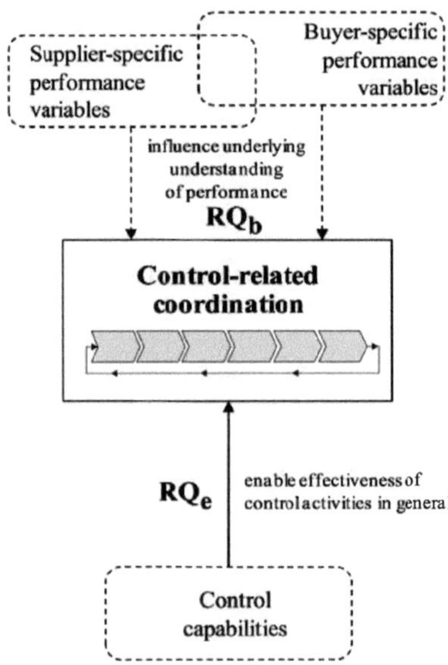

Figure 12: 3rd phase of analysis in the context of the research framework

4. Research design and positioning of research

This chapter describes the design of the research project by outlining the basic methodologies applied (chapter 4.2) and the underlying theories (chapter 4.3). The description of the research design will be embedded in the process of classifying the research project's scientific-theoretical features, which terminates in a meta-methodological categorization (chapter 4.4). Theoretical fundamentals, connecting theory, methodology and meta-methodology are provided in chapter 4.1.

4.1. Theoretical fundamentals – The three levels of scientific research

"The choice of the research design is of great importance as it influences all the outcomes of the study" (Delbert et al.: 18). In general, research design can be understood as a blueprint for research activities to address the identified research questions (Blanche et al., 2006: 35). This covers methodological aspects, such as method selection and data gathering, as well as the identification of suitable theories serving as a rigorous basis for the research (Delbert et al., 2002: 18).[17] Strongly connected to characterizing a research project's design is the aspect of positioning research within scientific theory. However, scientific-theoretical positioning is of a more generic nature, as it is intended to describe the initial understanding of research to better assess the contribution of research findings (Schanz, 1990: 173). Drawing on existing approaches from Scherer (1999: 4) and Kirsch (1998: 281), Hofmann (2004: 11) discriminates three levels of scientific research, each building on one another and addressing specific aspects of research: the theoretical, the methodological and the meta-methodological level. The basic characteristics of the three levels and the relationships between them can be illustrated as follows:

[17] In their handbook of research design, Delbert at al. (2002: 18) provide a list of relevant dimensions of the research design that need to considered throughout the complete research process.

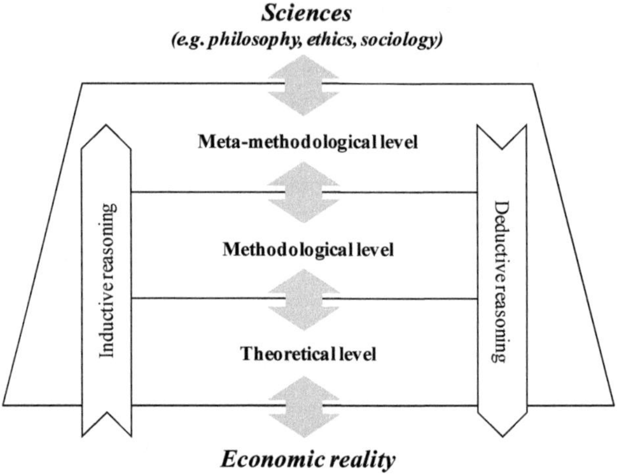

Figure 13: The three levels of scientific research

Due to the generic character of the approach, it can be considered well-suitable to classifying this research project and will thus serve as a basis for the following discussion. It covers design-related aspects such as methodological and theoretical features, and extends the scope to a meta-methodological level.

Thus, the discussion of the research design, applied in this thesis, will be embedded in the process of positioning the research project within scientific theory.

To characterize research simultaneously from both a design-related as well as a scientific-theoretical point of view, it is required to comprehensively address elements of all three levels. The levels can be further specified as follows:

- Theoretical level: This level categorizes research activities in terms of underlying scientific theories. Scientific theories represent consistent descriptions of economical models, applied concepts and instruments

(Hofmann, 2004: 18). As shown in chapter 4.2, deployment of theories is strongly related to the problem context of the phenomenon under investigation. Depending on the identified issues to be addressed by research, either a single- or multi-dimensional theoretical approach can be favorable. If several theories are adopted, two different approaches exist: a pluralistic one, applying several theories independently from each other, and an eclectic one, combining aspects from different theories (Kirsch, 1990: 114).

- Methodological level: Research methodology can be classified in different ways, for instance, according to the data gathering technique, analysis methods and the immediate purpose of the research (Sachan and Datta, 2005: 664). These attributes can be understood as different dimensions, which – taken together – comprehensively characterize the basic methodological pattern of a research activity (Meredith et al., 1989: 305). This allows defining research paradigms which are "a set of methods that all exhibit the same pattern or element in common" (Meredith et al., 1989: 305).
- Meta-methodological level: This level categorizes the scholar's thinking by describing his/her philosophical perspective in terms of ontology, epistemology and human nature (Burell and Morgan, 1979: 1-3). Within the meta-methodological level fundamental attitudes of scientific research are expressed. Thus, it is influenced by basic sciences, like philosophy, ethics and sociology (Hofmann, 2004: 11). Existing frameworks for categorizing the meta-methodological nature of research activities show (e.g. Beged-Dov and Klein, 1970; Meredith et al., 1989) that it is directly connected to the methodological level.

Design-related features are examined in chapter 4.2 (underlying theories) and 4.3 (methods applied and empirical basis). Scientific-theoretical discussion of meta-methodological aspects takes place in chapter 4.4.

4.2. Theoretical level

The aim of this doctoral thesis is to develop an integrated approach for analyzing and improving the design and use of formal MCSs in supply chain BSRs, primarily oriented to identifying and understanding interdependencies between performance capabilities, contingent performance-determining factors and performance variables. Also, knowledge on the conditions necessary for control to be executed effectively shall be gained by identifying relevant control capabilities and their influence on the effectiveness of control activities. In order to rigorously address stated objectives, research must be embedded in a theoretical context. Theories must be identified, suitable to describe the phenomenon of formal MCSs in BSRs.

When it comes to the use of formal performance control, *control theory* itself must by definition be considered as the dominant underlying theory. Control theory emerged in the 1940s and was strongly influenced by electrical engineering and mechanics (Aström and Murray, 2009: 32). It represents the basic idea of implementing decisions to guarantee that a device behaves as desired and "provides a rich collection of techniques to analyze the stability and dynamic response of complex systems and to place bounds on the behavior of such systems by analyzing the gains of linear and nonlinear operators that describe their components" (Aström and Murray, 2009: 18). Control techniques and mechanisms, in their basic meaning, are methodologies for regulating dynamic systems (Kirk, 1998: 3; Leigh, 2004: 1). Transferred to a managerial context, it can be understood as the control corporate-level managers exercise over other managers, i.e. midlevel managers, to ensure that organizational objectives and strategies are carried out (Fisher, 1995: 25).

However, it can be considered common sense that a formal control system which is applicable in all circumstances does not exist. Universal theoretical approaches explaining the use and effectiveness of formal MCSs do not hold in all settings (Fisher, 1995: 24). Each system must be tailored to the specific environment in which it is embedded (Otley and Berry, 1980: 233). Transferred to this research project, additional theories must be taken into account that help to explain the stated BSR-specific issues. In other words, supplementary theoretical approaches are required that are suitable for addressing coordination problems that occur in cross-company control activities between buyers and suppliers. Thus, an eclectic approach is appropriate to support research activities of this doctoral thesis, as several theories are adjoined (Kirsch, 1990: 114).

As the phenomenon relates particularly to the scientific disciplines of SCM, theories from this field will be considered in the following. Since it is not the intention to provide a comprehensive overview of existing theories, the following discussion will be limited to theories[18] that have been applied in either a BSR-specific or a control-related context. Theories will then be evaluated in their applicability to support the analysis of the designs and use of formal MCSs from a control-related perspective.

Buyer-supplier relationship-related theories in supply chain management

A wide range of theories applied in the context of BSRs can be found in literature, such as contingency theory (e.g. Ordanini and Rubera, 2008; Flynn et al., 2009), principal agency theory (e.g. Ketchen and Hult, 2007; Swink et al., 2007), relational view (e.g. Cousins et al., 2008; Paulraj et al., 2008), resource based view (e.g. Squire et al., 2009; Nakano, 2009), resource dependence theory (e.g. Eng, 2006; Paulraj and Chen, 2007) and transaction cost economics (e.g. Autry and Golicic, 2009; Sanders, 2008). However, suitability of these theories to address the stated problems must be assessed first. Several contributions to structuring and assessing theories in BSR-specific contexts can be found in literature. Stölzle (1999: 119), for instance, develops a set of criteria for systematic assessment of theoretical explanation patterns in BSRs. Focusing on transaction cost economics, agency theory, resource dependence theory, the IMP interaction approach, network theory and game theory, the author comes to the conclusion that in particular transaction cost economics, agency theory and game theory are (at least in parts[19]) suitable for supporting design and configuration of

[18] It may be the case that some of the discussed theoretical approaches do not meet the requirements of being a 'theory' in a strict scientific understanding. These approaches can be understood as, what Stölzle (1999: 5) calls 'theoretical explanation patterns'. As distinction is not crucial to the subsequent discussion, these patterns will be subsumed under the term 'theory' for reasons of simplicity.

[19] Stating that only transaction cost economics completely meets the defined criteria, Stölzle (1999: 129) stresses the need for also assessing the integration potential of the remaining patterns.

BSRs. However, game theory is found to have only a very limited adaptability to the research subject 'BSR' as the inter-organizational context is not considered in an adequate manner (Stölzle, 1999: 128). Accordingly, games theories will not be considered in the following; on the other hand, agency theory and transaction economics are, in principle, to be considered suitable. This is basically in line with Halldórsson et al. (2007: 291). Analyzing transaction cost economics, agency theory, network theory and resource-based view in the context of inter-firm relationships, the authors stress the general importance of all of the four theories and conclude that there is not a single ultimate theory and suggest that "depending on the concrete situation, one can choose one theory as the dominant explanatory theory, and then complement it with one or several of the other theoretical perspectives" (Halldórsson et al., 2007: 284). One basic finding consists in the recognition that the resource-based view complements transaction cost economics "by considering the resources, capabilities, and competencies both inside the individual firm and in the linkages between the firms in a supply chain" (Halldórsson et al., 2007: 291). As a resource-based view might be useful in the discussion of formal MCSs in BSRs as well, it will also be evaluated from a control-related perspective in the subsequent discussion. Another theory that appears basically suitable to explain the stated phenomenon is contingency theory. In its basic understanding, this theory states that companies adapt their structures in order to maintain fit with changing contextual factors in order to increase performance[20] (Donaldson, 2001: 23). As current contributions indicate, it has received increased attention in recent years; in particular in the empirical examination of performance-related topics. Analyzing interdependencies between SCM and the interactive performance between buyers and suppliers, Hsu (2005) applies a contingency-theoretical approach. He concludes that considering contingent impacts of environmental variables on performance outcomes in supply chains is of great importance (Hsu, 2005: 858). In summary, the following four theories will be assessed

[20] Referred to an intra-firm-specific use of contingency theory, "theoretical and practical contributions of this approach are achieved by (i) identifying important contingency variables that distinguish between contexts; (ii) grouping different contexts based on these contingency variables; and (iii) determining the most effective internal organization designs or responses in each major group" (Sousa and Voss, 2008: 698). Transferred to the cross-company-specific requirements of BSRs, this basic understanding of contingency theory's working principles will be adopted in the following.

from a control-related point of view: (1) transaction cost economics, (2) agency theory, (3) contingency theory and (4) resource-based view

Evaluation of the four identified theories from a control-related perspective

Transaction cost economics "offers a normative economic approach to determine the firm's boundaries and can be used to present efficiency as a motive for entering inter-organizational arrangements" (Williamson, 1996, cited in: Halldórsson et al., 2007: 287). The main addressed question can be formulated as "Which activities should be performed within the boundary of each firm, and which activities should be outsourced?" (Halldórsson et al., 2007: 287). This question is closely related to the cooperation problems, as transaction cost economics has argued that dependency from other companies increases with growing transaction-specific assets (Williamson, 1991: 282; Zenger and Hesterly, 1997: 219). Accordingly, transaction cost economics focuses on explaining the motives for companies to cooperate. However, its goal is not to explain the reasons and motives for cooperation problems, but to understand better the effect of existing cooperation problems on control activities' effectiveness. Concretely, the focus lies on analyzing causal relationships between control capabilities (resulting from these cooperation problems) and the effectiveness of formal control activities. Thus, these motives are not in the scope of this thesis and transaction cost economics cannot be considered appropriate for solving the stated issues.

The same restrictions apply to agency theory; it focuses on the explanation of reasons for a certain behavior that may result from issues, such as "asymmetric information between the principal and the agent, conflicting objectives, differences in risk aversion, outcome uncertainty, behavior based on self-interest, and bounded rationality" (Halldórsson et al., 2007: 287). In consequence, it also cannot be used to support this research project.

Contingency theory complements the previous theories and has argued that cooperating companies "need to establish division of labour, the modalities to carry out inter-organizational activities, the involvement required in the relationship, and the level of mutual satisfaction to be achieved" (Caglio and Ditillo, 2008: 891). Drawing a direct connection to coordination problems, Caglio and Ditillo (2008: 891) further specify this need by concluding that "resulting interdependencies require some form of coordination, and the joint actions should be aligned across organizational boundaries so as to guarantee a match between partners' interfaces." The potential of contingency-based approaches in the field of formal MCS in cross-company environments has also been recognized by other scholars. Chenhall (2007: 603), for instance, concludes that applicability of contingency theory for explaining the effectiveness of such control systems can be assumed. This is in line with Fisher (1995: 24), who states that examinations of control systems and mechanisms require the consideration of environmental circumstances. To conclude, the applicability of contingency theory to support the underlying research project can be fully assumed.

Resource-based view is the fourth theory under consideration. Focusing on resources and capabilities, this theory addresses appropriation problems such as the issue of ensuring "that the value of the joint output is perceived by the parties to be clearly and fairly distributed, and that the resources exchanged are not misappropriated by their counterparts" (Jarillo, 1988, cited in: Caglio and Ditillo, 2008: 891). Since misappropriation problems are out of the scope of this thesis, resource-based view can also not be considered suitable.

Combining control theory and contingency theory – An eclectic approach

Having discussed different theories, all more-or-less applicable to address BSR-related issues, it can be concluded that in particular contingency theory seems to be suitable in achieving the stated research objectives. In consequence, an eclectic approach combining control theory and contingency theory will be applied in the following. It represents the theoretical basis in each of the three phases of empirical analysis. Figure 14 gives an overview of the four theories in the context of the research framework.

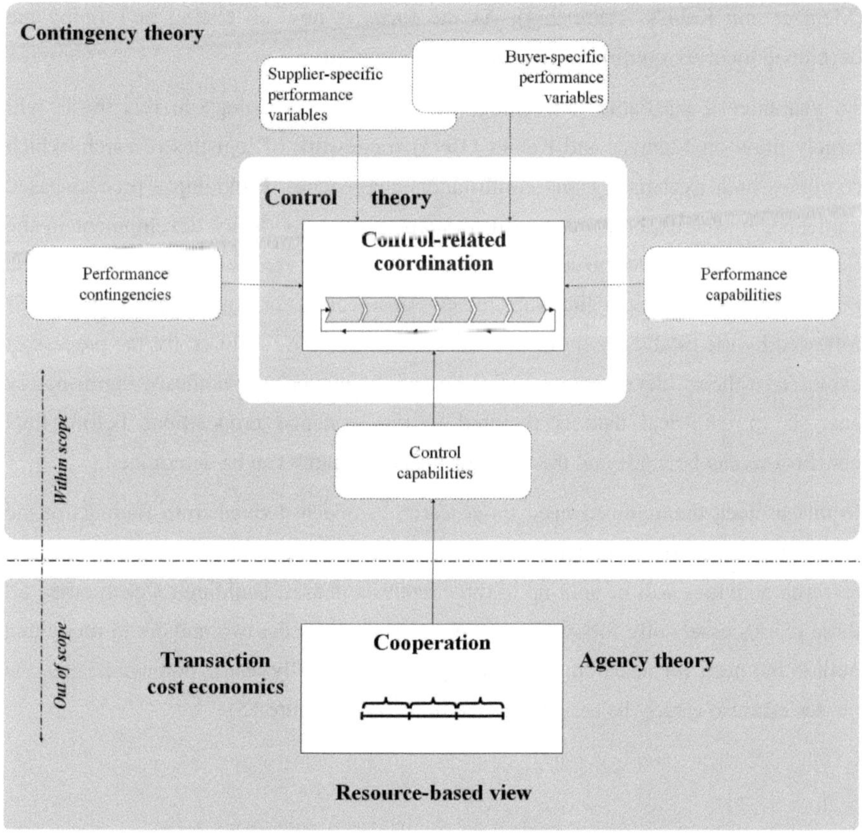

Figure 14: BSR-related theories in the context of the research framework.

4.3. Methodological level

Practical observation and additional literature review suggest that new propositions need to be developed to serve as a basis for further research activities, achieved by applying an explorative design (Kaplan, 1998: 97; Reason, 2006: 189). These theoretical constructs and assumed relationships then need to be addressed by further research in an iterative process to provide stronger evidence for initial findings

(Mentzer and Kahn's, 1995: 234). As the focus is now on testing or refining the developed theories, confirmatory methods are required.

To guarantee a verifiable proceeding, the applied methodology in this thesis will largely draw on Mentzer and Kahn's (1995) framework of logistics research, which combines both explanatory and confirmatory approaches. Providing a process-based guideline, it was explicitly designed to support rigorous theory development in the field. According to Mentzer and Kahn (1995: 234), research begins with 'idea generation' resulting from literature review, observation, or both. 'Idea generation' is followed by the establishment of 'substantive justification', required for the process of explorative theory development. After having developed a hypothesis, confirmatory analysis of empirical data is required to test assumed propositions before final conclusions can be made and the need for further research can be determined.

In this project, the assumed need for research has been derived from findings of the case study described in chapter 1.1. As the doctoral thesis is of cumulative nature, research activities will be split up in three analysis phases. Building on each other, all three phases essentially follow the process suggested by the two authors to prove and outline the need for research, and develop and empirically test hypotheses. Thus, the phases can also clearly be assigned to the framework (figure 15).

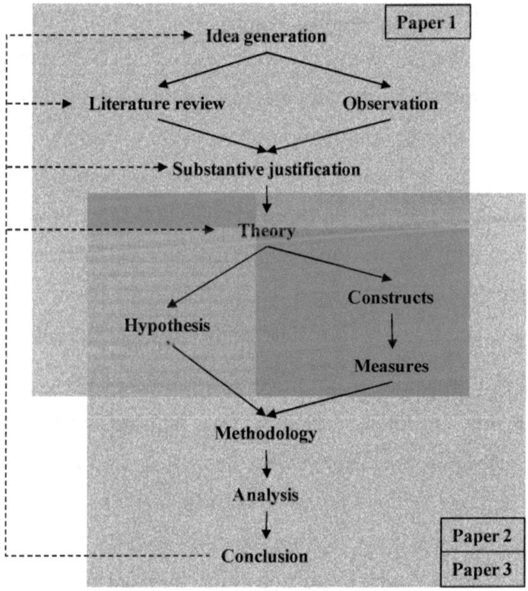

Figure 15: Conceptual proceeding in the research project

Characterization of the research project in terms of methodology

In the following methodology applied during the three analysis phases is briefly introduced. More detailed information about applied methods and the underlying empirical basis is provided in chapter 5, 6 and 7.

The applied methodology in phase I reflects the process steps from 'idea generation' to the development of theoretical propositions of Mentzer and Kahn's (1995: 233) suggested proceeding and basically represents the explorative part of the thesis. Substantiation is attained through several steps. A first review of relevant marketing, management accounting and SCM literature provides a historical overview of relevant contributions to the field. Also, it brings relevant research areas together to refine the research plan by strengthening scientific foundation and specifying the need for research for phases II and III. Based on these first findings, propositions for control-related interdependencies in supply chain relationships are derived and the conceptual causal model, as well as a guideline for analyzing formal MCSs is designed. An additional structured literature review of contributions to performance control in SCM-disciplines allows for specifying the model and structuring the field (Easterby-Smith et al., 2002: 159) by developing classification schemes for contingencies, capabilities and indicators of interface performance. The review process was based on the proposed proceeding from Halldórsson and Arlbjørn (2005: 111-113). Finally, in-depth semi-structured interviews with key informants of medium- and large-sized firms from the manufacturing industry are conducted to gather first empirical data about the propositions' validity and to assess practical applicability of the analysis framework.

Phase II research activities aim to improve assessment of performance in BSRs by identifying contingent influence factors on interface-performance that limit comparability of performance measurement values. Based on first theoretical findings, an exploratory literature review helps to identify eight appropriate performance indicators describing interface performance of BSRs. Furthermore, relevant contingencies are identified, which are not directly linked to transactional processes but significant in their impacts on interface-performance. Based on these findings, expected causal relationships between contingencies and performance are formulated and combined in a hypothesized model. Next, a conceptual contingency-based classification scheme for BSRs is developed and three specific BSR-types are defined. As subsequent empirical investigations focus on identifying differences between them, the BSR-types represent the basic unit of analysis. Several statistical methods are combined for confirmative analysis of the expected performance-determining impacts. First, mean comparison is done to show group-specific differences in interface-performance. Furthermore, BSRs within the same group are compared to identify relative causalities between the supplying and buying side of the same relationship type. Second, analysis of covariance (ANCOVA) is used to test impacts of contingencies for statistical significance, and to quantify their shares of variance explained. ANCOVA is selected for two reasons (Herrmann and Seilheimer, 2000: 267): first, the identified contingencies are expected to represent supplementary impacts of independent variables that lead to significant differences between the BSR-types. Second, selection of covariates is based on a reasonable suspicion about causal relations between outcome and predictor variables. Data collection for the statistical analysis is survey-based as recommended for statistical analysis (Meredith et al., 1989: 12). To follow the idea of analyzing the relationship from an unbiased point of view, as suggested by Caglio and Ditillo (2008: 885), the survey is based on two equally structured questionnaires. This way, both sides of the dyad can be considered and buyer- as well as supplier-specific KPIs are taken into account.

The third analysis phase focuses on the mediating role of cross-company control activities in systematically enhancing interface-performance in BSRs. To create a sophisticated theoretical basis, control capabilities are identified first by a broad review (Easterby-Smith et al., 2002: 159) of SCM and management accounting literature. Next, causalities between these capabilities and formal performance control activities in BSRs are formulated and brought together. The resulting hypothesized model then serves as a starting point for the empirical analysis. Structural equation modeling (SEM) is applied to empirically assess effectiveness of formal performance control activities on interface-performance in BSRs. SEM is selected for two reasons: first, the basic elements of the hypothesized model are represented by multi-dimensional constructs (Hardy and Bryman, 2004: 35). Second, SEM is required to simultaneously analyze multiple cause-and-effect relationships between these constructs (Shook et al., 2004: 397). For the same reasons mentioned in the previous paragraph, data collection occurs via a large-scaled survey based on two equally structured questionnaires to enable an unbiased dyadic perspective on interface-performance.

4.4. Meta-methodological level

Several widely accepted and still valid conceptual frameworks for categorizing research in terms of meta-methodology exist. These frameworks are usually tailored to specific research areas, such as the one of Beged-Dov and Klein (1970) classifying research in management science in terms of formalism or empiricism. Other frameworks can be found for research conducted in operations management (e.g. Chase, 1980; Meredith et al., 1989), business policy (e.g. Mitroff and Mason, 1984, cited in: Meredith et al., 1989: 305) or entrepreneurship (e.g. Paulin et al., 1982). This variety of approaches results from the fact that each scientific discipline usually has its own specific research traditions that in turn affect the methodological and theoretical level (Remenyi et al., 1998: 32; Weber, 2000: 23f.).

Inspired by Sachan and Datta (2005)[21], the framework of Meredith et al. (1989) will be applied to classify research activities of this doctoral thesis. This classification will then be used to describe the author's philosophical perspective in terms of ontology, epistemology and human nature.

One of the major advantages of the framework results from the fact that it directly connects methodological and meta-methodological attributes. Building on Mitroff and Mason (1984), the authors offer a matrix framework that enables meta-methodological categorization of research based on the underlying methodological principles in terms of information used and the nature of truth. Both dimensions are represented by continuums which enable a disjunctive assignment of the single research activities. The continuums range from natural to artificial information, respectively from a rational to an existential nature of truth; the matrix is illustrated in figure 16.

[21] Examining the state of logistics and SCM, Sachan and Datta (2005: 670), use the framework to categorize scientific contributions from a meta-methodological perspective. Accordingly, its applicability to classify this contribution to formal performance control in BSRs will be assumed as well.

Kind of information used (Natural ↔ Artificial); *Nature of truth* (Rational ↔ Existential)

	Direct observation of object reality	People's perception of object reality	Artificial reconstruction of object reality
Axiomatic			- Reason/Logic/Theorems - Normative modeling - Descriptive modeling
Logical positivist/ empiricist	- Field studies - Field experiments	- Structural interviewing - Survey research	- Prototyping - Simulation - Laboratory experiments
Interpretative	- Action research - case studies	- Historical analysis - Delphi - Intensive interviewing - Expert panels - Futures/Scenarios	- Conceptual modeling - Hermeneutics
Critical theory		- Introspective reflection	

Figure 16: A framework for classifying research methods in terms of meta-methodology.

The two dimensions are briefly introduced. Explanatory notes in the following two paragraphs draw on Meredith et al. (1989: 305).

The first dimension – the nature of truth – refers to the epistemological structure of the research activities, also describing benefits and limitations of the philosophical approach applied to generate knowledge. The spectrum ranges from rationalism, conforming to the traditional deductive approach by considering "formal structure and pure logic as the ultimate measure of truth" (Meredith et al., 1989: 305), to existentialism, relating to the traditional inductive approach by pretending "that knowledge is acquired through the human process of interacting with the environment" (Meredith et al., 1989: 305). This spectrum covers four generic perspectives that structure the research depending on their degree of formalism; these are axiomatic, logical positivist/empiricist, interpretive, and critical theory. The most formal perspective, an axiomatic one, represents the theorem-proof world of research; it is based on formal procedures, consensus and consistency of goals. The other extreme represents the viewpoint of critical theory, attempting to place knowledge in a wider context of its contribution to social evolution.

The second dimension – kind of information used – categorizes the information that is used in the research. Empiricism, on the one hand, requires 'natural' information consisting of concrete and objective data. Subjectivism, on the other hand, gains knowledge from interpretation and artificial reconstruction of reality. Thus, this spectrum reflects the researcher's perception of reality which can be split into three categories: object reality, people's perceptions of object reality, and artificial reconstruction of object reality. While object reality relates to a direct observation of a phenomenon, artificial reconstruction of object reality recasts the object reality "into another form that is more appropriate for testing and experimentation, such as analytical models, computer simulations, or information construct" (Meredith et al., 1989: 308). However, the information used in artificial reconstruction is usually drawn from one of the two less artificial categories of information. Between the two ends of the continuum, a third category is defined, reflecting the kind of information that is gained by people's perceptions of object reality.

Characterization of the research project in terms of meta-methodology

In order to characterize the research activities' meta-methodological nature, the methods applied in the different research phases, as described in chapter 4.3, must be treated separately. Then findings can be harmonized and the research project can be classified as a whole.

Although, it is not included in the following, the case study that was undertaken to assess the practical relevance of the research project (as described in chapter 1.1) is categorized as well as it represents the first element of this research project, during which research ideas were generated[22] through observation of a real-life phenomenon. As operations were studied in their natural settings and knowledge can be gained from

[22] This equals the first level of Mentzer and Kahn's procedure of sophisticated research (1995: 233).

the involved companies' data (Meredith et al., 1989: 311), the case study represents a direct form of observation. Also, a lot of 'how' and 'why' questions existed in this early phase of research. Accordingly, an interpretative perspective was taken to describe the identified issues and to develop concepts to address them.

In the first phase the identified issues were picked up and an integrated framework for analysis of formal MCSs in BSRs was developed. This required an intensive literature review to acquire an overview of the current state of research in the relevant scientific disciplines. Findings were used to structure the field and to build the framework for analyzing formal MCSs in BSRs. As meta-analysis was used to formulate a more integrated perspective of the phenomenon of formal MCSs in BSRs, this procedure can be understood as a conceptual modeling; showing an interpretative nature and having a more existential than rational perception of object reality (Meredith et al., 1989: 316). Next, semi-structured interviews with responsible managers helped in gathering first empirical evidence and in testing propositions of the conceptual framework. In a first part, a fixed format was applied for the interviews, meaning that questions referred to standardized scales (e.g. Likert scales) and were the same for all respondents. In the second part, open questions were used to complete the picture and to become aware of additional contentious issues in practice. Thus, structured and unstructured methods were applied to gain data from people's perceptions of object reality. The former falls into the logical positivist/empiricist cell (Meredith et al., 1989: 311), the latter into the interpretative one (Meredith et al., 1989: 312).

In phase II and III, the same three methods were applied to empirically assess the impact of contingencies on comparability of performance values in BSRs on the one hand (phase II) and to analyze causalities between control capabilities to enhance effectiveness of cross-company control activities on the other hand (phase III). First, a conceptual model was developed that can be classified in the same way as the framework for analysis in the first step. Second, a survey was conducted to gather the required data, based on people's perceptions of object reality. Due to the high rationality of the survey technique, the nature of truth of this method can be assigned to the positivist/empiricist cell (Meredith et al., 1989: 312). However, as objective performance data (e.g. delivery reliability ratio, average delivery time) was collected as well, the survey also included objective data originating from object reality. Third, statistical analysis was used next to empirically assess propositions of the conceptual model, again showing an artificial perspective on object reality.

4.5. Summary and positioning of research within scientific theory

In summary, it must be stated that research activities of the doctoral thesis at hand cannot be clearly assigned to one cell of Meredith et al.'s (1989) framework. However, mainly the logical positivist/empiricist and the interpretative perspective were used in the applied research methods. Also there is a strong tendency to the artificial viewpoint of object reality, as conceptual modeling is part of all three phases of empirical analysis. Although the logical positivist/empiricist perspective assumes "that the phenomenon under study can be isolated from the context in which it occurs" (Meredith et al., 1989: 306), it is the author's opinion that contextual conditions must be considered in the best possible way. Based on these classifications, the ontological and epistemological perspective taken in this doctoral thesis, as well as the perception of human nature, can be described as follows:

- Ontological perspective: Reality is understood as a contextual field of information (Morgan and Smircich, 1980: 496). Though being assumed existent and tangible (Cherryholmes, 1992: 14), an objective perception of this reality in the sense of truth "is impossible to grasp and thus is operationalized through the meaning that exists within the scientific community and its conventions" (Howe, 1988, cited: in Peters 2010: 10). Accordingly, a pragmatist position is taken. This understanding, which takes a medium stance between normalism and realism, originates from the understanding that business research is initiated by a problem identified in practice and supported by theoretical reasoning.

- Epistemological perspective: The underlying ontological position calls for epistemologies that emphasize the importance of understanding contexts in a holistic manner (Morgan, 1979, cited in: Morgan and Smircich, 1980: 496).

Accordingly, the thesis takes an epistemological perspective that is also concerned with the mapping of contexts and "facilitating understanding of the patterns of systemic relationships inherent in the ecological nature of those contexts"(Morgan and Smircich, 1980: 496). Thus, a strictly positivist perception is not appropriate and a medium stance between positivism and anti-positivism must be taken (Burrell and Morgan, 1979: 5).

- Perception of the human nature: Although it is assumed that humans are, in principal, free-willed and able to influence their environment, it is also expected it that human beings are, at least in parts, determined by environmental factors. Humans and the world within they act are expected to evolve together and "relationships are relative rather than fixed and real"(Morgan and Smircich, 1980: 496). Thus, humans are considered being adaptors in an interactive relationship with the environment, influencing as well as being influenced by their environment (Morgan and Smircich, 1980: 495).

PART II

Theory building & empirical analysis

5. Performance-control in buyer-supplier relationships: Development of a contingency-based framework for analysis

5.1. Current situation and challenges

Globalization has transformed the world into a highly integrated global market place, resulting in continuously growing customer orientation, shorter product life cycles and increasing competiveness. Companies deal with buyers and suppliers from different countries (Giunipero et al., 2008) and various functional activities have transcended companies' boundaries (Hsu, 2005). To compete in such a highly dynamic environment, enterprises have been - and are - continuously forced to find new ways of making business processes more flexible, reliable and responsive at a minimum total cost level, (Perea et al., 2000). One attempt to meet this challenge is to elevate inter-company competition to inter-supply chain competition (Lamber and Cooper, 2000; Tan, 2001).

Giunipero et al. (2008), also emphasize the relevance of performance control in an inter-firm context in their analytical review of existing trends and gaps in supply chain research. Analyzing ten years of supply chain management (SCM) literature, the authors list a number of sources (e.g. Gunasekaran et al., 2001; Lambert et al., 1998), confirming that company performance and competitive advantage are directly linked to supply chain performance. Giunipero et al. (2008) conclude that increased attention in the SCM community is driven by performance-oriented needs, as SCM is considered central to value generation in today's companies. Christopher (2005) and Meira et al. (2010) even call SCM one of the most powerful ways to enhance inter-organizational profit. Various efforts have been made to meet this challenge in the past, such as building strong alliances (McCutcheon and Stuart, 2000).

Although the term 'chain' in SCM is not always considered adequate, due to the network character of today's business environment (Meira et al., 2010, 151), it is widely accepted that processes, such as coordination and cooperation, play a decisive role in SCM competiveness, especially at the interface between buyers and suppliers.

Efficient and effective management of buyer-supplier relationships (BSRs): e.g. strengthening coordination and cooperation, has become a critical success factor in securing competition and improving involved companies' financial and operational performance (e.g. Ballou et al., 2000; Chenhall, 2005; Foggin and Mentzer, 2004; Hsu, 2005; Li et al., 2006; O'Toole and Donaldson 2002; Presutti and Mawhinney, 2007; Ross et al., 2009). Thus, performance management in companies cannot be achieved without paying attention to cross-company processes at the BSRs interface, due to their significant impact on a company's overall performance. Managing these relationships is an essential part of performance management and is one of today's biggest challenges for all kinds of supply chains.

In consequence, the following investigation will strictly refer to performance control in BSRs. This means that a dyadic perspective on single industrial business relationships between a buying and a supplying company will be taken. However, as BSRs in supply chains can be seen as an elementary trans-sectional component of SCM in general, the following research will draw on SCM literature where it is necessary. In these cases SCM-specific findings will be narrowed down again to BSR-specific needs.

The question of how to measure and control this kind of inter-firm performance is central to the discussion of BSRs performance management and the need for adequate management accounting tools has been formulated. Dwyer et al. (1987), for instance, pointed out the general importance of carefully defining and measuring exchange activities and processes. In line with this, Mouritsen et al. (2001) concluded that management controls were essential for developing systematic supplier relations. Also focusing on strategic supply relationships, Mahama (2006) stressed the suitability of MCS in fostering cooperation among exchange participants and enhancing performance. Assessing the applicability of MCS for performance management in BSRs, further explanation about the general nature of MCS is necessary.

Originating from Anthony's (1965, cited in: Otley, 1999) framework for 'management planning and control systems', MCS in general have been defined in many ways and used for varying purposes (Mahama, 2006). After more than four decades of MCS research, there is a wide range of MCS definitions in management accounting literature (Ferreira and Otley, 2009; Langfield-Smith, 2007), which often causes difficulties in comparing and integrating existing studies (Fisher, 1995). Recognizing the diversity of definitions, several distributions have been made aiming strictly at defining and classifying control systems (e.g. Brown, 2005; Green and Welsh, 1988; Malmi and Brown, 2008). In field literature, at least two basic types of control exist: control of subordinates and so-called formal control (Giglioni and Bedeian, 1974). According to the authors' understanding, direction of personnel by firm structure, firm culture and human resources policies differs from this second type of formal control mechanism, measuring performance and comparing it to predetermined standards. Numerous researchers have contributed to this view (e.g. Ansari, 1977; Eisenhardt, 1985; Govindarajan and Fisher, 1995).

Even though this classification has been refined and elaborated in recent years (e.g. Brown, 2005; Malmi and Brown, 2008), the basic distinction between formal and non-formal MCSs can still be identified within these typologies. Mentioned continuously in contributions to the field (e.g. Ferreira and Otley, 2009; Mahama, 2006), its wide acceptance and strong relevance in the management accounting community is obvious. Due to strong emphasis on performance control in the following analysis, focus will be narrowed down to formal MCSs; control of subordinates will not be addressed.

Based on the identified relevance of formal MCS for performance control in supply chain BSR, the following research activities aim primarily to develop a framework for the analysis of formal and BSR-specific MCSs (BSR-MCSs).

The following questions must be answered: what basic requirements must the framework meet? Can this study draw on suitable existing frameworks and approaches? Is there a need for further research? To answer these questions, this investigation follows a conceptual research method developed by McCutcheon and Meredith (1993). It is organized as follows: in section 5.2, contributions to performance-related issues in supply chain relationships will be analyzed to identify basic requirements for our framework. Moreover, existing frameworks and approaches will be critically assessed to ascertain whether they meet the identified requirements, and the need for research will be outlined. Section 5.3 describes the research methodology applied, followed by the actual development of the framework for analyzing BSR-MCS in section 5.4. The framework is designed to support academics by providing a research tool consisting of two basis parts: (1) a control process-oriented guideline on how to systematically identify and analyze weak points of performance control activities, and (2) a conceptual model bringing control processes and performance determinants in supply chains together in a systematic manner. Section 5.5 helps to assess practical relevance of theoretical findings; implications for future research are derived. The chapter closes with a brief conclusion and an outlook for future research activities in section 5.6.

5.2. Theory development

BSRs have been subject to academic research in different disciplines, such as marketing, SCM (Ross et al., 2009) and management accounting (Meira et al., 2010). Regarding performance-related topics in BSRs, the latter two are of particular importance. As subsequent reviews will show, the number of investigations has been continuously increasing in both disciplines over the last two decades. Thus, developing an integrated framework for analyzing formal BSR-MCSs from a supply chain perspective requires knowledge from both research streams to achieve scientific foundation for, and practical applicability of, the framework. But before these can be discussed, a theoretical foundation in terms of performance control in BSRs must be provided in order to identify the requirements for the framework.

5.2.1. Performance control in buyer-supplier relationships

Numerous performance-related topic investigations in BSRs can be found in scientific literature. Depending on the type of relationship and academic context, relational performance has been defined and actualized in many different ways (O'Toole and Donaldson, 2002). Entering the discussion on BSR-specific performance, a basic distinction needs to be made between performance capabilities and performance indicators, as Klein et al. (2007) did in their analysis of logistics relationships in supply chains. Capabilities, on one hand, reflect potential to achieve performance and can thus be understood as performance-limiting factors. Performance indicators, on the other hand, are crucial to the discussion of performance control. Moreover, the role of environmental circumstances (*contingencies*) must be discussed due to their performance-determining influence. All three aspects will be analyzed extensively before consequences of our framework are derived.

Performance in buyer-supplier relationships

Relationship-specific performance, basically defined, is a measurement for success of inter-firm relationships (Beugelsdijk et al., 2009; Bucklin and Sengupta, 1993; Gaski and Nevin, 1985; Kumar et al., 1992; LaBahn and Harich, 1997) and can be described as "an affective state resulting from the appraisal of all aspects of a firm's working relationship with another firm" (Anderson and Narus, 1990, p. 45). LaBahn and Harich (1997) and Mohr et al. (1996) went into further detail and defined relationship-specific performance as the degree to which the relationship is perceived to be productive and worthwhile, whereas Straub et al. (2004) called it the magnitude of outputs realized by two independent companies with recurring business exchange. These general definitions leave much room for interpretation (Beugelsdijk et al., 2009) and need further clarification about selection of performance indicators.

In terms of BSRs, two basic, mutually exclusive types of performance indicators can be distinguished (O'Toole and Donaldson, 2002). The first one focuses on the relationship itself, directly analyzing efficiency and effectiveness of relational processes and activities such as cross-company coordination and information sharing. These indicators reflect operational performance at the interface between two companies. Determined by these interface processes and the nature of the collaboration, indicators of the second type then abstract from the transactional level, and refer to firm-specific performance outcomes of both companies involved, by measuring the change in intra-firm-performance resulting from the relationship. The various impacts of BSRs on sales (Kalwani and Narayandas, 1995), inventory (Dyer, 1996) and profitability (Evans and Laskin, 1994) are some of these indicators (a more sophisticated overview can be found in O'Toole's and Donaldson's (2002) review of empirical studies on relational performance). Both types of indicators are thus directly linked to each other, as the firm-specific performance outcome (type one) results from efficiency and effectiveness of processes and activities at the inter-organizational buyer-supplier interface (type two). According to this differentiation and due to their mutually exclusive nature, *'interface-performance'* and *'relational firm-performance'* will be differentiated in the following.

It is important to note that performance assessment of the same relationship can differ, depending on which of the two companies is asked. Evaluating collaboration from a dyadic upstream perspective, the buying firm will probably not take the supplier's economical success into consideration, as it focuses on its own economical situation. The corresponding supplier takes the opposite view. In contrast, assessments of interface-performance by both parties refer to the same processes and activities and can thus be considered equal. In consequence, two assessments of relational firm-performance and one interface-performance for each BSR dyad exist and need to be distinguished. The following definitions explain the two different types of performance and will serve as a basis for our framework of analysis:

> *Relational firm-performance of BSRs in supply chains (type one) is a measurement for company-specific performance yield resulting from the relationship. Determined by the nature of the actual relational processes and activities, it quantifies the impact of BSRs on firm-performance of the two involved companies. Relational firm-performance, as defined by the buying and supplying company, will differ.*
>
> *Interface-performance of BSRs in supply chains (type two) is a measurement for the success of all relational processes at the interface between a buyer and its supplier. It will be defined by indicators measuring the efficiency and effectiveness of cross-company operations and cooperation activities.*

Interface-performance is equal for both the buying and the supplying company.

Performance capabilities in buyer-supplier relationships

In SCM, capabilities represent the potential of a company to identify, utilize and align internal and external resources and information to support supply chain activities (Amit and Schoemaker, 1993; Bharadwaj, 2000; Collis, 1994), as well as responding to environmental changes (Teece et al., 1997). Wu et al. (2006) built on this understanding and described them as "the ability to perform cross-functional as well as inter-organizational activities which are required in supply chain management." (p. 494). Analyzing the influence of supply chain capabilities on firm-performance, the authors conceptualize them as a second-order construct encompassing different capability dimensions. Information exchange capabilities, for instance, refer to supply chain partners' ability to efficiently and effectively share knowledge, whereas coordination capabilities mainly address transaction-related activities. Narrowing the focus from SCM to BSR by excluding purely intra-company-related activities, this understanding can be directly adapted and BSR-specific performance capabilities can be used to measure the potential to successfully organize transactional processes between buyer and supplier. Depending on the nature of the relationship, both partners involved need to develop different capabilities. In order to achieve the desired outcome, they need to, for instance, enable efficient and effective information sharing and process integration (Day, 2000). As an example, purely transactional exchanges require capabilities mainly related to coordination of physical delivery, whereas collaborative exchanges also require technology and process integration capabilities (Klein et al., 2007).

Contingencies for performance in buyer-supplier relationships

Another important analysis framework feature arises from the fact that a control system applicable in all circumstances does not exist. Each system must be tailored to the specific circumstances the company faces, contingent to the organization's environment (Fisher, 1995; Otley and Berry, 1980). Categorizing contingency research on MCSs, Fisher (1995) also stated that universal approaches to research on control systems design do not hold in all settings and companies, and thus cannot completely explain use and effectiveness. In his opinion, contingency-based frameworks should be the primary tools to address this deficit, as they also consider the role of interactions between contingent and control factors. Analyzing findings from more than 25 years of contingency-based studies on MCSs, Chenhall (2007) claimed that importance and applicability of this theory, especially for explaining the effectiveness of such control systems, is still proven.

Due to its generic nature, contingency theory has been a subject of research in many other management disciplines as well and, as current publications show, performance-related topics still seem to receive increased attention. Sousa and Voss (2008), for instance, analyzed the effect of contingencies on performance outcomes in operations management practices, while Cho and Lee (2005) conducted a study on contingency factors affecting R&D performance measurement. Delery and Doty (1996), in contrast, took a contingency-based perspective in strategic human resource management. Despite the potential importance of contingency-based research on performance control in general, it still can be considered under-developed in SCM in general (Buttermann et al., 2008). One of the few exceptions is Hsu's (2005) case study-based examination of interdependencies between SCM and the interactive performance between buyers and suppliers. Referring to the heterogeneous character of supply chains, he stressed the need to consider the contingent impacts of environmental variables on performance outcomes in supply chains.

Although, very little work exists applying contingency-theory to performance control in BSRs on the SCM side, we adopt Fisher's (1995) thesis that analyzing control systems and mechanisms cannot take place without considering environmental circumstances. Consequently, a framework for analyzing such systems must allow for identification of contingent performance-determining factors.

Summary

Developing the framework for this research phase, it is clear that integrated performance control in BSRs requires focusing not only on interface-performance but also paying attention to relationship capabilities and their limiting role on performance as well as the performance-determining impact of contingencies. Interdependencies between interface-performance, relational firm-performance and firm-performance need to be considered carefully as well. Based on these definitions and brought into a broader context, the resulting causal relationships and interdependencies are summarized in figure 17, integrating BSR-specific capabilities and contingencies' as well as both types of BSR-related.

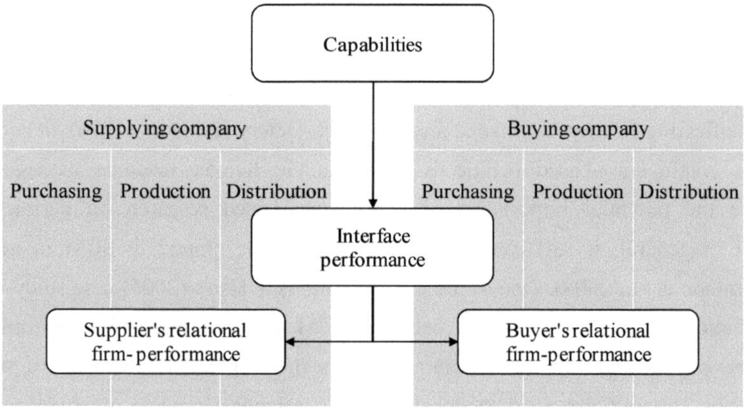

Figure 17: Interdependencies between capabilities, relational firm-performance (type one) and interface-performance (type two) in BSRs

After identifying issues to be addressed by our framework from an SCM perspective, the procedure needs to be repeated with a focus on control-related issues to complete the picture. As control in economics can be considered an essential part of management accounting, the literature basis for the following investigation will be extended to this research stream, to identify requirements resulting from a control perspective. Then, relevant material from both literature streams, SCM and management accounting, will be harmonized.

5.2.2. **Formal management control systems**

In this paragraph, formal MCS – and what constitutes them – will be discussed, and their potential role in inter-firm performance management will be analyzed. This is necessary to identify further requirements refer mainly to management accounting literature. To get a comprehensive overview of recent research on the use of such formal MCS in BSR in supply chains, recent literature reviews on MCS in inter-firm relationships will be analyzed in terms of supply chain-specific content.

For a formal definition of MCSs, this investigation will basically use Fisher's (1995) idea that a formal control system must be cybernetic (drawing on contributions from Giglioni and Bedeian (1974), Green and Welsh (1988) as well as Otley and Berry (1980)). Transferred to a BSR-specific context, formal MCSs can be defined as a cybernetic feedback process consisting of three basic steps:

> *First, performance standards for relevant activities and processes at the buyer-supplier interface are set reflecting the company's planned targets (1). Actual interface-performance is then measured and compared to these targets to identify variances and optimization potentials (2). Last, appropriate corrective action is taken addressing the identified performance issues (3) and the control loop starts again from the beginning.*

Following this process, the structure of our framework will reflect this feedback process by separately addressing the three sub-processes. Further literature review will also be limited to cybernetic control processes.

In recent years, several reviews with different perspectives on MCS in inter-firm relationships have been made in management accounting literature, not only to summarize, organize and classify the existing publications, but also to identify limitations, inconsistencies and indications for future research (e.g. Caglio and Ditillo,

2008; Håkansson and Lind, 2007; Meira et al., 2010). Analyzing these reviews, two of them turned out to be particularly suitable for this investigation and will be presented in more detail. The first, conducted by Meira et al. (2010) distinguishes between different types of inter-firm relationships, namely 'supply chain relations', 'outsourcing' and 'others' including joint ventures and unspecified further relationships. The second review, by Caglio and Distillio (2008), has been selected due to its functional view classifying papers by their breadth of the control solution. The typology they developed ranges from specific cost and accounting techniques, such as total cost of ownership, value chain analysis, target costing and open book accounting, up to more general management control mechanisms and so-called control archetypes, representing a combination of control mechanisms. Combining the two reviews and narrowing down the focus to supply chain relationships (in the first case) and performance-related management control mechanisms (in the second case) allows for directly identification of relevant literature on cybernetic performance control issues in BSR within supply chains. Accordingly, publications dealing only with specific control techniques (e.g. Mouritsen et al., 2001; Dekker, 2003) have been excluded. A list of relevant papers remaining, including a brief description of content and main findings, is given in table 2.

Reviewing these contributions and comparing them to our findings from SCM literature, one particular new implication for our framework could be derived. Although, both research streams deal with related performance issues, for instance by analyzing the role of coordination and cooperation, SCM literature is limited to measuring performance and analyzing interdependencies between performance elements, whereas management accounting also stresses the importance of performance evaluation and the need for taking corrective action to increase performance. A comprehensive framework for analysis thus needs to give clear advice on performance assessment and on how to derive implications for selecting and implementing appropriate countermeasures.

Table 2: Excerpt of relevant management accounting literature on performance control in supply chain relationships

Author	Contribution and findings
Free (2008)	Free (2008) presented a framework for conceptualizing the relationship between accounting and inter-organizational trust, based on an analysis of supply chain relationships in the UK retail industry. Findings: The role of trust in inter-firm relationships has not yet been explored in a satisfying manner, and trust as an explanatory variable has to be analyzed critically as it can be overestimated under certain circumstances. In addition, there should be put emphasis on examining the relationships between accounting, trust and trustworthiness.
Mahama (2006)	Mahama (2006) investigated the impact of two management control systems (performance measurement systems and socialization processes) on four different dimensions of cooperation (information-sharing, problem-solving, adaptability to changes, restraint from the use of power) in strategic supply relationships. Findings: There is a positive correlation between performance measurement systems and all four types of cooperation, whereas socialization processes were only linked to one type, namely information-sharing. Cooperation, in turn, is positively related to performance.
Coletti et al. (2005)	Coletti et al. (2005) investigated the effects of control on trust and cooperation in collaborative relationships by conducting two experiments. Findings: Control systems can enhance the level of trust and that increased trust can have a positive effect on the future level of cooperation between the companies Moreover, control-induced trust can also result in a growing financial benefit for the partners.
Dekker (2004)	Dekker (2004) studied the use of formal control mechanisms for managing appropriation concerns and the coordination of tasks, also considering interrelationships with informal (trust-based) mechanisms. Results are based on the analysis of strategic alliance between a buyer and supplier of railway safety equipment. Findings: The relationship is influenced by coordination requirements and the social context of the relationship, and management controls improve trust for partners.
Baiman and Rajan (2002)	Baiman and Rajan (2002) discussed incentive issues and managerial accounting in inter-firm relationships with a focus on buyer-supplier transactions. Findings: In line with Coletti et al. (2005), the authors come to the conclusion that the buyer can weaken supplier's ex ante investment incentives by expropriating surplus. Thus, buyer and supplier have unequal relative bargaining powers. By introducing control mechanisms that increase the level of information sharing among partners these issues can be addressed as the involved companies become more cooperative and trustworthy.
Tomkins (2001)	Tomkins (2001) analyzed concepts that relate to the needs for information in inter-firm relationships, alliances and networks, with a focus on the interaction between trust and information. Findings: The effectiveness of the use of information systems depends on the level of trust between the companies.
Seal et al. (1999)	Seal et al (1999) examined management accounting systems and their role in facilitating relationships between manufacturing companies by using a case. Findings: Cost data sharing is important for inter-firm negotiations, and accounting is essential for the development of trust.
Frances and Garnsey (1996)	This study that was conducted by Frances in Garnsey in 1996 highlighted the role of accounting information in UK supermarket supply chain relations. Findings: There are asymmetrical power relations, as supermarkets dominate relationships with their suppliers because of their buying power and their control over information on resource flows, prices and performance.

5.2.3. Identification of research gaps

Basically, our framework is intended to allow a company to comprehensively analyze and assess current cybernetic MCSs to improve performance control at the buyer-supplier interface. Discussing contributions to BSRs, performance and control in supply chain relationships, a number of relevant aspects to be addressed by such research tools could be identified. Although different issues seem to dominate discussions in SCM and management accounting, both perspectives can be brought together in a consistent set of requirements, valid for an interdisciplinary applicable framework for analysis. Harmonizing findings from the two literature reviews, the basic purpose of the framework is to provide assistance on identifying weak points in the cross-company's control activities with consideration of performance-determining contingency factors. Specifically, the following factors have been identified as crucial to performance control in BSRs:

- Within the involved companies' individual competitive strategies, level of alignment in terms of a common supply chain strategy.
- Level of cross-company integration, determined by relationship capabilities (IT-integration, information sharing, contractual basis, trust and developmental aspects).
- Suitability of the applied measurement system, depending on the dyad (buyer vs. supplier), strategy and interdependencies between capabilities, interface-performance and relational firm-performance.
- Suitability of the performance evaluation processes and comparison values, depending on contingent influence factors.
- Suitability of the control mechanisms initiating corrective action, depending on direct and indirect interdependencies between the performance elements addressed.

According to our understanding, the framework must consist of at least two components to being able to fulfill these requirements:

On one hand, *a control process-oriented guideline* needs to be developed, helping the user to systematically identify and analyze the weak points of his performance control activities. On the other hand, *a conceptual model* is required, bringing control processes and the relevant building blocks of performance control in BSRs together systematically to improve understanding of the contextual conditions where MCS are effective. This involves performance measurement and evaluation processes, as well as selection of adequate corrective measures in contingencies, strategic priorities and other business-related aspects. Providing such a guideline and the corresponding conceptual causal model assures applicability of the framework by allowing the manager to make the right connections and to draw relevant conclusions for his control activities.

5.3. Research methodology

To answer the research questions, Meredith's (1993) approach to theory building through conceptual modeling and McCutcheon and Meredith's (1993) procedure for hypothesis development and testing was followed. Starting with an investigation of existing analysis frameworks, the guideline and conceptual model have been developed, and propositions to be tested have been derived. Next, a structured review of SCM literature enabled developing BSR-specific classification schemes for the model's key elements by identifying relevant capabilities, contingencies and performance elements. Finally, semi-structured interviews with those responsible for supply chains and other key players helped in gathering first empirical evidence and to test propositions.

To guarantee consistency with existing analysis frameworks, fundamentally suitable approaches in SCM fields and management accounting had to be identified and assessed first. The literature basis was expanded to contingency-theoretical contributions to also cover relevant contingency research from the field of general management. To increase applicability of the guideline, a control-oriented structure was chosen, clearly addressing the cybernetic sub-processes of formal MCSs. For each sub-process, a set of questions was formulated, pointing out the main key success factors. Additionally, organizational preconditions to be met for successfully managing the respective control activities were outlined. The proposed relationships between key elements of performance control in BSRs and control processes served as a basis for proposition development and were also integrated in a conceptual model.

Before actually testing these propositions empirically, the different key elements needed to be further specified due to their generic nature. Thus, a structured literature review was conducted to structure the research field (Mentzer and Kahn, 1995; Easterby-Smith et al., 2002) by developing possible classification schemes for relationship capabilities, contingencies and performance variables. The review process was based on the proposed proceeding from Halldórsson and Arlbjørn (2005). Furthermore, it was referred to excellent reviews in the field of SCM conducted by Giunipero et al. (2008), Sachhan and Datta (2005) and Burgess et al. (2006).

Analyzing the thematic focus of journals selected in these reviews and combining them with Menachof et al.'s (2009) 'research usefulness index', eight peer-reviewed journals were chosen: (1) Journal of Supply Chain Management (JSCM), (2) International Journal of Physical Distribution and Logistics Management (IJPDLJM), (3) Journal of Operations Management (JOM), (4) International Journal of Logistics Management, (5) Journal of Business Logistics, (6) International Journal of Operations and Production Management, (7) Industrial Marketing Management and (8) Decision Sciences. Since the objective of this analysis is to identify recent trends and to also give implications for future research, the relevant period was set from 2000 to 2009. To create a comprehensive literature basis, a key word search helped to identify potentially suitable contributions. Two sets of key words were defined: the first, including the terms 'supply chain', 'buyer', 'supplier', 'inter-firm', 'inter-organizational', and the second, including 'performance' and 'control'. A basic search was then carried out, based on the presence of a combination of at least one term of each set in the abstract and/or title, to capture any articles focusing on the broader concept of either performance or control in an inter-organizational context. Searching the ten combinations of terms in the defined period led to a sample of 472 papers. To identify relevant articles, two data reduction processes followed, both conducted independently by two researchers to assure reliability of results. Pair-wise agreement was required regarding the subjective evaluation and analysis review activities. This means that the second researcher mirrored every process. In case of disagreement, the final interpretation was resolved via discussion. A first quick content check helped identify potentially suitable papers to the field and led to a preliminary count of 154 articles. Beside the requirement of focusing on performance- and/or control-related issues in supply chains, the following criteria had to be met to guarantee relevance for our framework development: articles have been eliminated that, despite having contained the search terms, solely focused on intra-firm issues or other disciplines such as logistics, marketing and operations research. Performance somehow needed to be addressed and measurement items describing performance had to be clearly outlined. Empirical evidence and contextual information about investigation circumstances was also considered crucial to our investigation, meaning that purely theoretical papers were excluded. Elimination of inappropriate contributions, according to these predefined criteria, resulted in a final sample of 109 articles, which served as a basis for the actual analysis.

Relationship capabilities and contingencies, as well as interface- and relational firm-performance, were identified and classification schemes, including definitions for each type, have been developed. Many articles focused on firm-performance in general instead of relational firm-performance. These papers did not focus on BRS-induced performance yields, but on a company's overall success. Instead of measuring relative performance changes, general cause-and-effect relationships between the nature of the relationship and companies' actual performance level were examined here. Strictly speaking, these papers did not address relational firm-performance, as defined here. However, they contained important knowledge about interrelations of BSRs-specific performance issues. Neglecting this research stream would have been detrimental; thus, the development of the framework will draw on selected findings from this as well. Based on findings from this extensive analysis, we will then complement and refine our analysis framework.

Finally, semi-structured interviews were conducted to provide a first empirical examination of the relevance and validity of the framework and the proposed relationships between the identified key elements.

5.4. The contingency-based framework for analysis

Although there are many articles analyzing interdependencies between single performance elements, various contingencies and sometimes even capabilities, we found no generic research tools for systematically conducting an analysis of performance control-specific issues in supply chains, in comparison to management accounting literature. Due to the maturity of the topic, much conceptual research exclusively on structuring MCSs exists, providing principally useful patterns for our analysis framework. Examples are Hopwood (1974) - categorizing control and controls, Otley (1980) - focusing on contingent approaches to MCSs, and others. In addition, frameworks designed specifically to analyze MCSs in general have been developed, such as Simons' (1995) levers of control framework, Otley's (1999) framework for MCSs research and, building on these two, Ferreira's and Otley's (2009) framework for analyzing performance Ferreira and Otley (2009) turned out to be particularly suitable in an extraordinary manner for several reasons. Most importantly, cybernetic MCSs for use in supply chain BSRs are captured by the framework, as performance management systems (in the authors' understanding) cover any type of formal and informal MCSs. Additionally, the five key aspects, are all addressed in a direct or indirect way, and the main control processes (measurement, evaluation and taking corrective action) are clearly outlined and can thus serve as a structural basis for the guideline. The selection of this framework is further motivated by the fact that the authors provide a sophisticated and up-to-date overview of relevant prior contributions to the topic.

Designed as a generic research tool for describing the structure and operation of performance management systems, the authors formulate twelve basic questions, helping researchers to systematically analyze the design and use of formal and informal control mechanisms, processes, systems and networks. However, because formal MCSs represent only a small part of the wide range of performance management systems addressed, not all of the twelve questions are equally important, and need to be refined to meet the specific requirements of cybernetic BSR-MCSs. Questions addressing informal control issues, like development and communication of plans and strategies, as well as subjective performance evaluation, will be excluded. Remaining questions must then be integrated into a cross-company context by shifting the focus from single companies to inter-organizational processes and activities, considering both buyer's and supplier's needs (dyadic both perspective). In addition, key elements of performance control in BSRs must be considered. With these constraints, four sets of questions have been developed, addressing the main control processes of cybernetic MCSs. For each set, necessary preconditions for answering these questions have been formulated. Building on each other, the preconditions of the previous question group must be addressed in order. If this is not the case, it is necessary to close existing gaps first, before continuing analysis. The question blocks follow:

A. *Measurement of buyer's and supplier's relational firm-performance (type 1)*

   Questions: What do individual competitive strategies of buying and supplying companies look like? Are there formal control mechanisms established, measuring outcome of the BSR for the respective companies? If so, do the performance indicators applied also adequately reflect the individual companies' goals ?

   Preconditions: Clear definition of the competitive strategy and firm-performance within each of the two companies, enabling the measurement of cross-company processes' influence on selected firm-performance elements.

B. *Measurement of interface-performance (type 2)*

Questions: Are the two companies' competitive strategies aligned and is there a common supply chain strategy formulated considering both sides' interests (dyadic both perspective)? Are there formal control mechanisms established to measure efficiency and effectiveness of cross-company processes and activities (interface-performance)? If so, do the performance indicators applied reflect the goals of the common supply chain strategy in a sufficiently?

Preconditions: Alignment of the two companies' competitive strategies. Development of a harmonized supply chain strategy. Identification and measurement of appropriate performance indicators at buyer-supplier interface.

C. *Evaluation of interface-performance*

Questions: Are measurements of interface-performance compared against predetermined standards to identify weak points and optimization potentials? If so, how have standards been developed? Are there reference values from comparable BSRs?

Preconditions: Knowledge about contingency factors determining comparability of performance measures to correctly identify appropriate business relationships. Ability to correctly define standards, for instance, through analysis of comparable business relationships within the same corporation or, if available, using comparison to best-in-class practices.

D. *Selection and implementation of corrective actions*

Questions: How much deviation from pre-determined standards is tolerated and when is corrective action initiated? Which corrective actions are available and how to decide, which one to take in address the identified interface-performance issue in the most effective manner?

Preconditions: Knowledge about relationship capabilities and their limiting influence on different interface-performance elements. Knowledge about how these relationship capabilities can be addressed most effectively.

As the guideline's structure and, especially, preconditions indicate, there are certain important order and cause-and-effect relationships between processes and building blocks. These must be integrated in a conceptual causal model to fully understand under which conditions MCSs are effective. This demands taking a contingency-based view of relevant MCSs entities and their causal relationships that, in turn, requires switching to a process- and variable-oriented perspective. In consequence, performance and performance-determining factors have to be classified and assigned to specific types of variables first. The classification will follow Luthans' and Stewart's (1977) general contingency theory of management, developed to offer a conceptual research-based framework for 'identifying and developing functional relationships between environmental, management and performance variables' (Luthans and Stewart, 1977, 182). It is not only an excellent and still valid conceptual framework for categorizing and integrating various different performance-related elements, but was also selected because the provided systems of variables enable a disjunctive assignment of our identified model entities. While fitting the author's basic understanding of the different variable types, their labeling will be slightly adjusted to guarantee consistency in wording.

Performance output is represented by performance variables. As our framework differs between interface-performance and relational firm-performance, two types of performance variables will be distinguished in the following as well. Performance-determining factors, not directly controlled by management, are represented by contingent environmental variables, labeled as 'contingency variables'. Controllable factors that can be addressed by management to increase performance are represented by resource variables. Due to our focus on BSRs in supply chains, this type of variable will be relabeled as 'capability variables'.

These variables and the three control sub-processes now must be brought together in a causal model, reflecting expected interdependencies. Based on literature review results, the first four propositions, resulting from the expected causal relationships between different types of variables, can be formulated:

P_{1a} Interface-performance (type 2) is positively associated to relational firm-performance (type 1).

P_{1b} Cross-company integration (reflected by capability variables) is positively associated with the maximum achievable interface-performance.

P_{1c} Contingent circumstances, the BSR faces (reflected by contingency variables), are positively linked to the maximum achievable relational firm-performance.

P_{1d} Contingent circumstances, the BSR faces (reflected by contingency variables), are positively linked to the maximum achievable interface-performance.

In terms of assumed causal relationships between the different types of variables and the actual control processes, four additional process-oriented propositions can be derived:

P_{2a} Selection and weighting of performance variables to be included in the MCS are determined by the view of the buyer-supplier dyad and the companies' strategic constraints.

P_{2b} Comparability of measurement results is determined by the contingent circumstances the BSR faces (reflected by contingency variables).

P_{2c} The range of suitable corrective action(s) to be taken by management is determined by the degree of cross-company integration already achieved (reflected by capability variables).

P_{2d} The effectiveness of corrective managerial actions is determined by how effectively they enhance capabilities.

The seven proposed relationships, describing how key elements of performance control in BSRs interact with control processes, are shown in figure 18. Before validating them empirically, the different types of variables need to be further specified due to their generic nature.

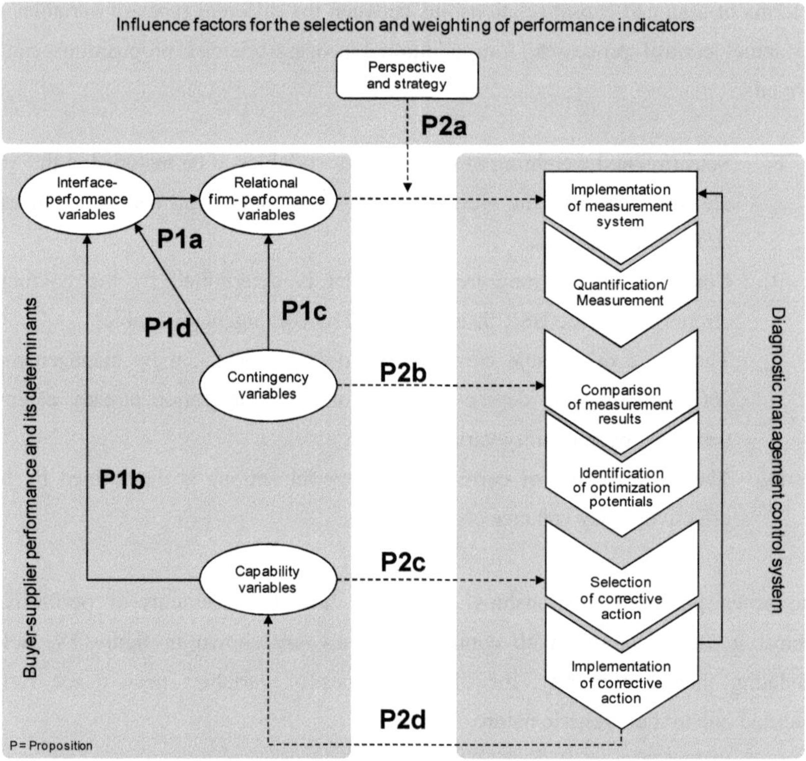

Figure 18: A contingency-based framework integrating key elements and processes of formal management control systems BSRs

The following subsections present possible classification schemes for the different key elements of formal performance control in BSRs. This includes relationship capability and contingency variables as well as interface-performance and relational firm-performance variables. Moreover, definitions are mentioned and variable-specific measurement items outlined. All findings are based on the structured literature review described in section A.4.

5.4.1. Classification scheme for relational firm-performance variables

In terms of relational firm-performance two variables were identified: financial performance, which is measured by profitability and profit, and market performance which refers to indicators measuring a company's behavior and success on the market as well as its competitive position. A list of papers addressing these dimensions and typical measurement items is given in table 3.

Table 3: Relational firm-performance variables

Selected variables for relational firm-performance variables	Papers addressing this variable (numbers refer to references in annex A)	Selected measurement items
Financial performance	1, 2, 6, 7, 9, 10, 13, 14, 16, 17, 18, 20, 21, 22, 23, 25, 26, 29, 30, 31, 32, 33, 34, 36, 38, 39, 42, 43, 44, 46, 47, 50, 55, 58, 60, 61, 62, 63, 66, 70, 71, 72, 73, 74, 76, 77, 78, 82, 83, 84, 85, 86, 87, 89, 90, 97, 98, 100, 101, 102, 106, 107, 109	- Return on investment (ROI) - Return on assets (ROA) - Earnings before interest and taxes (EBIT) - Net profit - Financial liquidity - Sales volume
Market performance	6, 12, 13, 17, 18, 21, 23, 26, 29, 31, 34, 38, 43, 44, 46, 47, 55, 62, 63, 73, 76, 78, 82, 84, 87, 90, 97, 98, 106, 107, 109	- Market Share - Sales Growth - Overall Competitive Position

5.4.2. Classification scheme for interface-performance variables

Three performance dimensions were identified reflecting interface-performance (table 4). Responsiveness refers to BSR associates' ability to react instantly towards changes in the environment. Not only does a BSR need to be able to perceive and implement changing customer demands, it also has to react effectively to variations in competitors' strategies. Processes and configuration of intersections with associated firms serve as a basis for high responsiveness. Delivery performance describes efficiency and effectiveness of transport and distribution transactions and indicates the company's ability to respond accurately to the supply chain partner's needs, for instance in case of demand variability. It can be ascertained in two different ways in a supply chain, upstream and downstream, and either refers to suppliers or a firm's own delivery performance. Customer satisfaction measures the supply chain partner's degree of satisfaction with the supply chain partner.

Table 4: Interface-performance variables

Selected interface-performance variables	Papers addressing this variable (numbers refer to references in annex A)	Selected measurement items
Responsiveness	5, 6, 8, 10, 16, 17, 18, 23, 25, 26, 27, 29, 30, 31, 32, 36, 37, 39, 41, 43, 44, 47, 50, 51, 53, 55, 56, 62, 63, 66, 68, 70, 71, 72, 73, 74, 77, 88, 89, 92, 93, 94, 95, 97, 100, 101, 102, 103, 106, 107, 108, 109	- Ability to achieve short time periods between design and market launch of a product - Response time for product design changes - Ability to react to competitors strategy changes quick and effectively - KPIs: Time-to-market, inventory turns, cash-to-cash cycle, throughput time, percent idle time
Delivery performance	1, 2, 5, 6, 7, 8, 9, 13, 15, 16, 18, 19, 23, 26, 27, 29, 30, 32, 33, 39, 40, 41, 43, 44, 45, 47, 50, 51, 53, 54, 56, 58, 59, 60, 61, 62, 66, 68, 70, 71, 72, 73, 74, 77, 81, 83, 86, 89, 90, 93, 94, 97, 98, 101, 102, 103, 106, 108	- Effectiveness of billing methods - Effectiveness of distribution planning - Flexibility of distribution system - Accuracy of order processing for customers - KPIs: Order fulfillment, on-time delivery, delivery speed, delivery reliability, reduction of response time for product volume changes
Customer/Buyer satisfaction	5, 12, 29, 30, 31, 39, 42, 47, 55, 62, 74, 78, 79, 89, 93, 97, 98, 100, 101, 103, 106	- Ratio of customers with recurring exchanges - Length of exchange relationship - Sales volume with customer

5.4.3. Classification scheme for capability variables

Four basic relationship capabilities have been identified. IT infrastructure reflects the degree of IT integration with customers and suppliers and determines supply chain member's ability to exchange knowledge and date efficiently and effectively within a supply chain. Information sharing refers to supply chain members' ability to exchange knowledge and data efficiently and effectively within a supply chain. This definition also addresses the skill to filter out and exchange which information is relevant. Coordination involves participatory behavior of supply chain agents that are trying to reach their own and shared goals effectively. Coordination addresses organizing and adjusting shared activities and structures with a focus on transaction-related aspects.

Hence, coordination calls for an active exchange of goals and opinions, as well as actively approaching each other. Contractual integration (often labeled as cooperation) refers to the extent of formalized contractual stipulations. They can range from single contracts with clearly defined content to long term agreements committing the supply chain partners to each others. In literature collaboration has been mentioned as an additional performance dimension in the context of BSRs. As collaboration is often referred to an aggregation of the dimensions information sharing, cooperation and coordination (e.g. Field and Meile, 2008) it cannot be clearly separated from the other dimensions and is not listed separately. Trust is a soft factor, describing the relationship with the supplier/customer which is not based on contractual agreements. It reflects the degree of understanding and willingness to change in favor of the partner. Moreover, the term supply chain integration can be found in SCM literature. Described as the process of acquiring and sharing operational, technical and financial information and related knowledge with the exchange partner (Swink et al., 2007), it can be considered of information sharing and cooperation and is not listed separately.

Table 5: Relationship capabilities

Selected relationship capabilities	Papers addressing this variable (numbers refer to references in annex A)	Relevant issues and selected measurement items
IT Infrastructure	2, 4, 6, 13, 21, 22, 23, 24, 26, 28, 29, 32, 36, 37, 40, 41, 43, 44, 45, 47, 48, 53, 54, 57, 61, 63, 64, 66, 68, 70, 71, 72, 76, 77, 80, 81, 82, 83, 84, 85, 86, 87, 93, 96, 99, 100, 102, 103, 107, 108, 109	- No standardized interface - Standardized interface - Data exchange processed manually - Standardized interface - Data exchange processed automatically
Information sharing	2, 3, 4, 6, 10, 11, 12, 13, 15, 18, 21, 25, 26, 27, 29, 30, 31, 32, 33, 36, 37, 38, 42, 43, 44, 46, 48, 50, 51, 52, 53, 54, 55, 56, 57, 58, 59, 60, 61, 62, 64, 66, 68, 69, 70, 71, 72, 73, 76, 79, 81, 82, 83, 84, 85, 86, 87, 90, 92, 93, 95, 96, 97, 100, 101, 102, 104, 105, 107, 108, 109	- Information about customer's purchase orders - Information about supplier's delivery orders - Amount of informally and personally transmitted knowledge - Extent to which standards of information exchange and knowledge transfer are implemented - Frequency and regularity of information exchange - Share of strategically important data - Data quality and punctuality
Coordination	2, 8, 11, 14, 15, 23, 24, 25, 31, 32, 37, 38, 42, 44, 46, 55, 59, 63, 64, 70, 71, 73, 81, 87, 88, 90, 93, 94, 96, 100, 102, 106, 107, 109	- Frequency of meetings with partners for reconciliation - Amount of exchange and reconciliation of targets - Amount of idea exchange - Reconciliation of processes and structures - Effectiveness of reconciliation
Contractual integration (Cooperation)	2, 5, 14, 21, 32, 36, 37, 38, 42, 44, 46, 56, 64, 70, 72, 82, 84, 94, 100, 102, 103, 104, 105	- Anonymous ad hoc transactions - Recurring exchange - Long term strategic framework contracts - Permanent sales contracts
Trust	1, 2, 3, 5, 7, 8, 10, 11, 12, 14, 15, 16, 17, 18, 19, 20, 21, 26, 30, 31, 33, 34, 36, 37, 38, 40, 41, 42, 44, 46, 47, 49, 50, 53, 54, 55, 57, 59, 61, 62, 64, 65, 66, 68, 69, 70, 71, 73, 76, 81, 82, 84, 85, 86, 87, 88, 89, 92, 93, 95, 97, 98, 100, 101, 102, 104, 106, 107, 108, 109	- Short-term (impersonal, ad-hoc basis) - Mid-term (recurring exchanges) - Long-term (trustful partnership)

5.4.4. Classification scheme for contingency variables

In terms of contingent factors, two basic types of contingency variables have been identified in articles, with the first reflecting the general background of the companies (e.g. industry sector, position in the supply chain and company size), while the second is determined by specific product attributes (e.g. product value, demand uncertainty and market-specific conditions). A comprehensive overview is given in table 6.

Table 6: Contingency capabilities

Selected contingency variables	Papers addressing this variable (numbers refer to references in annex A)	Potential scale(s) for this variable
Position in the supply chain	1, 2, 3, 4, 5, 6, 7, 8, 9, 10, 12, 13, 14, 15, 16, 17, 18, 19, 20, 21, 22, 23, 24, 25, 26, 27, 28, 29, 30, 31, 32, 33, 34, 36, 37, 38, 39, 40, 41, 42, 43, 44, 45, 46, 47, 48, 49, 50, 51, 53, 54, 55, 56, 57, 58, 59, 60, 61, 62, 63, 64, 65, 66, 68, 69, 70, 71, 72, 73, 74, 76, 77, 78, 79, 80, 81, 82, 83, 84, 85, 86, 87, 88, 89, 90, 91, 92, 93, 94, 95, 96, 97, 98, 99, 100, 101, 102, 103, 104, 105, 106, 107, 108, 109	- Miner/Raw material extractor - Raw material manufacturer - Component manufacturer - Final product manufacturer - Manufacturer (not further specified) - Wholesaler - Retailer - Logistics Service Provider
Industry sector	1, 2, 3, 5, 8, 9, 10, 11, 12, 13, 14, 15, 16, 17, 18, 19, 20, 21, 22, 24, 25, 26, 27, 28, 29, 30, 31, 32, 33, 34, 35, 36, 37, 39, 40, 41, 46, 47, 48, 49, 50, 51, 54, 56, 57, 58, 59, 60, 61, 63, 65, 66, 67, 68, 69, 70, 72, 73, 74, 75, 76, 77, 78, 79, 80, 81, 82, 83, 84, 85, 86, 87, 88, 89, 90, 91, 92, 93, 94, 95, 96, 97, 98, 99, 100, 101, 102, 103, 104, 105, 106, 107, 108, 109	- NACE Rev 2 Code (Europe) - US-SIC (USA)
Firm size: employees	2, 4, 5, 6, 7, 10, 11, 13, 14, 15, 16, 20, 22, 23, 25, 27, 28, 30, 31, 32, 34, 36, 37, 38, 39, 41, 42, 43, 44, 46, 47, 48, 53, 54, 55, 57, 60, 63, 65, 66, 68, 69, 74, 78, 79, 81, 82, 85, 86, 87, 89, 90, 96, 97, 98, 100, 101, 102, 103, 106, 107	- Small (<50) - Medium-sized (<500) - Large (<5000) - Very large (>5000)
Firm size: sales	1, 2, 4, 5, 6, 7, 9, 10, 11, 14, 15, 16, 18, 20, 22, 23, 26, 27, 32, 33, 34, 36, 37, 38, 41, 43, 44, 45, 46, 47, 50, 51, 53, 55, 56, 57, 58, 59,	- Small (<50) - Medium-sized (<500) - Large (<5000) - Very large (>5000)

	65, 66, 68, 69, 70, 72, 78, 80, 83, 84, 85, 86, 87, 90, 92, 94, 96, 97, 100, 101, 102, 103, 105, 106, 107	
Supply chain strategy	2, 9, 11, 14, 21, 23, 25, 31, 37, 39, 41, 44, 47, 51, 60, 63, 73, 74, 76, 77, 78, 82, 83, 92, 93, 94, 95, 98, 101, 103, 104, 106, 108	- Efficient / Lean - Responsive / Agile
Place of business	1, 2, 3, 4, 5, 7, 10, 12, 13, 14, 15, 16, 17, 18, 19, 20, 22, 23, 25, 26, 27, 28, 29, 30, 31, 33, 34, 36, 37, 38, 40, 41, 43, 45, 46, 47, 50, 51, 52, 53, 54, 55, 56, 58, 59, 61, 62, 63, 64, 65, 66, 67, 68, 69, 70, 72, 73, 74, 78, 79, 81, 82, 84, 85, 86, 87, 89, 90, 91, 92, 93, 94, 95, 96, 97, 98, 100, 101, 102, 103, 104, 106, 108	- Continents - Counties
Demand uncertainty	12, 22, 25, 32, 36, 38, 40, 45, 48, 49, 59, 61, 63, 67, 74, 82, 90, 100, 103	- Strong and unpredictable demand fluct. - Regular fluctuations in demand - Stable demand
Supply uncertainty	5, 25, 36, 38, 48, 64, 79, 92, 100	- Strong variances of product availability - Medium variances in product availability - Continuous product availability
Dependency on customer / sup.	1, 5, 7, 14, 25, 31, 37, 43, 50, 79, 86, 92, 100, 104	- Low - Moderate - High
Sales and supply markets	2, 14, 17, 20, 21, 25, 30, 36, 37, 40, 44, 45, 49, 59, 64, 68, 88, 96, 97, 105, 108	- Regional sales markets - National sales markets - International sales markets - Global sales markets
Competitiveness	1, 2, 3, 17, 20, 21, 23, 24, 25, 26, 34, 37, 41, 46, 47, 48, 49, 51, 56, 58, 59, 60, 63, 68, 71, 73, 74, 80, 83, 88, 89, 95, 96, 103, 104, 106,	- Small competition - Average competition - Intense competition
Market structure	3, 72	- Monopoly / Oligopoly / Polypoly
Trading conditions	2, 21, 37, 45, 48, 56, 58, 59, 60, 63, 72, 73, 74, 80, 82	- Niche, Emerging, Saturated - Stable, Dynamic
Turnover rate	6, 20, 21, 32, 37, 57, 74, 82, 85, 95	- Fast-moving - Not fast-moving
Customization	1, 11, 13, 21, 29, 74, 78, 82, 86, 92, 95	- No (standard goods, commodities) - Moderate - High
Designated use	5, 9, 29, 78, 104	- Consumer goods - Capital goods
Manufacturing penetration	17, 74	- Raw materials - Semi finished products - Finished products

5.5. First empirical examination of propositions

After developing an analysis framework, six in-depth semi-structured interviews were conducted to gather first empirical data about the propositions' validity. The interviews were also intended to help assess the guidelines' practical applicability, highlight need for adjustments and derive indications for future research. The interviews were conducted with key informants of four medium- and large-sized firms from the manufacturing industry in Germany and Switzerland. Each company's background is summarized in table 7.

Table 7: Company background of the respondents

Background	Company A	Company B	Company C	Company D
Industry sector	Machinery and equipment n.e.c.	Motor vehicles, trailers and semi-trailers	Machinery and equipment n.e.c.	Electrical equipment
Primary actor of analysis	Final product manufacturer	Final product manufacturer	Component manufacturer	Final product manufacturer
Firm size employees	5'000-10'000	>10'000	5'000-10'000	>10'000
Firm size sales (in mio. EUR)	5'000-10'000	500-5'000	500-5'000	500-
Internationalisation of sales markets	Global	Global	Global	Global
Trading conditions	Dynamic/-	Dynamic/Emerging	Stable/Niche	Dynamic/Saturated
Market structure	Oligopoly	Oligopoly	Polypoly	Polypoly
Buyer perspective	x	x	x	x
Supplier perspective			x	x

During the interviews, two outline protocols were developed examining upstream and downstream firms along the supply chain. The respondents were questioned about their supplier interface (buying perspective - dyadic upstream). These questions were mainly focused on operational and strategic aspects of procurement-related activities, such as supply planning, supplier management and purchasing processes. The respondents were also questioned about their buyer interface from a sales and distribution perspective (supplying perspective - dyadic downstream). Both outline protocols were identically structured and addressed the same two areas from each perspective.

In a first part, respondents were asked to assess the general validity of statements regarding the expected limiting impact of identified capability variables on three selected interface-performance variables. A five-point Likert scale type ranging from 1 (strongly disagree) to 5 (strongly agree) was then used to assess these statements' correctness. This determined, for example, to what extent the efficiency of transactional processes was related to the amount of shared information between supply chain partners. Questions were also asked about performance-determining impacts that specific relationship contingencies (e.g. buyer or supplier dependency) have on interface-performance indicators (e.g. delivery reliability). This enabled validating propositions P1a, P1b, P1c and P1d.

The survey's second part consisted of open questions referring to the control process. There, enquiries were made about which performance measurement and evaluation mechanisms firms use for specific product categories, focusing on reference values' availability during performance evaluation and mechanisms that assist selecting and implementing corrective actions. In doing so, indirect propositions about basic issues of performance control could be derived to test the P2b, P2c and P2d propositions. Comparing the interviews from both perspectives then allowed for testing proposition P2a by matching answers from both sides.

All respondents expected a strong positive impact of interface-performance on relational firm-performance, showing that proposition P1a is widely supported, with the same results for propositions P1b, P1c and P1d, as all six interviews basically agreed on expected causal relationships between relationship capabilities and interface-performance, as well as contingencies and both types of performance. Because outcomes differ strongly between contingency variables, the results are not universally valid. Three out for interviews, for example, assume, from a buying perspective, that the supply chain level shows no correlation with interface-performance. Increasing variability, however, is expected to lead to a decline of interface-performance. The same applies to capability variables. Respondents predominantly attest that a positive impact exists between the degree of information sharing and performance, but they do not see lasting effects from contractual relations with partners.

The interview's evaluation of perspective showed clear results. Several connections exhibited differences between buyers and suppliers; within those groups, however, the questions were answered homogeneously. For suppliers, efficient and successful transactions were considered to be much more important than having information about their client's inventory levels and order situation.

The anticipated correlations about process-related propositions also appeared to be valid. As expected, reference values were either company-internal values from previous periods or benchmark data from competitors within the same industry and usually even the same product category during cross-company comparisons. Thus, proposition P2b can be considered valid. No clear statements can be made about P2c and P2d, because the respondents often did not have exact knowledge about corrective actions' implications. Although the results confirmed that interface capabilities must be enhanced to improve cross-company performance, the impact of modified interface capabilities on interface-performance is difficult to assess.

It can be stated that all interviewed firms conduct standardized performance measurements and comparisons regarding reference values. The assumption that almost no information about comparable BSRs of competitive supply chains exists was, however, confirmed. Reference values were computed on the basis of values from previous periods or contractual guidelines and 'real' inter-supply chain comparisons were not possible in most cases. In addition, significant lack of knowledge about corrective actions' actual effect on performance was recognizable.

Except for P2a, which to be tested by comparing interviews from the buying-side to interviews from the supplying side, a comprehensive and more detailed overview of respondents' answers in terms of validity of the propositions is given in table 8.

Table 8: Validity of propositions

Respondent / Perspective	P_{1a}	P_{1b}	P_{1c}	P_{1d}	P_{2b}	P_{2c}	P_{2d}
A / Buyer perspective	++	+	+	+	++	+	+
B / Buyer perspective	+	-	-	-	++	-	-
C / Buyer perspective	++	++	+	+	++	+	++
C / Supplier perspective	++	++	+	+	+	+	++
D / Buyer perspective	+	+	+	+	++	-	-
D / Supplier perspective	-	+	-	-	++	-	-

++ validity strongly confirmed
\+ validity basically confirmed
\- validity not confirmed

To summarize this first empirical examination; none of the seven proposition were clearly proven wrong. Thus, the developed theoretical framework for analysis of BSR-MCSs can be considered a sound foundation for future research activities. The topic is practically and scientifically relevant because supply chain competitiveness is widely accepted as important. The correlations are not universally valid, due to the heterogeneity of answers arising from different contingencies and capabilities, as well as the small sample size. This calls for a differentiated analysis allowing systematic conclusions about control activities. Two aspects should be highlighted: first, a perspective-specific quantitative analysis of causal relationships between specific contingencies, capabilities and performances should be performed in order to identify performance-driving variables. Second, interactions between performance elements should be studied to find the optimal selection of corrective actions while considering contingent circumstances.

5.6. Summary 1st phase of analysis

In summary, it can be said that interface-performance, resulting from efficiency and effectiveness of processes at the buyer-supplier interface, is directly linked to overall performance and competitiveness of the two interacting companies. There is also a broad consensus about the basic interdependencies between relationship capabilities and their limiting impact on the companies' interface-performance. The performance-determining role of contingencies can be considered valid as well. Moreover, the decisive role of managing performance at the buyer-supplier interface to improve overall performance and competitiveness of the two interacting companies has been widely accepted in various scientific communities. In line with this, an urgent need for appropriate control mechanisms and techniques meeting the specific requirements of BSRs has been expressed in SCM. Reviewing SCM literature led to the assumption that two particular aspects are considered underdeveloped from an inter-company perspective. First, evidence that interface processes and activities impact both buyer's and supplier's firm-performance has not been adequately credited. With only few exceptions, analysis of BSRs in supply chains has focused on performance of either the buying or the supplying company. This differs with an opinion widely held in the SCM community, purporting that inter-company competitiveness is today's most important challenge. In reality, the need to analyze interface-performance in supply chains from an unbiased point of view is a current issue. This also implies that causal relationships between relationship capabilities and interface-performance (similar for both partners) and the respective companies' relational firm-performance (which differs) must be better understood to improve cross-company performance control activities. Second, a lack of sophisticated analysis frameworks has been identified.

On the other side, the potential role of formal MCSs in inter-firm relationships has been recognized in management accounting research and various scientific contributions to the debate of management control directly addressing BSRs in supply chains have been made. But despite all this discussion, configuration of formal MCSs in supply chains seem to have been neglected in prior research. A systematic and comprehensive analysis of relevant influence factors on performance, for instance, still seems to be missing. Interdependencies between these performance-determining factors and control processes in BSR-MCS have been only marginally explored and a framework for analyzing such systems did not exist because existing approaches did not fully consider specific BSRs characteristics.

A major advantage of this framework is its ability to systematically connect contingency theory to control processes of formal MCSs by embedding the main control processes in an inter-organizational context. Due to the general acceptance of these interdependencies, the guideline for systematically identifying key aspects affecting formal control systems could be applied to other areas of management accounting by researchers as well.

However, the discussion and conclusion of this investigation are limited. Only eight journals have been reviewed. Including more journals might have led to additional findings. The list of capabilities, contingencies and performance variables (both types) should not be considered exhaustive. This conclusion also applies to semi-structured interviews, as a sample size of six caused a strong heterogeneity in the findings. The empirical evidence needs to be strengthened to verify the framework and to assess applicability of the implementation guideline. This could be achieved by analyzing expected interdependencies quantitatively. As an example, statistical analysis of causal relationships between performance and its determinants, such as contingencies and control mechanisms, can help to assess effectiveness of different MCSs types, depending on the organizational context.

6. Analysis of environmental influences on comparability of reliability, flexibility and inventory efficiency

6.1. Current situation and challenges

Buyer-supplier relationships (BSRs) and their efforts to derive value have become more and more complex over last two decades (Terpend, 2008). In particular, coordinative and cooperative processes between buyers and suppliers have a growing impact on companies' profitability, customer satisfaction, competitive capability and other performance areas (Cousins et al., 2008; Hult et al., 2007; Swink et al., 2007; Vickery et al., 2003). Consequently, the larger a company's number of suppliers (upstream perspective) and customers (downstream perspective), the larger an effect can be assumed. However, a high proportion of inter-firm relationships[23] fail to achieve their intended objectives (Meira et al., 2010) due to the special challenges for management when company's boundaries are transcended (Mouritsen and Hansen, 2006; Dekker, 2004; Cooper and Slagmulder, 2004; Håkansson and Lind, 2004; Seal et al., 2004). Referred to performance management on BSRs, especially the sub-process of evaluating performance appears to cause major difficulties as the following explanations show.

Effective performance evaluation generally requires determining reference values to correctly identify performance gaps and optimization potentials (Fisher, 1995). In practice, a BSR can be evaluated in two different ways (figure 19). In its simplest form, assessment is made using an isolated view of the relationship, strictly focusing on reference values originating from the relationship itself: e.g. resulting from contractual agreements (e.g. in terms of the buyer's requested delivery reliability) or from historical data. Another way to assess BSRs, using a wider focus, additionally compares the relationship with other BSRs. In this case, BSR evaluation draws not only on contractual or historical reference values, but also on differences between

[23] Different kinds of cross-company relations are sub-summated under 'inter-firm relationships', such as joint ventures, alliances and BSRs in supply chains. Accordingly, it will be used as a higher-order term for relationships between two companies in general, including BSRs.

relationships: for instance, actual performance values of the related BSRs (e.g. achieved delivery reliability of the reference relationship).

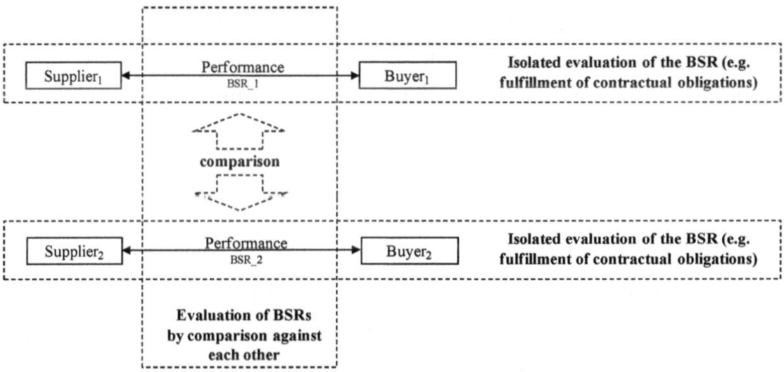

Figure 19: Two ways to evaluate performance of BSRs

From a managerial point of view, the second approach is particularly interesting as it might reveal additional information about actual potential still remaining in the relationship.[24] Especially in companies with a large number of suppliers (upstream) and/or customers (downstream), moving away from analyzing isolated business relationships to a more potential-oriented approach could reveal substantial additional possibility for improvement, i.e. by enabling powerful BSR benchmarking.

However, in practice, BSRs cannot simply be compared to each other. Relationships often show an enormous heterogeneity (Hsu, 2005; Terpend et al., 2008) due to various contingencies on exchange activities (Fawcett et al., 2008). To correctly evaluate performance, knowledge about these environmental influence factors limiting comparability of BSRs - and thus of performance values - is required. Scholars have long acknowledged this basic issue. Analyzing connectedness of dyadic business

[24] In the simplest case, comparison of two BSRs would emerge a 'high' and a 'low' performer in case the relationships show different levels of performance. Gaps between the two relationships can be interpreted as improvement potentials for the low performing BSR which then could be systematically addressed by appropriate corrective actions.

relationships, Anderson's et al. (1994) state that examination of such BSRs must capture 'the embedded context within which those relationships occur' (p. 1). As recent contributions show, this is still a contentious issue in research. In analyzing contributions to BSRs over two decades, Terpend et al. (2008) conclude that future research on performance improvement in BSRs should consider more contextual influence factors moderating relationships. The authors amplify this need by stating that 'the effects of many buyer, supplier and market characteristics, as well as product characteristics have yet to be explored (Terpend et al., 2008: 43), as stated by Hsu (2005). Analyzing effects on performance of buyers' and suppliers' interaction from a contingency-based view, the author empirically confirms the need for adequately considering contingent environmental impacts on performance outcomes. These statements and conclusions are in line with the review of BSR-related literature conducted for this study. Numerous examinations of performance-related aspects in BSRs exist. However, very few role relationship studies analyzing interdependencies between differences of relationships and performance-related aspects – e.g. Van Nyen et al. (2007) – investigating the impact of BSR-types on costs, were found. No empirical examination was identified that systematically analyzed external impacts on comparability of BSR performance.

This study addresses the need for research by addressing issues identified in performance evaluation of BSRs from a contingency-theoretical point of view. To aid practitioners, findings will also be embedded in a conceptual approach for improvement of their own performance evaluation processes. Accordingly, the primary objective of this study can be described as follows:

> *This study aims to improve inter-firm performance management by developing a conceptual procedure to correctly compare performance of BSRs. This requires identification of potential influence factors on performance comparability as well as quantification of their biasing impacts.*

In detail, development of such a procedure enabling correct comparison of BSRs requires several steps. First, a general theoretical background of performance evaluation in BSRs is provided to further define the need for research (section 6.2). Next, applied methodology is described to address identified issues (section 6.3). Then, statistical models to empirically analyze factors determining BSR comparability are developed. Different model elements (entities) relevant to performance evaluation are specified next (section 6.4). After designing the models, statistical analysis of expected causalities must be done to check significance and quantify actual impacts of expected causalities. For this, a survey of about 200 business relationships was conducted (section 6.5) and empirical analysis was undertaken by applying mean comparison and analysis of covariance (ANCOVA) (section 6.6). Finally, research findings, limitations and managerial implications are presented (section 6.7).

6.2. Theory development

Before being able to empirically analyze comparability of BSRs, several aspects should be discussed to provide a sound theoretical basis. When discussing performance evaluation in BSRs, further definition of this term is required to create a common ground and to allow selection of appropriate measurement indicators. Based on this understanding, discussion of performance-determining influence factors is then required to enable development of the hypothesized model. This addresses two basic types of contingencies: those directly connected to the nature of the BSR,[25] reflecting the way the companies interact and the material and information flows are organized, and those resulting from the economic business environment[26] where BSRs are embedded.

Performance in buyer-supplier relationships: interface-performance

A review of contributions empirically examining various performance-related issues in inter-firm contexts helped identify relevant categories of performance in BSRs

[25] Analogous to Van Nyen's et al. (2007) analysis of impacts from relationship types on costs in BSRs.

[26] As suggested by Terpend et al. (2008) and Hsu (2005).

(labeled as 'interface-performance'). In particular, the following relationship-specific performance categories seemed to play a significant role in overall firm-performance of the companies involved, and will thus serve as basis:

(a) Delivery reliability: Often the most important performance attribute in BSRs, reflecting effectiveness of transportation and distribution processes. Direct and indirect effects of delivery reliability on both companies' overall success have been proven in various studies (e.g. Beamon, 1999; Gunasekaran et al., 2001; Tracey, 2004; Swink et al., 2007). On the supply side, delivery connects companies to their customers and directly impacts customer satisfaction (Gunasekaran et al., 2004). This, in turn, affects suppliers' competitive capability and long-term firm-performance (Swink et al., 2007). On the buy side, delivery reliability of suppliers also plays an important role. Depending on applied procurement and production concepts, insufficient availability of supply materials in the incoming goods warehouse can incur enormous costs in production downtimes. The risk of supply gaps increases with the degree of inventory optimization, for instance if a just-in-time concept is followed.

(b) Delivery flexibility: In the context of SCM, the basic definition of flexibility is the partners' 'ability to respond to a changing environment' (Beamon, 1999: 281).[27] Transferred to BSRs, this broad definition needs to be refined, as this examination addresses only flexibility of operational processes at the cross-company interface with a major focus on speed. Accordingly, delivery flexibility in BSRs will be defined as supplying companies' ability to satisfy planned and unplanned customer demand for already existing products in the supplier's portfolio. Flexibility allows suppliers to differentiate from competitors. In dynamic business environments, this can be a significant competitive factor (Wu et al., 2006). Delivery flexibility of suppliers, in the next step, also determines flexibility of their buyers, as it influences the buyer's response time to fulfill new orders of his own downstream customers.

[27] This understanding is in line with so-called 'responsiveness' reflecting the capabilities 'to respond quickly to environmental changes and to meet customer demand (e.g. Eng, 2006; Wu et al., 2006).

(c) Inventory efficiency: This performance dimension involves costs associated with inventory held, such as costs for obsolete inventory and capital-tied up (Beamon, 1999). Adapted to BSRs, this addresses inventory levels of the supplier's finished goods warehouse, as well as buyer's storage for incoming goods. In consequence, this attribute must be analyzed separately for each end of the dyad. Inventory efficiency of a supplier is a measure of how well its production is aligned to the actual demand. However, it must never be considered independently from delivery flexibility and reliability, as these attributes are negatively correlated to the level of provided inventory (Beamon, 1999). On the buy side, inventory efficiency refers to the alignment of supply and production processes. The same restrictions apply to significance for the buyer's firm-performance.

The nature of BSRs and implications for comparability of interface-performance

Discussions about how attributes of a BSR are connected to its interface-performance and how transactional processes and activities at the cross-company interface are organized are closely connected. Following Giannakis' (2007) framework for measuring performance of relationships, buyer-specific as well as supplier-specific characteristics of the relationship must be differentiated. On one side, a minimum performance level must be achieved to guarantee that the buyer's downstream processes are not affected by poor delivery performance (Beamon, 1999), e.g. in case of production down-time due to supply gaps. On the other side, maximum achievable performance level is determined by the supplier's production and distribution capabilities (Wu et al., 2006). Both levels can be taken as lower and upper bound of a corridor of fit, in which the range of the supplier's performance potential exceeds the buyer's requirements (figure 20). Accordingly, performance will be considered 'sufficient' if it falls within this corridor, whereas buyers won't be satisfied with a misfit. A wide fit range, in contrast, indicates supplier's capabilities designed to meet higher performance requirements that could possibly indicate a waste of resources.

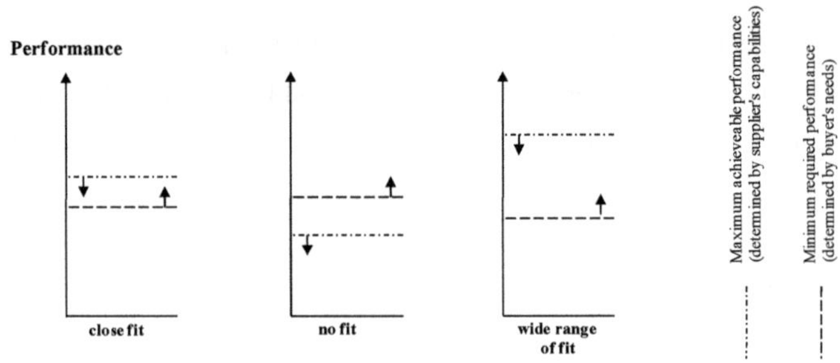

Figure 20: Performance fit in BSRs

As a first conclusion, it can be stated that the organization of transactional processes and activities at the buyer-supplier interface reflects performance standards to be met. In other words, how companies are connected in terms of interface-performance capabilities (supplier side) and requirements (buyer side), can be an indicator for the relative assessment of the BSRs interface-performance. Moreover, interface-performance-related capabilities and requirements are closely connected to each other. Especially in long-term relationships with periodic demands, suppliers are expected to adjust their capabilities according to the buyer's needs, leading to the following basic implications for BSR performance evaluation:

> *Supplier- and buyer-related relationships-specific attributes cannot be considered independently when characterizing BSRs. Comparison can only be made between BSRs with similar performance capabilities and requirements characteristics. Accordingly, if relationship types with comparable characteristics are defined, comparison of interface-performance allows us to quantify the contingent impact of the relationship's nature on its interface-performance.*

Accordingly, types of relationships with comparable interface-performance capabilities and requirements need to be identified and a classification scheme developed. Performance values of relationships from the same type can then be compared and treated as 'true' reference, and implications for performance evaluation can be derived.

The role of the economic business environment of the BSRs and implications for comparability of interface-performance

Despite the major performance-determining influence of the relationship's nature, determined by supplier-related capabilities and buyer-related requirements, review of the contributions above also showed that additional environmental circumstances need to be considered even though they are not directly linked to the business relationship. Analyzing performance in supply chains, Defee and Stank (2005) support this assumption by stating that performance is generally influenced by contingent environmental factors such as customer requirements, competition and industry structure. Analysis of these external effects has been subject of numerous contributions to the field of performance management in inter-firm relationships. As a result, a wide range of different company-related[28] and product-related[29] contingencies can be found in literature. The more the examination actually focuses on relational processes and activities, the greater the role of more product-specific contingencies appears.

As interface-performance strictly refers exclusively to a certain product or commodity group, only product-specific contingencies will be investigated, meaning that. a direct link to delivery reliability, flexibility and inventory efficiency must be given. This allows control of supplementary non-relationship-specific effects, as well as

---

[28] Contributions, for instance, account for external company-specific contingencies such as industry sector (e.g. Eng, 2006; Tracey, 2004, da Silveira and Arkader, 2007) or firm-size in terms of sales volume or number of employees (e.g. Sanders , 2005; Hsu et al., 2008). Other examinations put focus on the company's position in the supply chain (e.g. Curkovic et al., 2000; Gimenez and Ventura, 2005) in their analysis.

[29] The economic environment (e.g. Curkovic et al., 2000; Eng, 2006) is considered as well as product-related characteristics like product value (e.g. Eng, 2006) or target group (e.g. Stevenson and Spring, 2009). Also production conditions such as the level of customization (e.g. Squire et al., 2009; Sengupta et. al., 2006) seem crucial to performance issues in inter-firm relationships.

significant influence factors on interface-performance. One can draw the following implication for the hypothesized model:

> *Grading performance values cannot be done without considering the economic business environment in which the companies interact. This requires taking variables not directly linked to the BSR into account, like up- and downstream production characteristics, as well as environmental market conditions. Thus, criteria for situations when BSRs face homogenous environmental conditions (in terms of interface-performance) will be developed.*

Summary of expected causalities

In summary, before being able to empirically analyze the influence of the relationship type and supplementary contingencies on interface-performance, the following research questions can be formulated:

(i) What are suitable interface-performance indicators reflecting reliability, flexibility and inventory efficiency at the buyer-supplier interface?

(ii) Which are the constitutive factors for categorizing the nature of BSRs and what types of comparable relationships exist?

(iii) Which are significant non-relationship-specific influence factors on interface-performance resulting from environmental market and production conditions?

A summary of assumed causalities affecting evaluation of actual interface-performance of business relationships is shown in figure 21 and entities addressed by the three foregoing questions are marked.

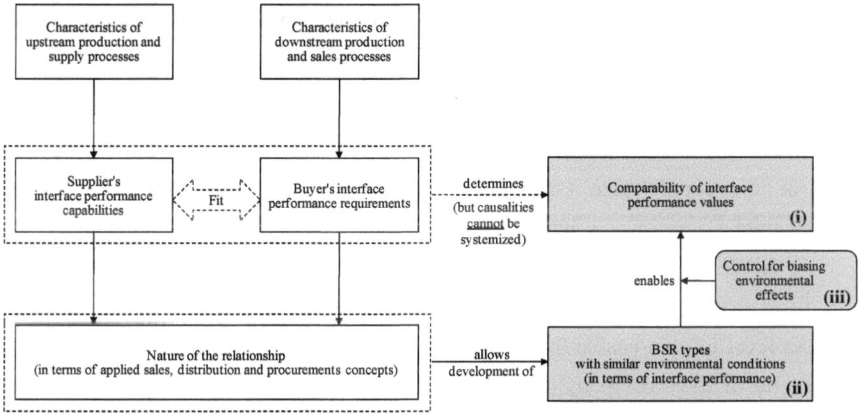

Figure 21: The determinants of interface-performance and the role of the relationship's characteristics for comparability

6.3. Research methodology

To answer research questions and provide empirical evidence for the expected causalities, a sequential procedure, combining exploratory and confirmatory steps has been applied. This research design is line with the logistics research framework of Mentzer and Kahn (1995), which allows systematic and rigorous theory development and testing.

Based on first theoretical findings and the identified need for research, a second exploratory, and more selective, literature review will be conducted to identify appropriate performance indicators describing reliability, flexibility and inventory efficiency of business relationships (section 6.4.1). Moreover, it better defines existing external influences on these indicators. Distinction is made between relationship-specific and non-relationship-specific contingencies to split up influences. These findings are used in two ways. First, a target-oriented classification scheme for BSR types is developed from existing typologies (section 6.4.2), serving as grouping variable in the empirical analysis. Second, additional market- and production-specific contingencies are identified, not directly linked to the companies' interaction processes but significant in their impacts on interface-performance (section 6.4.3).

After having structured the field from a theoretical perspective, two equally structured questionnaires were designed: one for the buy side (procurement and purchasing) and one for the supply side (sales and distribution). This way, knowledge about environmental impacts on interface-performance from both ends of the dyad was gained. As delivery reliability, flexibility and inventory efficiency within a company can differ sharply for different sales/supply products, it was necessary to go down on product level to gain usable information. In consequence, respondents were asked to select one of their company's specific commodity groups for which the questions should be answered. To later enable classification of BSRs, additional product-specific data was collected describing the nature of the relationship. Classification was done using only characteristics of cross-company material flows without considering any general industry- or company-specific attributes: i.e., not directly linked to the commodity group. After a pretest, scales were further developed based on the respondents' feedbacks and the survey was run. The sample statistics are described in section 6.5.

Several statistical methods then were combined to also provide empirical evidence. First, mean comparison was done to show group-specific differences of the eight performance indicators. Furthermore, intra-group comparison of average storage time and value of stored goods was conducted to identify relative causalities between supplying and buying side of the same relationship type.

Then, contingent impacts on performance were tested for statistical significance and explained variance share was calculated using analysis of covariance (ANCOVA) with one categorical factor (relationship type) and several continuous covariates[30] (non-relationship-specific control variables). Each performance indicator was analyzed separately to isolate effects in the best possible way. As relevance of covariates for

[30] Consideration of covariates seems in particularly suitable in cases where significant differences between groups exist, resulting from supplementary impacts of one or more independent variables. Due to the method's confirmative character, selection of covariates is supposed to be based on a reasonable suspicion about causal relations between outcome and predictor variables (Herrmann and Seilheimer, 2000).

outcome variables was expected to vary, several tailored model designs were used to improve the basis for managerial implications for inter-firm performance assessment. In contrast to mean comparison, inventory values were not included to account for diverging average values of goods among the three relationship types, which would render an unbiased analysis of variance impossible.

As the main goal of both statistical analyses was to prove the effect of the relationship's characteristics on performance, the classification scheme of relationship types was crucial to all kind of examinations (also reflected in the results structure shown in section 6.6). All calculations were done in PASW Statistics 18 (release 18.0.1). The survey gathering the required data for the analysis above is described in section 6.5. Fulfillment of methodical assumptions is described in the subsequent paragraph.

ANCOVA - Validity of methodological assumptions

Before analysis was conducted, evaluation of general methodological assumptions of ANCOVA was done to appraise result validity related to basic requirements of regular variance analysis[31] for the categorical variable (relationship type), as well as specific requirements for the regression part[32] (covariates). Because ANCOVA was executed independently for each performance item, it was also necessary to check assumptions item-wise. The following discussion centers around observed violations to determine whether ANCOVA is appropriate in this study.

In looking at relationship types, assumptions of normal distribution and population variances homogeneity were violated in almost all eight settings. Consequently, violation severity was assessed next by analyzing group sizes[33] and the ratio between

[31] The basic assumptions can be summarized as follows: normally distributed observations in each group, homogeneity of variance between groups and independency of observations (Stevens, 1990).

[32] In methodological literature a number of different aspects impacting result validity are discussed. Hereby, the different criteria vary in their severity of consequences in case of violation. Discussion different criteria, Stevens (1975: 163) comes to the conclusion that the most important checks to be made are 'to see whether there is a linear relationship between dependent variable and the covariates and whether homogeneity of regression slopes is tenable'.This is basically in line with Bortz (2005)

[33] Drawing on Bock (1975), Stevens (1990) states that sums of 50 or more observations approximate to normality even if the distribution departs strongly from normality. For moderately non-normal distributions 10 to

largest and smallest group[34]; these parameters can measure how serious the effect of violations on type one and type two error rates can be. Referring to the three groups of relationships, both aspects indicate that variance analysis can basically be applied without any restrictions. However, some peculiarities in terms of group size must be considered for the four inventory-related items. Performance values for reliability and flexibility in the BSR are the same for information collected on both sides of the dyad, so that all records of one group can be used for analysis. This does not apply to the four items measuring inventory efficiency, as these were only collected for one side of the dyad, from which the questionnaire was completed. Accordingly, data records from suppliers include only inventory information on their own finished goods warehouse and vice versa. This leads to lower group sizes when analyzing inventory levels and storage times, as the three main groups have to be split up depending on the dyad perspective. Although group sizes were still in an acceptable range, this led to increased ratios of largest/smallest group of about 2.0. To double-check for the effect of unequal group sizes, calculations were also done with reduced groups[35] (records selected by random). As only very minor deviations of results were observed, the original groups were kept.

To check appropriateness of covariates, Pearson's R[36] was used to test significant correlation with dependent variables. As covariates were solely selected on a theoretical basis, few of the expected correlations turned out to be not significant. To double-check whether results of the affected ANCOVA models were biased to prevent misinterpretation, these models were calculated in two ways, one including these covariates and one without. Comparison of model results showed very slight deviations in terms of variance explained and did not lead to changes in any other

20 observations can be considered sufficient. This is line with Bortz (2005) who, referring to a number of corresponding examinations such as the one of Glass et al. (1972), summarizes that one should switch to nonparametric tests in case of violations of normality if groups sizes are smaller than 10.

[34] If the groups sizes are approximately equal, variance analysis is robust for unequal variances (Bortz, 2005; Stevens). Stevens (1975) names a ratio of largest/smallest<1.5 as upper bound.

[35] Glaser (1978) suggests eliminating observations in larger groups to get equal-sized groups. Reduction has to be done by random selection. This way it can be guaranteed that variance analysis can be applied despite violation of assumptions (Eschweiler et al., 2007).

[36] As recommended by Backhaus et al. (2011).

variables' significance. Thus, no methodological adjustments to the models were necessary. As non-significant variables were also expected to provide useful information, especially for managerial practice, original designs were used. However, special attention will be paid to these cases in the discussion of results.

Moreover, homogeneity of the covariates' regression slopes was analyzed. As ANCOVA can be considered a method quite robust for violation of this assumption in case of equally sized groups[37], analysis was limited the following two aspects: first, a visual control of effect directions was done. Second, maximum differences between standardized regression coefficients[38] were calculated separately for each setting and each covariate within the setting. Maximum discrepancies were below 0.2 in most cases, and none crossed the barrier of 0.35.

In conclusion, ANCOVA seems basically applicable for examining the described causalities, despite partially violated methodological conditions; most issues are counterbalanced by group characteristics (minimum sizes and ratios). In cases where violations were still considered potentially serious, additional double-checks were made to test severity of biases to guarantee validity of model results.

---

[37] Bortz (2005) claims that ANCOVA is very robust for violation of this assumption in terms of type 1 and type 2 errors in case of equally sized groups. He also lists a number of studies having proved this statement (e.g. Dretzke et al., 1982; Hamilton, 1977; Rogosa, 1980).

[38] Drawing on Wu (1984), Bortz (2005) names an upper bound of 0.4 as reference value under which deviations can be considered negligible in their biasing effect.

6.4. Model development

Drawing on the theoretical findings, three kinds of model entities need to be differentiated in the statistical model (ANCOVA) examining the effect of the industrial relationship's characteristics on performance of cross-company activities:

1. *Interface-performance indicators* describing reliability, flexibility and inventory efficiency of business relationships (represented by continuous outcome variables).
2. *Type of relationship*, reflecting the relationship-specific contingencies, whose influence on interface-performance is to be analyzed (represented by a categorical factor variable).
3. *Non-relationship-specific influence factors* such as market and production conditions which also are expected to have a significant impact on interface-performance and thus must be considered (represented by continuous control variables).

6.4.1. Interface-performance in buyer-supplier relationships

Various indicators for all three identified dimensions of interface-performance have been defined in different ways in logistics and operations literature, depending on the underlying understanding of performance and the questions to be answered. As diversity and general reliability of existing measurement scales are not within our frame of reference, subsequent sections do not try to give a comprehensive overview of variety of existing scales in literature[39]. Rather, discussion will focus on the measurement indicators actually selected from a broad range of existing contributions. An overview of the eight identified items for interface-performance is given in table 9.

[39] For exhaustive discussion of key performance indicators in inter-firm relationships see, for instance, Gunasekaran et al.(2001), Beamon (1999) or Toni and Tonchia (2001).

Table 9: Performance dimensions and indicators at the buyer-supplier interface

Performance dimension	Performance indicator	Shortcut
Delivery reliability	On time delivery	REL_1
	Average delay	REL_2
Delivery flexibility	Average delivery time	$FLEX_1$
	Delivery speed for replacement supplies	$FLEX_2$
Inventory efficiency (supplier)	Average storing time	INV_{S1}
	Average inventory level (value)	INV_{S2}
Inventory efficiency (buyer)	Average storing time	INV_{B1}
	Average inventory level (value)	INV_{B2}

Delivery reliability

In particular two measurement items are commonly used to measure delivery reliability: on-time delivery and perfect order fulfillment (e.g. Gunasekaran et al., 2001; Swink et al., 2007; Tracey, 2004;). On-time delivery can be understood as a pre-condition for perfect order fulfillment which can be extended to consider aspects like product quality (correct amount at the right time in the right quality and at the right place). As these additional aspects focus mainly on production-related topics outside the scope of this investigation, perfect order fulfillment is not taken into account.

Another important reliability measure for interface-performance, strongly connected to on-time delivery, is what Beamon (1999: 283) calls 'average lateness'. Lateness, defined as delivery date minus due date, provides essential additional information for control activities as it also indicates the severity of late deliveries.

Delivery flexibility

In general, operational flexibility measurement items in industrial business relationships are strongly time-related. However, the time periods indicators refer to may vary. For instance, time periods can refer to the time slot between order placement by customer and delivery (e.g. Tracey 2004), to the time-slot between order confirmation and delivery (e.g. Gunasekaran et al., 2001) or to response time for order quantity changes (e.g. Kim 2006). To derive useful managerial implications, it must be ascertained whether the supplier's production is based on customer orders or decoupled from actual demand. As supplier's production concept is one of the classification criteria for the relationship types, defined in the subsequent section, there is no need to treat order confirmation date separately at this point. Therefore, customer response time is selected, defined as average time from incoming order to delivery at the buyer's incoming goods department (Toni and Tonchia, 2001).

A second important performance indicator for the supplier's delivery flexibility is its ability to quickly react to unplanned orders,[40] when deliveries were insufficient and compensation delivery was necessary (labeled as delivery speed of replacement supplies).

Inventory efficiency

Because required delivery reliability and flexibility are expected to strongly correlate with safety stocks and average inventory levels, neither can be analyzed without considering this efficiency dimension of interface-performance. Capital tied up in inventory is an important cost factor, directly affecting the company's profitability. It is a common and appropriate indicator applied to measure efficiency (e.g. Beamon, 1999; Toni and Tonchia, 2001; Gunasekaran, 2001). To gain more differentiated conclusions, distinction is made between supplier's and buyer's inventory. For both sides, average value of inventory held is measured.

Moreover, average storage time of goods is collected to allow for additional analysis of turnover rates and to enhance conclusions in terms of risk-bearing and inventory efficiency.

---

[40] Only few researchers recognized the importance of separately measuring the severity of unplanned orders like response time for product returns (Kim 2006). Even though, no contributions were found explicitly considering delivery speed of replacement supplies, this item will be included as it is expected to have a non-negligible influence on customer satisfaction.

Summary

Performance of operational processes and activities at the buyer-supplier interface must sufficiently represent attributes of both partners in order to draw a comprehensive picture of the relationship's performance. It is required to come from two company-specific views to one dyadic perspective, commonly taken by buyer and supplier. This double perspective is visualized in figure 22.

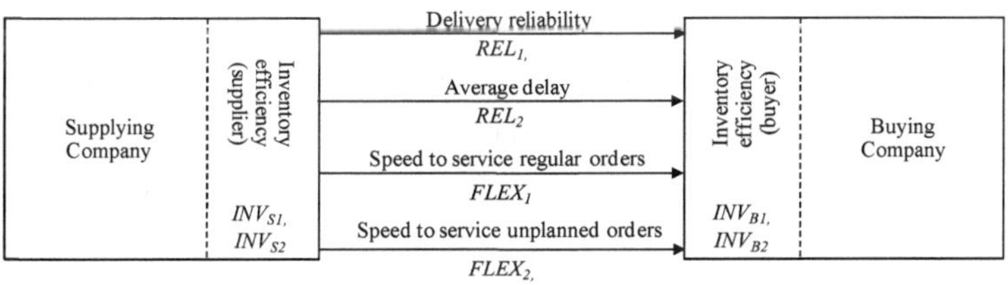

Figure 22: Performance indicators at the buyer-supplier interface

6.4.2. Types of buyer-supplier relationships

As discussed in section 6.4.2, relationships of the same type should show comparable supplier-specific capabilities and buyer-specific demands to be comparable to each other. Focusing on actual physical movement of goods, the nature of BSRs' attainable and required performance is reflected by the way cross-company material flows are organized (Meyer and Stadler, 2005; Schweicher and Jursch, 2006). In consequence, classification of BSRs must also consider these logistics aspects adequately. This affects concepts of supplier-specific, as well as buyer-specific, logistics activities. To clearly identify conditional influences resulting from relationship-specific characteristics, a goal-oriented classification scheme for BSRs needs to sufficiently consider logistics configuration of the whole dyad. Logistics conditions should ideally be homogenous within all relationships of the same type, whereas they should be as heterogeneous as possible between different types. Both are necessary to isolate type-specific effects on the identified performance indicators and – in the next step – to draw valid conclusions for the evaluation of interface-performance BSRs.

Constituent attributes of buyer-supplier relationships

BSRs represent an elementary trans-sectional component of supply chains of any kind. Analysis of relationship-specific attributes of existing supply chain typologies thus serves as a basis for the development of a tailored BSR classification scheme.

Several such typologies[41] can be found in literature. The one of Meyr and Stadtler (2005) seems particularly suited from a logistics point of view. The authors delineate two basic types of attributes: 'functional attributes' of the involved supply chain entities (companies) and 'structural attributes' reflecting the relations among these entities. A single entity is described by four functional categories (procurement, production, distribution and sales concept) whereas the relationship between two companies is defined by topography and the level of integration and coordination between them. Adapted to a single business relationship with one supplying and one buying company, the two companies' functional attributes and the structural attributes of their transactional remain to characterize this business relationship. As the focus of the new classification scheme is set on logistics related to cross-company material flows, characteristics directly connected to the joint interface are further limited. This means that neither supplier's upstream attributes (procurement and production concepts) nor buyer's downstream attributes (production, sales and distribution concepts) are considered. In consequence, the supplier's sales and distribution concepts, as well the buyer's procurement concept, will serve as a basis for the classification scheme for relationship types. The connections between the different types of attributes are represented in figure 23.

[41] Lejeune and Yakova (2005), for instance, distinguish communicative, coordinative, collaborative and co-opetitive supply chains, whereas Fine (1998) differs between integrated and modular supply chains. Another widely accepted typology is provided by Vonderembse et al (2006). Drawing on contributions from Fisher (1997) and Christopher (2000) the authors propose a concept of lean, agile and hybrid supply chains.

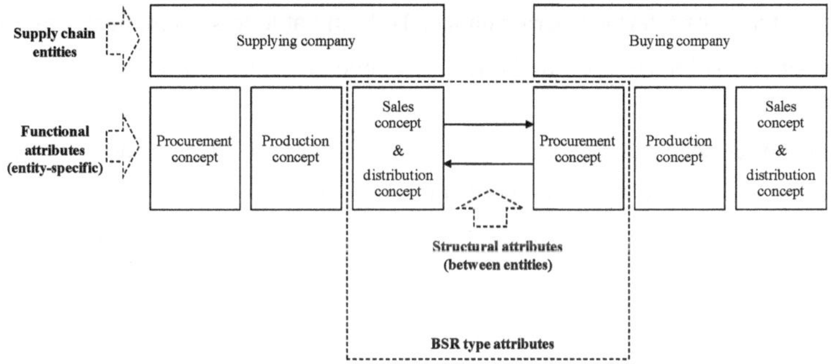

Figure 23: Relationship type attributes in the context of functional and structural supply chain attributes In principal, the underlying concepts for the different attribute categories can be combined in any possible ways. A classification scheme for mutually exclusive relationship types needs to group combinations expected to have similar effects on performance. An overview of different production, sales and procurement concepts is shown in table 10.

Table 10: Concepts describing sales, distribution and procurement types

Concept category	Selected attributes (concepts)
Procurement concept (buyer-specific)	- Just in time - Just in sequence - Vendor managed inventory - Delivery at warehouse and storage
Sales concept (supplier-specific)	- Make-to-stock - Make-to-forecast - Make-to-order - Engineer-to-order
Distribution concept (supplier-specific)	- Direct delivery - Singe- and multi-level cross-docking concepts - Singe- and multi-level storage concepts

A conceptual approach to classifying types of buyer-supplier relationships

Having identified three basic concept categories defining a relationship's nature, types of BSRs with similar business environments need to be defined. In other words: combinations of the supplier's sales and distribution concepts and the buyer's procurement concept must be found, with a comparable fit of capabilities and requirements in terms of interface-performance. To being able to systematically assign these concept-combinations to specific BSR types, several steps must be taken.

- First, supplier-specific concepts must be graded to what degree they limit the maximum achievable interface-performance (upper-bound of fit), and buyer-specific concepts must be classified to what degree they determine the minimum required interface-performance (lower-bound of fit).
- Second, precedence constraints between the three categories of relationship attributes must be identified (Ahlert and Evanschitzky, 2003) as some concepts are expected to play a more dominant role in characterizing BSRs than others. In these cases, the general level of the corridor of fit is determined primarily by one side of the BSR.
- Third, combinations that do not make sense from an economic point of view must be excluded, for instance a 'JIT' procurement concept with 'engineer-to-order sales concept'.
- Fourth, based on the identified precedence constraints, combinations with the same dominant concept can be aggregated because distinction between the dominated concepts is no longer necessary.

Development of a framework for systemizing the conceptual approach

Regarding *procurement concepts,* the example of a manufacturer dealing with a broad range of supplied goods (e.g. an OEM in automotive industry) will be used illustrate how comparability of BSRs vis-à-vis buyer's performance requirements may vary. It is easy to imagine that high-value components being daily delivered just-in-time directly to the assembly line (e.g. car seats) need to fulfill higher performance requirements, for instance in terms of delivery reliability, than parts or liquids being irregularly delivered to the manufacturer's stock (e.g. paint for coatings). In consequence, a comparison of types of BSRs can be done roughly as the required effort to achieve 'sufficient' performance strongly differs. Especially JIT- and JIS-based BSRs relationships require intense information exchange and often go along with IT and infrastructural integration of suppliers. This also applies somewhat to VMI-based concepts. In these cases, distinction of the supplier's order and distribution concepts is of minor importance as both features are aligned to procurement's needs. All of these kinds of relationships require a high degree of reliability by simultaneously minimizing inventory levels on the supplying side. Depending on the demanded response times, the risk of supply gaps due to production and delivery times must be compensated by safety stocks on the supplying side. In case the buyer applies a delivery-to-warehouse concept, a supplementary differentiation must be made in terms of responsibility for inventory control in the customer's incoming goods warehouse. If the supplier is in charge of inventory and carries out the orders, requirements for information sharing and integration to a buyer's supply processes similar to the ones of VMI concepts occur. The way, the two companies interact fundamentally changes, if inventory is managed by the buyer himself. If this is the case, more emphasis needs to be put on supplier -specific features of the relationship as order and distribution concepts gain increasing importance for characterizing the whole BSR.

The *sales concept* indicates how much supplier's production is linked to the actual demand. Two basic forms exist: supplier's production can either be strictly decoupled from customers or initiated by supplier order (standardized or customized products). Both forms can further be split into sub-forms such as make-to-stock or make-to-forecast (decoupled concepts) and make-to-order or engineer-to-order (customer order-based). As far as interface-performance, capabilities required to achieve a certain response time or reliability ratio as well as the supplier's weighting of the different performance aspects are expected to vary between the different concepts because the sales concept often results from product attributes like the degree of standardization. Decoupled sales concepts, for instance, can only be applied in case of standardized products[42] whereas customized products can only be initiated by customer orders as additional information from the buyer is required. As order processing for customized goods tends to take longer than for standardized version of the same product (provided this even makes sense), it makes it difficult to compare relationships with different

[42] However, production of standardized goods can also be based on customer's orders. In this specific case, it can be assumed that products are extremely valuable and complex which, in turn, makes them again comparable to customized goods in terms of attainable reliability and flexibility ratios. For this reason, the sales concepts based on customer orders will not further be distinguished in customized and non-customized goods.

sales concepts. The same restriction in terms of comparability applies to attainable reliability levels because on-time delivery is expected to be harder to meet the bigger the level of customization is. Moreover, sales concepts have extremely different impacts on supplier's inventory management, as future demands are available in case of order-based production and inventories can be handled more efficiently.

The applied *distribution concept* reflects features like delivery and storage concepts and the deployment of transportation means. Depending on product specifics and additional factors like geographic proximity of sales markets (supplier's point of view) respectively supply markets (buyer's point of view), distribution structure can have a considerable impact on interface-performance. Time-sensitive indicators and inventory efficiency are particularly affected by number of distribution stages and modes of transportation. However, as it can be assumed that the characteristics of distributional processes are usually somewhat aligned to either sales or procurement concepts, the distribution concept is dominant in any case. Consequently, it will not be considered separately in the framework of the classification approach shown in figure 24.

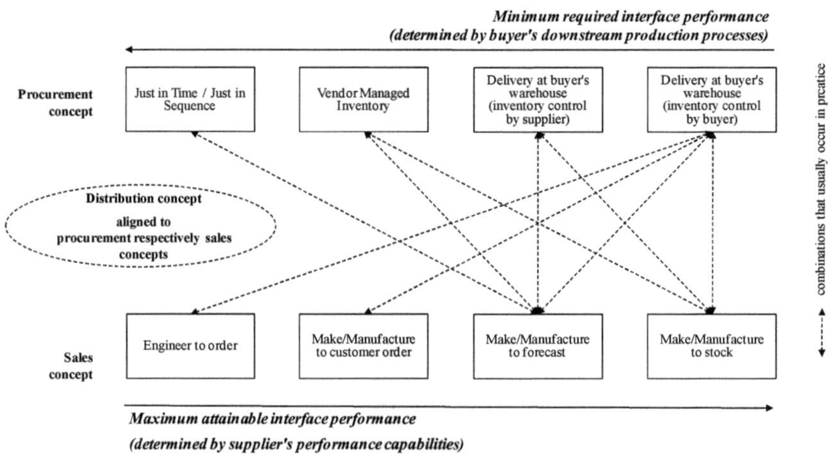

Figure 24: Framework for classifying types of BSRs

Development of classification scheme for buyer-supplier relationships

Based on the developed conceptual approach and framework for classifying BSRs, three specific types are now defined to serve as a basis for the empirical analysis. The first type unites BSRs with a strong domination by procurement concepts. In these relationships, suppliers are usually highly integrated. Consequently, sales and distribution concepts generally play a subordinated role because transactional processes are aligned to procurement requirements. The second type includes BSRs moderately connected, meaning that the sales concept is order-based. Here, no clear precedence constraints procurement and sales concept can be assumed. Companies in relationships of the third type, in contrast, are loosely connected to each other, meaning that production is completely decoupled from actual demand. An overview of the three types is given in table 11.

Table 11: Basic types of BSRs

Relationship type	**Description**	**Classification criteria**
A Highly integrated BSRs	The supplier is highly integrated in the buyer's procurement and production processes. He needs access to production-specific information of your customer like current stock levels and the production plan. The buyer's sales concept and distribution processes are clearly aligned to the buyer's needs.	All BSRs with a JIT, JIS or VMI concepts are included. Furthermore, relationships where control of the buyer's inventory is performed by supplier are taken into account.
B Moderately connected BSRs	The supplier is not in charge of the buyer's inventory management as orders are normally placed by the buying company. The supplier's production is based on incoming customer orders, directly linked to the actual demand.	The buyer follows a delivery-at-warehouse procurement policy. Supplier's production is directly linked to a customer order, either by make-to-order or engineer-to-order concept.
C Loose BSRs	The supplier is not in charge of the buyer's inventory management as orders are normally placed by the buying company. The supplier's production is decoupled from incoming customer orders, not directly linked to the actual demand.	The buyer follows a delivery-at-warehouse procurement policy. Supplier's production is not directly linked to the actual demand. Production is based on either a make-to-stock or a make-to-forecast concept.

6.4.3. Market- and production-specific contingencies

To gain a more comprehensive picture and to better isolate the effect actually caused by the relationship's characteristics, supplementary influences on efficiency and effectiveness of transactional activities must be considered in the analysis. One one hand, this addresses effects caused by the market conditions where the two companies interact. On the other hand, performance-determining effects resulting from production-specific characteristics need to be extracted. Statistical models must consider both kinds of contingent influences in forms of covariates to improve implications for the role of the three defined relationship types for interface-performance. Table lists the identified control variables of both kinds of contingencies. Discussion of the variables and their expected impacts for the four categories of interface-performance follows.

Table 12: Contingency categories and control variables at the buyer-supplier interface

Contingency category	Control variables (covariates)	Shortcut
Market-specific	Stability of demand	MAR_1
	Geographic magnitude	MAR_2
	Competitiveness between suppliers	MAR_3
Production-specific	Standardization of supplier's production processes	$PROD_1$
	Standardization of buyer's production processes	$PROD_2$

Market-specific contingencies

One of the most import market characteristics impacting interface-performance of BSRs can be found in *stability of demand*. Analyzed in many ways in an SCM context (e.g. Simatupang and Sridharan, 2005; Nakano, 2009; Germain et al., 2008), direct causalities between demand uncertainty and performance have been proven; forecasting abilities are strongly connected to supplier's performance capabilities. Discussing delivery reliability of suppliers, Meyr and Stadler (2005) emphasize that continuity in demand particularly affects supplier's ability to react in a reliable manner to unplanned demand. Furthermore, suppliers acting in volatile markets will provide higher inventory levels as the ability to satisfy short-term demand can be considered a major competitive factor. To guarantee comparability of business relationships acting on markets with different levels of demand uncertainty, the intensity of demand fluctuations must be taken into account when analyzing supplier's reliability and inventory efficiency.

Another important performance determinant lies in the *geographical magnitude*[43] of the BSRs. The range of sales markets (supplier's perspective)/supply markets (buyer's perspective) can vary from regional to global which affects interface-performance in several ways. Most importantly, time needed for transportation processes increases with growing internationalization (Behr and Semlinger, 2004). In addition to extending response times for planned and unplanned orders, requirements for fulfilling reliability promises also rise due to the growing complexity of distribution activities. To compensate risk of production downtimes resulting from the time delay between order placement and arrival of goods, buyers will probably show a tendency to keep higher safety stocks in cases of long transportation distances. So, in contrast to demand fluctuation, geographical magnitude impacts safety-stock levels on the buying side and thus needs to be considered when analyzing supplier's inventory efficiency.

Discussing the role of market and environmental circumstances for performance in business relationships, the *degree of supplier competition*[44] must be considered; it represents a major driver for performance levels provided by suppliers. This concerns the general situation on the supply side and is reflected by the number of suppliers offering the same products and, in turn, the dependency of the supplier on its buyer. Especially in competitive environments, suppliers are forced to guarantee relatively high reliability and flexibility standards in order to prevail on the market. Evaluating the influence of a business relationship's characteristics on delivery reliability and

[43] For a more thorough discussion on the role of internationalization of supply chains for relationship management see Kutschker and Schmid (2008) and Behr and Semlinger (2004).

[44] The need for considering competition when analyzing performance-related issues in SCM, is reflected by the high share of contributions paying attention to competitiveness in their empirical analysis (e.g. Curkovic et al., 2000; Eng, 2006; Daugherty et al., 2003; Defee and Stank, 2005)

flexibility thus must account for the intensity of competition on the market to diminish bias.

Production-specific contingencies

When analyzing suppliers' upstream production and supply activities effects on BSR interface-performance, focus must center on any kind of activities affecting delivery time. Especially when supply company production is triggered by customer order placement; e.g. if a make-to-order or engineer-to-order concept is followed, delivery flexibility is largely determined by upstream processes like supply of materials and manufacturing of goods. In order to correctly control for such impacts, a meta-variable aggregating the differing production characteristics is needed. The importance of production characteristics for a company's performance capabilities has been widely recognized by researchers. Meyr and Stadler (2005) name repetitiveness of operations as a major aggregate attribute in characterizing the influence of production on response times. The authors state that lead time is negatively connected to the standardization level[45] of production processes, arguing that time need for mass products, manufactured constantly and over a long period, is usually lower than for goods produced in batches or even one by one. In consequence, flexibility is assumed to go up with an increasing level of process standardization and time interval between order-placement and its arrival at the buyer's warehouse tends to become shorter. At the same time, inventory levels and storing time in the supplier's finished goods warehouse are expected to decrease. The level of standardization of production processes will thus be taken as a control variable for flexibility indicators. Moreover, it will be used to monitor production-specific effects on the supplier's inventory efficiency.

On the other side of the dyad, standardization of buyer's production must be equally considered when analyzing buyer-specific inventory efficiency, for the same reason;

[45] Several contributions to performance management in dyadic inter-firm relationships or supply chains can be found, indirectly addressing production characteristics by considering the product's level of customization (e.g. Claycomb et al., 1999; Squire et al., 2009; Sengupta et. al., 2006; Dehning et al., 2007, Christiansen et al., 2005; Autry and Golicic, 2009; Sanders, 2007). As the level of customization limits the maximum achievable level of standardization both issues are strongly connected to each other.

the buyer's planning ability is expected to positively correlate with the standardization level of his downstream production processes. An exception occurs if the downstream end of the dyad (buyer) is a wholesaler or retailer with no production. As production-related influences completely omit these, buyers can be treated as 'production concept with the maximum possible standardization'. A direct connection between buyer's production (for a producing company) characteristics and the remaining performance categories is not assumed; reliability and flexibility requirements to guarantee stable and unbroken production are already reflected by the buyer's procurement concept. The same applies to wholesaling and retailing companies.

Model development

All of the identified contingencies – though not directly linked to the relationship – are expected to have a significant impact on interface-performance and thus have to be considered as control variables in the empirical analysis. However, as the foregoing discussion made apparent, not every control variable is relevant to every performance indicator in the same way. Particularly between the four categories of interface-performance indicators, impacts are expected to vary. To sufficiently consider these differences, four adjusted ANCOVA model design with varying sets of covariates are to be developed for (a) delivery reliability, (b) delivery flexibility, (c) supplier-related inventory efficiency and (d) buyer-related inventory efficiency. An overview of expected causalities between contingencies and performance categories is given in table 13. A schematic illustration of the four model designs can be found in figure B-7 in section 6.6.

Table 13: Expected impacts from non-relationship-specific contingencies on interface-performance categories

Model design	Performance Category	$PROD_1$	$PROD_2$	MAR_1	MAR_2	MAR_3
(a)	Deliver reliability	-	-	X	X	X
(b)	Delivery flexibility	X	-	-	X	X
(c)	Inventory efficiency (supplier)*	X	-	X	-	-
(d)	Inventory efficiency (buyer)*	-	X	-	X	-

An 'X' indicates that the control variable is expected to have a significant impact on indicators of the respective performance category.

* In contrast to mean comparison, ANOVA will be limited to average storage time, as inventory value is not comparable between groups due to diverging average values (for further explanations see section 6.3).

6.5. Survey development and sample description

Due to the dyadic perspective taken in the analysis, two equally structured surveys[46] were designed to gather the information required of the identified model entities. A description of measurement items can be found in the annex in table 25 (performance items), table 26 (BSR-specific contingencies) and table 27 (environmental market- and production-specific influence factors). The one addressing relationship-specific issues from the supplier's perspective was sent to sales departments and company units in charge of distribution activities. The equivalent questionnaire for the buy side was dispensed to procurement and purchasing departments. In total, the survey was mailed to about 2'500 manufacturing companies, wholesalers and retailers from ten different industries. As the survey was conducted in cooperation with the German Association for Materials Management, Purchasing and Logistics (AMMPL), it was also available online on the official websites of AMMPL and the author's university. Following Dillman's (2007) Tailored Design Method for web surveys, we sent up to three reminders including a personalized link to the survey.

[46] As answering the questions referred to a specific commodity group, to be selected by the respondent, comprehensive knowledge about sales respectively distribution channels was required as well as a basic understanding of production characteristics and market conditions of the goods. Thus, the actual position of the respondent was of minor importance and the corresponding information was not collected.

Responses were received from 210 companies. Because the relationship type had to be classified for every respondent, nine who had not completely specified the applied sales, distribution and procurement concepts could not be considered in the analysis. Additionally, five records had to be excluded,[47] as at least one of the eight collected performance values exceeded the predefined interval scales. In these cases, the actual value was not known and comparability to measurement values within the predefined range was not given. Statistics for the remaining sample of 196 are shown in table 14.

According to the classification criteria, described in section 6.4.2, the BSRs could be assigned to three predefined groups of highly integrated relationships (60), moderately connected relationships (59) and loose relationships (75). The three groups served as basis for empirical analysis (mean comparison and ANCOVA) of the eight identified performance indicators.

[47] This practice is also in line with recommended standard procedures from Backhaus et al. (2011) and Eschweiler et al. (2007) who suggest eliminating strong outliers to improve validity of measurement results in variance analysis.

Table 14: Sample statistics

Demographics and attributes of relationships (N=196)		Supplier	Buyer	Total
Perspective on the dyad	Supplier's point of view			46.8%
	Buyer's point of view			53.2%
Industry in which the BSR acts	Machinery and equipment			16.4%
	Food, beverages			14.9%
	Coke and refined petroleum products			2.0%
	Electronics, electronic equipment			21.9%
	Chemicals, pharmaceuticals, cosmetics			9.0%
	Paper and printing industry			7.5%
	Automotive industry			17.4%
	Metals, heavy industry			5.0%
	Textiles			2.0%
	Agriculture, forestry, wood-processing			1.5%
	Other			2.5%
Respondent's position	CEO or other member of mgt. board			16.7%
	Head of logistics			33.3%
	Head of SCM			6.0%
	Head of purchasing			1.2%
	Head of sales			6.0%
	Logistics manager			1.2%
	Sales manager			9.5%
	Area manager from other divisions			20.2%
	Experts (e.g. in finance, product development)			6.0%
	Other experts (e.g. in finance, product development)			6.0%
Company turnover (2009)	< 7.5 Mio. CHF	1.1%	1.0%	1.0%
	7.5-15 Mio. CHF	5.4%	3.9%	4.6%
	16-75 Mio. CHF	25.0%	24.5%	24.7%
	76-150 Mio. CHF	12.0%	10.8%	11.3%
	151-750 Mio. CHF	31.5%	20.6%	25.7%
	751-1'500 Mio. CHF	7.6%	7.8%	7.7%
	1'501-3'750 Mio. CHF	4.3%	6.9%	5.7%
	>3'750 Mio. CHF	13.0%	24.5%	19.1%
Company employees (2009)	< 10	1.1%	0.0%	0.5%
	10-50	7.7%	2.9%	5.1%
	51-100	8.8%	9.5%	9.2%
	101-500	34.1%	30.5%	32.1%
	501-1'000	18.7%	12.4%	15.3%
	1'001-5'000	12.1%	14.3%	13.3%
	>5'000	17.6%	30.5%	24.5%

6.6. Results and discussion of empirical analysis

Empirical analysis results are presented as follows; first, a summary of performance indicators' means is provided, showing actual average values to get an impression of group-specific differences. Then, ANCOVA model results are discussed, showing significance of expected causalities and shares of variance explained. Scientific and managerial implications are derived in section 6.7 and need for future research is specified.

6.6.1. Mean comparison

While comparison of the four reliability and flexibility values is useful to analyze basic differences between BSR types, indicators for both partners' inventory efficiency primary help to better understand conditions within relationships of the same nature. Table gives an overview of group-specific means and standard deviations of the interface-performance indicators under investigation. The most important observations are summarized below.

Table 15: Group-specific means and standard deviations of performance indicators

BSR type		REL_1 (%)	REL_2 (days)	$FLEX_1$ (days)	$FLEX_2$ (days)	INV_{S1} (days)	INV_{S2} (mio. CHF)	INV_{B1} (days)	INV_{B2} (mio. CHF)
A	Mean	92.47	6.83	21.98	6.56	13.18	2.967	5.90	1.565
Highly	N	60	59	58	55	40	32	20	14
integrated	Std. Deviation	5.170	7.870	27.282	8.187	12.074	3.216	5.230	2.057
B	Mean	84.93	8.60	31.79	13.34	6.75	1.923	14.51	2.852
Moderately	N	75	72	71	71	24	21	43	39
connected	Std. Deviation	14.875	8.802	26.643	12.362	6.556	2.540	12.627	2.690
C	Mean	89.95	5.29	15.41	8.71	14.78	4.485	14.94	2.765
Loosely	N	59	58	56	55	18	14	35	34
connected	Std. Deviation	10.562	4.801	16.637	9.134	12.693	3.251	13.068	3.023
Total	Mean	88.79	7.03	23.76	9.87	11.65	2.957	12.91	2.611
	N	194	189	185	181	82	67	98	87
	Std. Deviation	11.701	7.566	25.109	10.633	11.254	3.120	12.125	2.749

Type A – Highly integrated buyer-supplier relationships

Analyzing reliability ratios of the three groups, highly integrated relationships show the highest average rate with about 92.5% on-time delivery: plausible, as these forms of cooperation normally occur in cases where reliability is of extraordinary importance for the buyer's production processes. Because these relations are mostly dominated by buyers needs, a second basic tendency can be observed: inventories are held by suppliers as long as possible and consigned inventories (in case of VMI) respectively work-in-progress inventories (in case of JIT/JIS) on the buy side are reduced to a minimum. This is reflected by two figures: an average storage time of 5.9 days, in comparison to about 15 days for the other relationship types and, second, an inventory level half the amount of average inventory values stored by suppliers. This rate strongly diverges from both other groups where buyers have to carry a greater share of the relationship's overall storage costs.

Type B – Moderately connected buyer-supplier relationships

The group of moderately connected relationships includes all kinds of BSRs where supplier's production is directly linked to a customer's order. This variable affects interface-performance in several ways. First of all, by far the lowest on-time delivery rates and the longest average delivery delays can be observed. With only around 95% and almost nine days, both figures indicate that these forms of cooperation are, especially in contrast to type A relationships, mainly determined by the suppliers' capabilities. Looking at flexibility, the longest periods are required for compensation deliveries, with an average customer response time of more than 30 days and a 13 days delivery time. As already mentioned, a basic reason for these relatively low performance levels can be found in the typically occurring need for product customization. The more customized the products are, the harder to fulfill reliability promises due to growing impacts of upstream production and supply processes. However, the picture changes when looking at the comparatively low values of inventory efficiency items. As the produced goods are already sold, suppliers can basically limit storage time for finished goods to time needed for transport consolidation. With an average storage time of less than seven days and the lowest share of inventory held, type B relationships showed the highest performance in this category.

Type C – Loose buyer-supplier relationships

BSRs where supplier's production is decoupled from the actual customer demand showed relatively high rates for on-time delivery, with an average value of almost 90%. Furthermore, the shortest customer response time - with slightly more than 15 days - was measured. The two figures support the assumption that reliability and flexibility play a more important role than in type B relationships, as the influence of both performance categories on a supplier's competitive ability is comparatively strong, especially in markets where suppliers can easily replaced. For the same reason, level of inventory held is the largest of all three groups, with the longest average storage time and the highest type-specific share of inventory held: almost inverse to the ratio in type A relationships.

6.6.2. Analysis of covariance

After examining the group-specific differences of actual performance values, six of the eight performance indicators were analyzed by ANCOVA to estimate significance of deviations. As described in section 6.4, four different model designs were used due to performance category-specific differences. Model designs and entities are illustrated in figure 25.

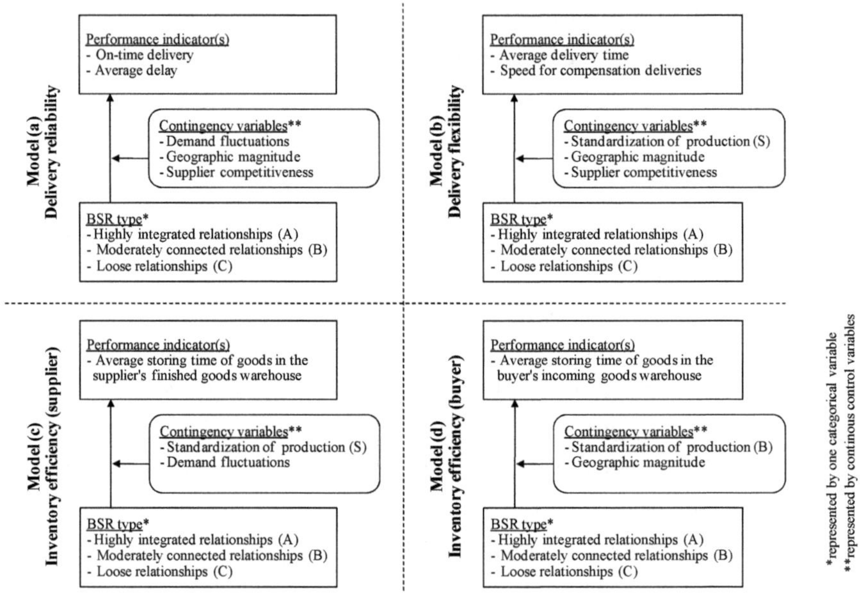

*Figure 25: The four applied ANCOVA model designs for analyzing the delivery reliability, flexibility and inventory efficiency*The model results are summarized in table 16 listing F-values, significances and shares of variance explained for the group-variable and covariates. Moreover, the adjusted R squared is given to assess the models explanatory power.

Table 16: ANCOVA model results

Model design	Outcome variable	Adjusted R^2		BSR type	$PROD_1$	$PROD_2$	MAR_1	MAR_2	MAR_3
(a) Delivery reliability	REL_1	.143	F-value	5.584**			13.337***	.175	6.659*
			Partial Eta Squared	.057			.067	.001	.035
	REL_2	.073	F-value	2.118			5.175*	5.817*	.592
			Partial Eta Squared	.023			.028	.031	.003
(b) Delivery flexibility	$RESP_1$	.184	F-value	6.872***	2.957(*)			16.344***	8.256**
			Partial Eta Squared	.072	.016			.084	.044
	$RESP_3$	.208	F-value	8.370***	.026			10.266**	24.930***
			Partial Eta Squared	.088	.000			.056	.125
(c) Inventory efficiency (s)	$INVS_1$	.153	F-value	6.183**	5.516*		4.461*		
			Partial Eta Squared	0.138	.021		.038		
(d) Inventory efficiency (b)	$INVB_1$	.070	F-value	4.466**		.132		1.970	
			Partial Eta Squared	0.088		.001		.021	

F-values significant at p-level: *** $p<.001$, ** $p<.01$, * $p<.05$, (*) $p<.10$

Delivery reliability – Model design (a)

Analysis of impacts on on-time delivery reveals the significance of the BSR type. As mean comparison showed, differences between highly integrated and relationships are primarily responsible. As far as supplementary effects, demand fluctuations seem to play an important role for suppliers in being able to fulfill reliability promises. As expected, competitiveness between suppliers also to slightly impacted this performance item. No significant influence could be proven for geographic range of the markets where relational exchanges take place, leading to the assumption that even wide-ranged transportation and distribution processes can be scheduled exactly. All in all, a proportion of on-time variability of about 14.3% is accounted for by model (a).

The second performance indicator, examined with model design (a), measures average delay when goods are delivered late. As expected, transport distances, as well as intensity of demand fluctuations are significant to this item. However, neither systematic impact from the level of competiveness between suppliers nor from the BSR type is verifiable. In consequence, the overall model's explanatory power is also limited, reflected by an adjusted R^2 of 7%. This could result from the fact that there are other performance-determining sources causing variability of average delay not considered in the model. Possibly, relationship-specific characteristics, such as distribution structure and transportation means, are not sufficiently differentiated.

Delivery flexibility – Model design (b)

As assumed, the BSR type is highly significant for average customer response rates (effect size: 7.2%) and speed of compensation deliveries (effect size: 8.8%). The two market-related contingencies included also showed strong effects on both flexibility items, so that in both models about 20% of the indicator's variance is explained in total. The influence of standardization on the supplier's production processes (additionally considered in the applied model design (b)) cannot be statistically confirmed; only very low shares of variability can be traced back to this contingency.

This could indicate that production-specific characteristics are already part of the relationship features - more than previously expected.

Inventory efficiency (supplier) – Model design (c)

Examination of average storage times in the suppliers' finished goods warehouse statistically confirmed a systematic effect resulting from the group-specific difference in the way the companies interact. With almost 14%, this is the performance indicator with the highest share of variance explained by relationship type. In addition, both expected performance-determining impacts from environmental variables turned out to be significant as well. The model's total amount of variance explained lies slightly above 15%.

Inventory efficiency (buyer) –Model design (d)

With an adjusted R^2 of 7%, explanatory power of this model is limited. Although the impact of relationship type is tested significant, no causalities between both of the contingent influence factors and inventory efficiency on the buyer's side of the dyad could be confirmed. Notably, the poor role of the buyer's production process standardization indicates that storage times are mainly determined by relationship-specific attributes (i.e., buyer's procurement concept). More room for interpretation is possible for influence of geographic magnitude. Comparable to on-time delivery, transportation distance does not seem to play a decisive role, indicating that even transportation over very long distances causes little trouble for scheduling.

6.7. Summary 2nd phase of analysis

After outlining basic issues of performance evaluation in BSRs and suitable performance indicators and potential supplementary contingencies have been identified. A classification scheme (providing empirical evidence for the expected causalities and to explain variability and significance of performance items' value) has been developed from existing typologies and can serve as a basis for subsequent empirical analysis. Based on these findings, conclusions for practitioners will be derived in the following. In addition, limitations of quantitative analysis and the need for future research will be discussed.

Managerial implications

As mentioned initially, this research phase basically aims at improving performance evaluation in BSRs. Conceptual and empirical findings addressing this 'higher-order' goal can be divided into two basic parts.

First, a statement on the relative nature of performance and its environmental determinants (not comparing 'apples and oranges') was created. This represents the fundamental precondition for effective performance evaluation because it helps achieve more correct reference values and to define ranges when corrective action is triggered. This can be easily illustrated with an example of empirical analysis; a moderately connected BSR with an on-time delivery rate of 90%, which is actually quite 'good', would be assessed 'bad' if compared erroneously to highly integrated relationships. Despite its simplicity, this example clearly demonstrates the need for situational and customized performance evaluation.

Second, these findings provide a conceptual procedure for systematically identifying potential influence factors and quantifying their actual impacts by applying scientific statistical methods. The procedure can be seen as part of a comprehensive control approach, basically following what Fisher (1995), calls formal management control systems. The procedure consists of the following basic steps:

> *(1) Identify and measure appropriate performance indicators (2) identify types of comparable business relationships and additional environmental influence factors, (3) compare performance values of relationships from the same type while controlling for the identified contingencies, (4) analyze high performing and underachieving relationships in more detail to find reasons for performance gaps, and (5) take suitable corrective action to address the identified performance issues.*

This procedure, in principle, can be adapted to any other areas of performance control. Thus, it is the procedure itself which represents actual additional value for management control in dyadic business relationships. Additional potential areas of opportunity include product portfolio management, site assessment or evaluation of customer profitability, or other performance aspects.

Limitations and future research

However, this research is not without limitations that must be considered when interpreting results of the quantitative analysis. First of all, selection of performance indicators and contingent influences is not complete, because of further possibilities to refine theoretical models, a condition that also applies to the choice of relationship attributes.

Moreover, types of relationships actually considered in the empirical analysis remain on an abstract level. On the buy side, it would also have been desirable to differentiate between JIT/JIS. On the supply side, a more detailed analysis of sales concepts, as well as consideration of distribution structure and transportation means, would have improved findings and managerial implications. Further, a more differentiated treatment of wholesaling and retailing companies (only performed on the buy side) would enhance the findings' value.

Drawing from these limitations, future research is needed. One recommendation is to refine dyadic performance evaluation in BSRs by conducting more detailed empirical studies. Especially in large companies with a large supplier (or customer) base, information would be available in the detail required. Moreover, it is important to gain further knowledge about how effectiveness of corrective actions, as part of cross-company control activities, can be improved.

Furthermore, it is the author's conviction that this form of 'customized performance control' is readily adaptable to other performance management disciplines. Applications could also be useful in other areas of performance management, such as research on product portfolio or customer analysis, or assessment of site or sales locations.

7. Analysis of dyadic control activities' mediating role in delivery reliability and flexibility

7.1. Current situation and challenges

Successfully managing inter-firm relationships in today's globalized business environments is a formidable challenge (e.g. Christopher, 2005; Presutti and Mawhinney, 2007; Meira et al., 2010). Efficiency and effectiveness of transactional processes at the buyer-supplier interface are particularly important due to their direct impact on customer satisfaction (Gunasekaran et al., 2004) and the company's intra-firm-performance (Swink et al., 2007).

Numerous approaches for enhancing performance of these relationships have long been acknowledged, such as systematic supplier selection and development (Carter and Elram, 2003) or integration of processes and resources (Klein, 2007) to name a few. Recent reviews[48] of supply chain management (SCM) literature explore the wide range of performance-related issues in industrial business relationships investigated within the last two decades. Besides SCM, performance improvement in inter-firm environments has also come under increased scrutiny in management accounting recently. As a growing number of examinations[49] on performance control activities shows, the mediating potential of managerial control systems (MCSs) for performance in business relationships has been more and more recognized in this scientific discipline. Mahama (2006), for instance, confirms that the use of adequate control approaches is a powerful way to systematically enhance efficiency and effectiveness of industrial business relationships.

[48] For a comprehensive overview of performance-related topics addressed in SCM literature see Giunipero's et al (2008) meta-analysis of existing reviews on SCM literature. Additional useful reviews with diverging focuses have been conducted by Sachan and Datta (2005), Terpend et al. (2008) and Ross et al. (2009).

[49] Analyzing literature on management control systems in different forms of inter-firm relationships, Meira et al. (2010) gives an overview of studies on the use of performance control approaches and their effect on relationship-specific aspects.

However, despite existing awareness and various efforts - made in both SCM and management accounting research - to gain knowledge about performance improvement and control approaches, interdisciplinary examinations integrating comprehensive existing knowledge are still underrepresented. Knowledge about use and effectiveness of two-sided, so-called dyadic performance control approaches in buyer-supplier relationships (BSRs) is very fragmented.

In SCM literature, the contributions applying a dyadic or even a supply chain perspective could not be proven to sufficiently address control-related issues. On one hand, several studies could be identified that at least principally addressed control-related issues, for instance by analyzing cross-company coordination in different research contexts (e.g. Cousins et al., 2008; Hsu et al., 2008; Hult et al., 2007; Wu et al., 2006). On the other hand, none of these contributions took an unbiased point of view[50] in the analysis, integrating buyer's and supplier's perspective. Moreover, no contribution was found that specifically examined the role of dyadic control activities, commonly executed by buyer and supplier, to systematically enhance performance of transactional processes in BSRs.

The same limitations apply to management accounting in the opposite way. On one side, the mediating potential of managerial control approaches for performance in business relationships has been recognized in principle and empirically proven in some contexts (e.g. Baiman and Rajan, 2002; Coletti et al., 2005; Dekker, 2004). On the other side, no examination assessing the appropriateness of dyadic control approaches for systematically enhancing performance in industrial business relationships on an operational level was found. Based on findings of field reviews[51] (e.g. Caglio and Ditillo, 2008; Håkansson and Lind, 2007; Meira et al., 2010) and analysis of identified

[50] This can be considered a general deficit of SCM research. Ross et al. (2009), for instance, state that most scientific studies still either adopt a buyer or a supplier firm view instead of joining a two-sided perspective. This is in line with Sachan and Datta (2005), clearly outlining the need for further intensifying research on what Halldórsson (2002) called 'flow thinking'. He recommends to overcome company boundaries by directly focusing on the flow of materials, information and services along the supply chain.

[51] Focusing on different aspects on management control in inter-firm relationships, the reviews aim to structure the field and to also identify limitations and indications for future research. Caglio and Ditillo (2008), for instance, generally state that even though a broad range of issues concerning the use of controls in inter-firm relationships has been covered, 'the extant literature is still in the process of being developed' (p. 890).

contributions to control mechanisms in inter-firm relationships, no research exists on systematic assessment of how MCSs enhance performance in industrial business relationships on operational levels.

Because efficiency and effectiveness of operational processes at the buyer-supplier interface is crucial to the whole supply chain's success, lack of knowledge about the usefulness of integrated control activities in industrial business relationships should be considered a current issue requiring attention in both literature streams. To gain further information about when dyadic performance control is reasonable and effective, causalities between control-specific capabilities (labeled as 'control capabilities') and performance outcome need to be empirically analyzed considering intensity of control activities (figure 26).

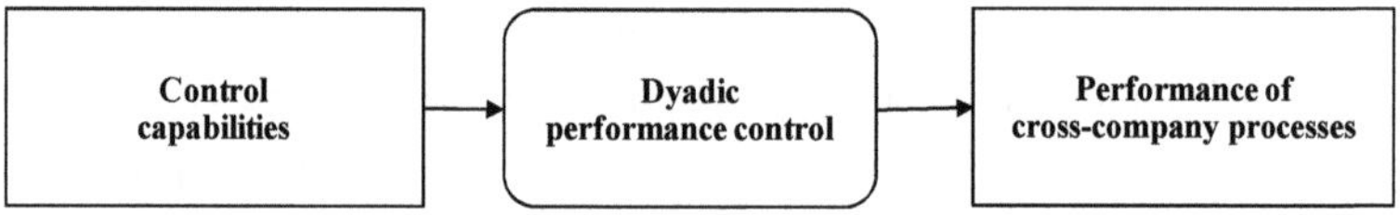

Figure 26: Basic research framework – The mediating impact of dyadic performance control for performance of BSRs

Findings would be helpful in several ways. Hidden potentials could be unlocked by implementing new or improving existing control activities. Unnecessary costs for inappropriate use of control systems could be avoided. An increased understanding about the capabilities that limit control effectiveness, for instance, would allow systematic development of cross-company control engagements. Also, detailed managerial implications for designing control activities could emerge. Thus, the general goal of the following examination can be summarized:

This study will empirically assess effectiveness of dyadic performance control in BSRs by (1) identifying control capabilities, (2) analyzing causalities between these capabilities, and (3) by determining the effect of control activities on performance of cross-company processes.

To address these research areas, the remainder of the study is split in four parts. First, a hypothesized theoretical model is developed, based on a review of relevant literature in the fields of supply chain performance management and management accounting in inter-firm relationships (section 7.2). After this, data collection procedure, sample statistics and data analysis methods are discussed (section 7.3) before results of the empirical analysis are presented (section 7.4). Finally, managerial and theoretical implications are outlined and propositions for future research are given (section 7.5).

7.2. Theory development

To gain a comprehensive picture of relevant performance dimensions and control capabilities, SCM and management accounting literature was analyzed and findings were combined. Due to the wide range of relevant sub-disciplines for performance management in SCM, a broad review of eight peer-reviewed SCM journals was conducted. The following journals were included: (1) Journal of Supply Chain Management, (2) International Journal of Physical Distribution and Logistics Management, (3) Journal of Operations Management, (4) International Journal of Logistics Management, (5) Journal of Business Logistics, (6) International Journal of Operations and Production Management, (7) Industrial Marketing Management and (8) Decision Sciences. Selection was based on the journals' thematic focus and Menachof et al.'s (2009) 'research usefulness index', with a timeframe from 2001 to 2010. In contrast, literature analysis of management accounting contributions draws primarily on existing reviews of management control systems in inter-firm relationships, affecting only a very specific area of this research stream. Based on these reviews, further studies on cross-company performance control in industrial business relationships were identified and included in the analysis.

This way, a wide range of studies from both disciplines could be identified, empirically analyzing selected causalities between relevant capabilities in BSRs and its performance. In addition, knowledge about potentially suitable managerial control activities was gained, serving as a basis for measuring the intensity of dyadic performance control activities. Findings of the review are discussed in the following (section 7.2.1), before elements of the theoretical framework are brought together and the hypothesized model is developed (section 7.2.2).

7.2.1. Elements of the research framework

Interface performance

When discussing the role of dyadic performance control in BSRs and its mediating impact on relational exchange activities' success, the term 'performance' must be better defined. Performance in inter-firm relationships has been analyzed in many different ways[52] and existing definitions often leave much room for interpretations (Beugelsdijk et al., 2009). However, review of existing definitions reveals that a fundamental distinction between two basic types of relational performance can be made by classifying: one that directly reflects success of the actual exchange activities between companies (e.g. delivery speed and reliability), and one that abstracts from the transactional level by measuring the indirect effect of a relationship on intra-firm-performance outcome (e.g. profitability, sales volume and growth in market share). To focus on cross-company operations and coordination activities, this study will be strictly limited to the first definition of performance, with a major focus on actual physical material flows (labeled as 'interface performance'). To allow for a more differentiated discussion, interface performance will be split up in sub-dimensions. Two major categories could be identified and will thus be considered in the theoretical model, delivery reliability and flexibility of the relationship:

> Delivery reliability: Reflecting actual effectiveness of all transactional activities between two companies, delivery reliability is particularly significant for characterizing the overall quality of distribution and transportation processes (Beamon, 1999). In competitive markets where suppliers can easily be replaced, being able to keep reliability promises represents a decisive success factor. Numerous studies, empirically confirm its mediating effect on both partners'

[52] For an extensive review of existing definitions see O'Toole and Donaldson (2002).

firm-performance and the relationship's overall success (e.g. Droge et al., 2004; Tracey, 2004; Swink et al., 2007). In this study, delivery reliability will serve as the ultimate outcome variable on which the moderating effect of dyadic performance control will be tested.

Delivery flexibility: The second essential dimension of interface performance in assessing operational performance in industrial business is a relationship's flexibility. Delivery flexibility, in general, reflects the supplier's ability to quickly respond to market demands[53] (Gunsekaran et al., 2001; Beamon, 1999), and can be considered a major competitive advantage (Bower and Hout, 1988; Christopher, 1992), directly influencing customer satisfaction level (Towill, 1997). Another additional important aspect is the transport distance to be overcome, as time needs for transportation processes increase with a growing internationalization (Behr and Semlinger, 2004). In consequence, the relationship's geographical magnitude must be considered when evaluating flexibility of material flows.

Dyadic performance control in buyer-supplier relationships

Formal control systems[54] generally follow a cybernetic loop consisting of three sub-processes: measuring performance, assessing measurement results and – if needed – taking corrective actions to address performance issues (Fisher, 1995). What sounds obvious from a theoretical perspective can be hard to realize in an inter-firm environment for several reasons. These cross-company-specific challenges for the design and uses of MCSs have been recognized and formulated by management

[53] Measured by time-related performance indicators, delivery flexibility is determined by various factors such as upstream production and supply processes (Beamon, 1999). However, the time which elapses between receipt of the customer's order and the delivery of the goods is also affected by transactional activities between a buying and a supplying company. Gunsekaran et al. (2001) name order entry time, order planning time and finished goods delivery time as relationship-specific elements of order cycle time as an overall measure of flexibility.

[54] Control systems have been extensively discussed and numerous different classification approaches can be found in literature (e.g. Brown (2005); Giglioni and Bedeian (1974); Green and Welsh (1988) and Malmi and Brown, 2008). However, as the nature of control systems is not in the scope of this study, no further distinction is made at this point and the understanding of 'control system' will draw on what Fisher (1995) calls 'formal control systems'.

accounting scholars. Drawing on a number of related contributions[55], Meira et al. (2010) conclude that managing cross-company activities in general creates specific requirements because organizational boundaries need to be transcended. Caglio and Ditillo (2008) further specify shortcomings of existing research to the field by categorizing them. In their in-depth review, particular two basic control problems in inter-firm relationships are identified: cooperation and coordination concerns.

Coordination can be understood as cross-company management of information and material flows between source and drain and requires "active participation in joint activities, information sharing and synthesis of expertise" (Eng, 2006: p. 763). Cooperation, in contrast, serves as a basis for building up business relations, reflecting, among other factors, the way two companies work together and invest in the relationship (Morgan and Hunt, 1994; Morris and Carter, 2005), alignment of strategic goals of both partners (Chen at al., 1998, Morris and Carter, 2005), as well as amount of information systematically shared and the contractual basis of the relationship vis-à-vis timeframe of the cooperative commitment (Arshinder and Deshmukh, 2007; Nyaga at al., 2009). Accordingly, coordination is closely connected to the actual control activities themselves while cooperation represents a prerequisite for being able to coordinate by providing an appropriate cooperative business environment. The level of control-related coordination activities systematization between two companies can thus be taken as an indicator for the intensity of dyadic performance control activities. Consequently, the role of dyadic performance control in BSRs will be considered in the theoretical model as follows:

> Control-oriented coordination activities: Reflecting intensity and systemization of cross-company control activities in dyadic business relationships, this characteristic is a specific sub-dimension within the broad range of coordination activities, drawing on control-specific aspects of existing contributions to coordination in inter-firm environments. It will be used to measure to what

[55] Among others, the authors list the following studies: Mouritsen and Hansen, 2006; Langfield-Smith and Smith, 2003; Roslender and Hart, 2003; Dekker, 2004; Cooper and Slagmulder, 2004; Hakansson and Lind, 2004; Seal et al., 2004).

degree buyers and suppliers participate together in systematically enhancing their relationships performance. This includes the amount of resources provided by both partners, as well as well as the systemization of control mechanisms: e.g. frequency of meetings (Kim, 2006), and whether clear rules are defined indicating what degree of deviation from nominal values prompts initiation of corrective measures.

Control capabilities

Capabilities in the basic SCM understanding reflect the potential to effectively support supply chain activities with existing resources (Bharadwaj, 2000) and can be further specified as "ability to perform cross-functional as well as inter-organizational activities required in supply chain management" (Wu et al., 2006: p. 494). Limited to potential factors affecting dyadic performance control in BSRs, this broad definition can be cut down to capabilities that enable cross-company control activities, commonly executed to enhance performance of physical material flows. As mentioned before, these control capabilities particularly addresses cooperation-related aspects since control activities can only take place in a cooperative environment.

The decisive element of any control activities is information. If there is no reference base, control is impossible. Much evidence confirms that information sharing among partnering companies is directly connected to both coordination and cooperation (e.g. Barratt and Oliveira, 2001; Bowersox et al., 2000; Vereecke and Muylle, 2006; Xu and Beamon, 2006). Analyzing coordination mechanisms in supply chains, Arshinder and Deshmukh (2007) state: "to communicate frequently and effectively, the partners are required to have good information systems and capability to share information" (p. 420). The authors name contracts, information technology and information sharing as essential capabilities[56] to implement coordination mechanisms effectively.

[56]Arshinder and Deshmukh (2007) also name collaborative initiatives such as ECR and VMI as a fourth capability. As this study is limited to control -related coordination capabilities, collaborative initiatives will not be considered.

To conclude, the amount and quality of available information, as well as the level of automation with which relevant information is provided, determine the power and effectiveness of control activities. Both availability of information and technology integration of partners represent major capabilities for coordination in general and will be taken into account in the hypothesized model.

> Availability of information: Due to the focus on operational processes of cross-company material flows, this consists of any information helpful in improving delivery flexibility and reliability of the supplier. As both performance aspects are strongly influenced by knowledge about expected future demands of customers (Meyr and Stadler, 2005), availability of forecasts and demand fluctuations can be considered the decisive buyer-specific in-house information to be shared. From the supply side, data concerning recent and expected utilization of production capacities, as well as lead and distribution times, could help to improve the buyers supply planning activities (Kim, 2006) and enhance the supplier's flexibility and reliability performance.
>
> Information system support: This capability reflects the extent of IT support for all kind of control-relevant information data exchanges, affecting different domains like order processing (e.g. in form of quick ordering system) and follow-ups on customer orders (e.g. tracking and tracing) (Kim, 2006). Also, automated exchange of market information (e.g. in terms of expected demands and capacity utilization) and tools are strictly maintained to support supplier and customer evaluation (e.g. supplier development tools).

When discussing expected demands information availability and IT support for information exchange in industrial business relationships, the extent to which suppliers are integrated in the buyers supply planning must be considered as well. This usually is directly connected to the contractual basis of the relationship, reflecting the timeframe of the cooperative commitment (Arshinder and Deshmukh, 2007). This assumption is confirmed by Meyr and Stadler (2005), stating that availability of future demands must either "be known (by contract) or have to be forecast" (p. 68). In consequence, neither aspect can be neglected in the theoretical model, because they determine whether in-house information about future demand is shared between partnering companies, and whether dyadic control mechanisms can be implemented.

> Supplier integration in the buyer's supply planning: This capability reflects how much sensitive in-house information is exchangeable and determines the theoretically available amount of information within the BSR that will be controlled by both partners, i.e. supplier integration into regular demand forecasts (Meyr and Stadler, 2005), and buyer's timetable in updating suppliers on unpredictable demand fluctuations (e.g. through large new orders or singular marketing campaigns) (Kim, 2006).
> Moreover, this capability must be seen in combination with duration of contractual agreements, as integrated supply planning only makes economic sense in mid- and long-term relationships (Arshinder and Deshmukh, 2007).

Summary of the research framework

This section outlined elements relevant to the research framework when analyzing the mediating role of dyadic performance control in BSRs. Delivery reliability and flexibility are relevant performance criteria for measuring efficiency and effectiveness of cross-company material flows. Intensity and systemization of control-related coordination activities have been selected to serve as a basis for 'dyadic performance control in industrial business relationships'. And last, supply planning integration, available control-related information and IT support have been identified as the major determining capabilities for effectiveness of cross-company performance control. An overview is given in figure 27.

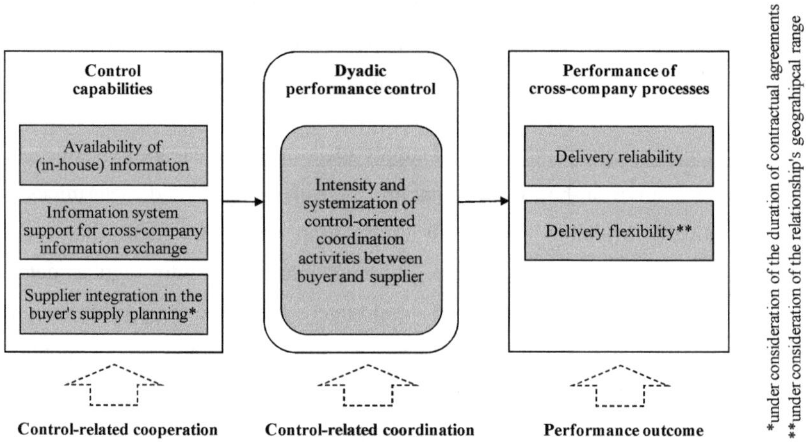

Figure 27: Research framework – Control capabilities, control-related coordination and interface performance

7.2.2. Development of the hypothesized model

After identifying major factors for effective usage of dyadic performance control in industrial business relationships, research framework elements now must be brought together by developing propositions about expected causalities between them. Findings from the previous section will serve as a starting point.

Hypotheses between the different control capabilities

The identified control capabilities reflect characteristics of three selected cooperation aspects. As mentioned, integration of suppliers in buyers' supply planning is fundamental to the two remaining capabilities 'information-sharing' and 'IT integration'; it determines the amount of potentially shared information in the BSR (Meyr and Stadler, 2005). Many studies confirm that a longer planning horizon positively affects relationship-specific investments of both partners and level of cooperation (Bensaou and Anderson, 1999; Kim, 2006; Sheu et al., 2006). Empirically analyzing determinants of supply chain architecture Sheu et al. (2006) specifically confirms the influence of long-term orientation on information sharing and IT capabilities. The literature allows us to hypothesize:

H_{1a} Supplier integration into the buyer's supply planning is positively associated with the amount of control-related information available in the BSR.

H_{1b} Supplier integration into the buyer's supply planning is positively associated with the level of cross-company IT integration in the BSR.

Hypotheses between control capabilities and dyadic performance control

Due to the strong coordinative nature of dyadic performance control activities, the two capabilities directly connected to actual transmission of information between buyers and suppliers should directly influence control coordination: actual amount of information shared, as well as degree of automation in processing this information (Arshinder and Deshmukh, 2007). Both assumptions are supported by studies such as Sheu et al. (2006) and Kim (2006), directly proving the relationship between capabilities and coordination. Cooperative aspects, such as computerization level and information processing automation, as well as information available for cross-company control activity, can be considered crucial. Our reasoning follows:

H_{2a} The amount of control-related information available in the BSR is positively associated with control-related coordination activities in the BSR.

H_{2b} The level of cross-company IT integration in the BSR is positively associated with control-related coordination activities in the BSR.

Hypotheses between dyadic performance control and interface performance

As shown in the previous section, the mediating role of dyadic coordination activities, (executed to systematically enhance delivery performance in industry) is supported in the studies of Kim (2006) and Sheu (2006). Simatupang and Ramaswami (2005) further distinguish and stress the importance of coordination for responsiveness and flexibility in cross-company relations. This result is also supported by Eng (2006), drawing on studies from Narasimhan and Mahapatra (2004) and Varadarajan and

Jayachandran (1999). Iyer (2004) puts more focus on reliability-related issues by confirming a positive relationship between automated communication and time-based delivery performance in business relationships. This is in line with Lee (2004), who states that coordination, communication quality and information-sharing are associated with partnerships' success. Analyzing coordination investments in BSRs, da Silveira and Arkader (2007) provide empirical evidence for the positive impact of customer coordination investment on both delivery flexibility and reliability. Although these studies focus more on general coordination than on performance control, basic causalities between coordination and delivery reliability, as well as delivery flexibility, will be assumed valid in the hypothesized model as well.

H_{3a} The intensity and automation of control-related coordination activities in the BSR is positively associated with delivery flexibility.

H_{3b} The intensity and automation of control-related coordination activities in the BSR is positively associated with delivery reliability.

Hypotheses between the different dimensions of interface performance

Gunsekaran et al. (2001) confirm a positive connection between delivery flexibility and delivery reliability, as short response times enable easier and more reliable scheduling of order processing times. This assumption is supported by Meyr and Stadler (2005) who state "...usually, the shorter lead times are, the more reliable the promised arrival dates are" (p. 66). Thus, the following proposition is derived:

H_4 Delivery flexibility is positively associated with delivery reliability.

Additional control variables

To detect additional external effects, biasing validity and quality of model results, two more aspects to consider in the model have been identified: impact of the longitude of agreements as a determinant of supply planning integration, and the BSR's geographical situation in terms of transport distance.

As supplier integration in buyer's supply planning activities reflects a long-term commitment between both companies, it is usually closely connected to long-term agreements (Arshinder and Deshmukh, 2007),: e.g. form of framework contracts and master agreements. Accordingly, the longevity of the relationship's contractual basis is a major determinant in supply planning integration and cannot be neglected in the theoretical model. However, no direct connection from longevity of contractual agreements to information sharing and IT integration is assumed, as both capabilities result solely from the need to efficiently and effectively execute integrated demand planning. In other words, there can also be long-term master agreements between two companies without any information sharing or resource integration. This understanding of the contractual basis' indirect role is supported by Kim (2006), who developed a scale for measuring integration between two companies. He mentions the influencing role of contract duration for technical integration, although he does not include it as an indicator for cross-company integration in general. We will include it as a control variable.

As mentioned, one significant additional aspect in evaluating time-based performance indicators for delivery flexibility is the geographical range of the BSR. It is obvious that international or even global deliveries cannot be compared without considering transport distance of the material flows; causalities between control-related coordination (H_{3a}) and flexibility, as well as between flexibility and reliability (H_{4a}), might be incorrectly analyzed. Thus, geographical magnitude of the BSR will also be included in the model to compensate for these biasing differences in transportation distance.

Summary of the hypothesized model

In conclusion, seven hypotheses have been developed integrating capabilities, control-related elements and performance in one framework. Furthermore, two control variables have been added to consider impacts resulting from both varying longevity of contractual agreements and differing geographical extensions of the BSR. The resulting hypothesized model is shown in figure 28.

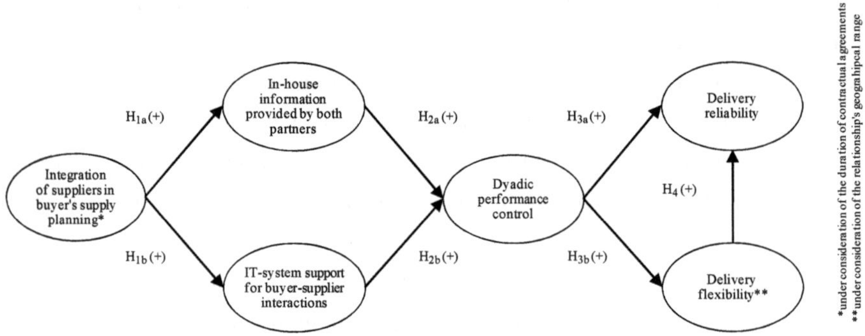

Figure 28: Hypothesized structural equation model for analyzing the mediating role of dyadic performance control for interface performance in buyer-supplier relationships

7.3. Research methodology

Structural equation modeling (SEM) was applied to test the theoretical model because core elements of the hypothesized model are multi-dimensional constructs (Byrne, 2010), and it was necessary to simultaneously test multiple interrelated causalities between these latent variables (Hardy and Bryman, 2004; Shook et al., 2004; Hair et al., 2006). Accordingly, research methodology was aligned to SEM needs and the following steps were taken. First, a survey was conducted to gather the required empirical data for the analysis. Development of the corresponding questionnaires is described in section 7.3.1 and sample statistics are given in section 7.3.2. Next, data quality in terms of self-reporting, key informant, non-respondent and common-method bias was checked (section 7.3.3). In a last preparing step, performance figures (having been measured as absolute values) were relativized to guarantee validity of model results following a contingency-theoretical approach (section 7.3.4). All software-based calculations were done using PASW Statistics 18, release 18.0.1, respectively AMOS 18, release 18.0.0.

7.3.1. Development of the survey instrument

This study analyzes the mediating impact of dyadic control activities on interface performance in BSRs. To gain meaningful information, one must sufficiently consider both sides of industrial business relationships (Caglio and Ditillo, 2008; Ross, 2009). Accordingly, two equally structured questionnaires were designed: one for the buy side (procurement and purchasing) and one for the supply side (sales and distribution), each addressing exactly the same issues within the BSR from a mirrored point of view. Consequently, identical scales were used for both questionnaires.

Beside the duality of the survey, the main difference in this study is its strong operational focus, implicitly connected to actual material flows. In reality, control capabilities, control-related coordination and, most importantly, interface performance cannot be measured for a company overall, as the three aspects can differ radically between different product types. Thus, the whole questionnaire was for a specific product group, and all measurement items strictly referred to BSRs of one and the same group of goods, to be selected by the respondent. Due to the heterogeneity of products, additional product-specific data was requested describing basic characteristics of cross-company material flows. This enabled retroactive classification of respondents' BSRs in peer-groups with comparable general relationship attributes, needed to relativize absolute performance values as described in section 7.3.4.

Scale development

Scale development was based on the procedure suggested by Churchill (1979). First, the understanding of the constructs was clarified and clearly defined. Then, literature review identified scales of prior research relevant to the field. Appropriate measurement items were adopted or, if necessary adjusted. When no suitable scale could be found, new measures were developed.

Supply planning integration of buyers was adapted from Kim (2006), measuring the general level of supply chain integration. As some of his items were strongly related technically, they also figured in development of the IT integration scale. For the latter, Wu's (2006) scale for IT alignment was also taken into account. Items for both scales were measured using 7-point Likert scales. Information sharing was measured by two five-step index variables, reflecting the amount of available buyer or supplier-specific in-house information in the relationship; necessary because sequencing of different information types was not feasible. Definition of different information types draws on Arshinder and Deshmukhet's (2007) classification of various kinds of information shared between supply chain members. The measurement scale for dyadic performance control is based on Eng's (2006) scales for cross-functional coordination and information-sharing and was adapted by transferring items to an inter-firm context and strengthening control-related aspects. Certain elements were also inspired by Arshinder et al.'s (2007) framework measuring the extent of supply chain coordination. Again, a 7-point Likert scale was used. Scales for delivery reliability and flexibility were based on a selection of key performance indicators (KPIs). For selection of reliability items, indicators from Beamon's (1999) and Gunsekaran et al.'s (2001) scales for supply chain performance were adopted. Moreover, Beamon's (1999) indicator for delivery lateness was used to measure flexibility performance by average delays of planned and unplanned orders. Selection of items for delivery flexibility was also inspired by Droge et al.'s (2004) analysis of time-based performance in inter-firm relationships. In contrast to coordination and control-related constructs, performance indicators were measured by actual performance values[57] such as response times (in days) or reliability rations (in percent). Items further measuring characteristics of BSRs to enable their classification were based primarily on Schweicher and Jursch (2006).

All items and scale were then intensively discussed with six managers from manufacturing companies to check for relevance and validity of items for each construct; any were included showing a strong relation to either purchasing and procurement or sales and distribution. As a result, slight adjustments were made: for instance, items measuring 'information sharing' also included aspects related to future product developments as part of long-term integration. Then, a web-based prototype questionnaire was designed and a final pretest was conducted with twelve companies,

[57] It was purposely avoided to measure performance by subjective self-assessments in order to minimize self-reporting bias. See section C.3.3 for further discussion.

five answering from a supplyi and seven from a buy perspective on the BSR. Due to the small number of the pretest sample, tests mainly focused on descriptive analysis of answers to test data quality and wording and comprehensibility of items. Results were also double-checked with other researchers from the field of logistics management. Additionally, response behavior of the participants was checked, revealing that questionnaires for both sides were completed in an adequate timeframe – maximum time for completion 35 minutes – and average resting time on different pages was quite uniformly distributed. Because quality checks and response behavior revealed no issues, the large scale-survey was initiated as described in the subsequent paragraph. Final scales for control capabilities, dyadic performance control and interface performance are listed in table 28. Attributes characterizing the BSRs are listed in table 29. Both tables can be found in the annex.

7.3.2. **Sample description**

The survey was mailed to about 2'500 manufacturing companies, wholesalers and retailers from different industries in Switzerland, Austria and Germany and took place from October 2010 to January 2011. the survey was also available online, as it was promoted by the German Association for Materials Management, Purchasing and Logistics (AMMPL). Following Dillman's (2007) Tailored Design Method for web surveys, we sent up to three reminders, including a personalized link to the survey. In total, responses were received from 210 companies; nine had to be excluded because respondents had not completed the additional information required for characterizing general attributes of the BSRs (e.g. the applied sales, distribution and procurement concepts). 201 records remained.

As shown in table 17, the sample includes industrial business relationships from a wide range of industries; 46.8% have been described from the supplier's and 53.2% from the buyer's perspective. The majority of participants held positions in middle and upper management, mostly in the area of logistics and supply chain management. CEOs and other members of the management board were also well represented. The differentiated analysis of buyers' and suppliers' annual turnover and number of employees confirmed that companies of all sizes participated in the study. Given this strong heterogeneity and broad coverage of different types of relationships, it is assumed that expected causalities of the hypothesized model, if tested significant, will not be limited to single industries or to specific positions in the supply chain.

Table 17: Sample statistics

Demographics and attributes of relationships (N=201)		**Supplier**	**Buyer**	**Total**
Perspective on the dyad	Supplier's point of view			46.8%
	Buyer's point of view			53.2%
Industry in which the BSR acts	Machinery and equipment			16.4%
	Food, beverages			14.9%
	Coke and refined petroleum products			2.0%
	Electronics, electronic equipment			21.9%
	Chemicals, pharmaceuticals, cosmetics			9.0%
	Paper and printing industry			7.5%
	Automotive industry			17.4%
	Metals, heavy industry			5.0%
	Textiles			2.0%
	Agriculture, forestry, wood-processing			1.5%
	Other			2.5%
Respondent's position	CEO or other member of mgt. board			16.7%
	Head of logistics			33.3%
	Head of SCM			6.0%
	Head of purchasing			1.2%
	Head of sales			6.0%
	Logistics manager			1.2%
	Sales manager			9.5%
	Area manager from other divisions			20.2%
	Experts (e.g. in finance, product development)			6.0%
	Other experts (e.g. in finance, product development)			6.0%
Company turnover (2009)	< 7.5 Mio. CHF	1.1%	1.0%	1.0%
	7.5-15 Mio. CHF	5.4%	3.9%	4.6%
	16-75 Mio. CHF	25.0%	24.5%	24.7%
	76-150 Mio. CHF	12.0%	10.8%	11.3%
	151-750 Mio. CHF	31.5%	20.6%	25.7%
	751-1'500 Mio. CHF	7.6%	7.8%	7.7%
	1'501-3'750 Mio. CHF	4.3%	6.9%	5.7%
	>3'750 Mio. CHF	13.0%	24.5%	19.1%
Company employees (2009)	< 10	1.1%	0.0%	0.5%
	10-50	7.7%	2.9%	5.1%
	51-100	8.8%	9.5%	9.2%
	101-500	34.1%	30.5%	32.1%
	501-1'000	18.7%	12.4%	15.3%
	1'001-5'000	12.1%	14.3%	13.3%
	>5'000	17.6%	30.5%	24.5%

7.3.3. Data quality

Self-reporting bias

This study is intended to provide quantitative empirical evidence for causalities between dyadic control activities and interface performance of BSRs. In consequence, objective measurability and controllability of performance items must be given for the sake of results' validity and usability for practitioners. However, large-scale quantitative examinations are often based on subjective self-assessments – not verifiable from other sources – and self-reporting is done by the managers or staff in charge – assessing their own organization or department. Both issues are widely known and extensively discussed in literature.[58] They can cause enormous bias due to lack of knowledge, missing controllability or self-aggrandizement, that can often compromise validity of measurement results. To minimize bias caused by self-reports, relationship perceptive operational performance indicators will be excluded. The quantitative analysis thus is exclusively limited to continuous and verifiable interface performance indicators as listed in table 28 (part 3) in the annex.

Key-informant bias

As the survey referred to a specific commodity group to be selected by the respondent, we assumed that he/she would have comprehensive knowledge in this area. The actual position and department of the respondent were not considered important; we tried to minimize key-informant bias by requesting the person with the most comprehensive knowledge to complete the questionnaires (Kumar et al., 1993). Consequently, the contacts were asked to forward the link to the online-survey to the corresponding experts within their organization. To guarantee the suitability of persons addressed, a

---

[58] Podsakoff and Organ (1986), for instance, discuss problems of self-report methodology in organizational research. Differing between six question categories the authors state that especially questions referring to respondents' perceptions can cause enormous bias. Furthermore it is emphasized that bias can even increase in case the answer directly affects the respondent's standing, for instance if it presents the person in a favorable light.

detailed description of knowledge required[59] was given in the covering letter. Following Seidler (1974), the informant was scrutinized on his ability to cover the broad range of aspects. As almost 98% of the respondents were corporate managers, such as head of logistics, head of sales or head of purchasing (see table 17 in section 7.3.2), it is reasonably certain that they could provide the required background.[60] Thus, the key-informants were considered knowledgeable and suitable to participate to the survey.

Non-response bias

Potential non-response bias was evaluated by comparing answers of early and late respondents (Armstrong and Overton, 1977). Following the procedure applied by Li and Calantone (1998) and Wu et al. (2003), the first 75% of the respondents were considered 'early respondents' whereas the remaining 25% were classified 'late respondents'. Accordingly, late-response bias was used to check for non-response bias. T-tests were conducted to statistically test whether there were significant differences between two groups in terms of company demographics, e.g. turnover and number of employees and the total purchasing/sales volume. Due to the focus on a specific commodity group, selected by the respondent, the share of this commodity group in the company's total purchasing/sales volume was also checked And all six constructs were compared between both groups. Results of the t-tests did not show any significance differences. Assuming that late-response bias can be considered representative for non-response bias (Armstrong and Overton, 1977), it appears that non-response bias is small.

---

[59] To being able to sufficiently complete the questionnaire from a supplier's perspective, it was clearly stated that the respondent's knowledge was required to cover the following aspects: operational distribution processes (storage, ordering, transport), sales planning/forecasting (for products generated in the production process), and customer relationship management (networking, communication, strategic integration). From the buyer's perspective, knowledge about operational procurement processes (ordering, transport, storage), demand planning (for products or commodities intended for further processing), and supplier management (networking, communication, strategic integration) was pointed out to be required.

[60] This argumentation is in line with Wu et al. (2006), conducting a survey to analyze the impact of information technology on supply chain capabilities and firm performance.

Common method bias

In order to minimize common method bias, several preparatory measures were taken. Anonymity was assured and a guarantee was given to keep sensitive information confidential (Podsakoff et al., 2003). As suggested by Huber and Power (1985), the usefulness of the study was also clearly pointed out and a study report was offered to respondents. In addition, Harman's single factor test[61] was utilized to test for common method bias, as suggested by Podsakoff and Organ (1986). Principal component analysis of all items included in the model indicated no dominant factor. The first factor accounted only for 27% of the total variance; at least three factors were needed to reach 50%. Six factors had an eigenvalue greater than one.

7.3.4. **Relativization of performance values**

For the above reasons, performance items were measured on continuous scales in days (delivery flexibility) and in percent (delivery reliability). However, inspired by several contingency-based approaches to managerial performance control in inter-firm relationships (e.g. Chenhall, 2007; Ferreira and Otley, 2009; Fisher, 1995; Otley and Berry, 1980), it is assumed that performance evaluation cannot be done without considering contingent environmental factors influencing the comparability of performance measurement values.[62] Inter-firm relationships often show extremely heterogeneous characteristics, depending on their economic environment. Accordingly, criteria must be defined when BSRs belong to the same category. This way, peer-groups with comparable BSRs can be defined in a next step. Within the groups, BSRs can now be evaluated against each other and their relative performance assessed. Definition of criteria, building of peer-groups with comparable respondents

---

[61] Podsakoff and Organ (1986) describe Harman's single factor test as follows: The basic assumption of this technique is that if a substantial amount of common method variance is present, either (a) a single factor will emerge from the factor analysis, or (b) one „general" factor will account for the majority of the covariance in the independent and criterion variables' (536).

[62] Heavily simplified, this means that an actual value, e.g. an on-time delivery ratio of 93% does principally not bear any information about if it is reflects 'poor' or 'high' performance. To guarantee validity of analysis results, this absolute figure needs to be translated into a relative one which indicates, how good 93% really is in comparison to similar industrial business relationships.

and group-specific relativization of actual performance values is described in the subsequent paragraphs.

Definition of criteria and building of peer-groups

When BSRs are characterized in terms of performance, buyer-specific as well as supplier-specific characteristics of the relationship must be differentiated (Giannakis, 2007). Focusing on efficiency and effectiveness of material flows in BSRs, this means that two basic types of external determinants exist: Those defining minimum required performance (demanded by buyer) to guarantee that downstream processes of the supply chain are not affected (Beamon, 1999), and those limiting maximum achievable performance (provided by supplier) resulting from upstream production and distribution capabilities (Wu et al., 2006). Both aspects are reflected by structural features at the cross-company interface: e.g. applied logistics and production concepts of buyers and suppliers (Meyr and Stadler, 2005). Thus, the relationship's character results from a combination of attributes, affected from both sides of the dyad. Taking a contingency-based view on performance, only BSRs with related relationship-specific attributes can be considered comparable to each other, as they operate in the same corridor of achievable and required performance.

To define clear criteria for how to characterize BSRs, this study will draw on existing typologies[63] from SCM literature, systematically characterizing inter-firm relationships in supply chains. Particularly well-suited from a logistics point of view, Meyr and Stadtler (2005) will serve as the main basis. The authors distinguish four categories of concepts, characterizing each single company in the value chain: (1) procurement, (2) production, (3) sales and (4) distribution concepts. Adapted to the situation at the interface between a (S)upplier and a (B)uyer, the relevant concepts of both sides must be combined to reflect characteristics of the business relationship between them. This

[63] As characteristics of these approaches is not in the major scope of this study, discussion will be limited to selected aspects of the typology of Meyr and Stadler (2005) as it seems particularly suitable to this investigation. For further reading to the topic, e.g. see contributions of Christopher (2000), Fisher (1997), Lejeune and Yakova (2005), and Vonderembse et al (2006).

particularly[64] affects the supplier's production (S2) and sales (S3) concepts as well as the buyer procurement (B1) and production (B2) concept. Eight groups were defined by combining concepts[65] of both sides as shown in table 18.

Table 18: Peer groups and relationship-specific attributes

Peer group	Production concept supplier (S2)	Procurement concept buyer (B1) and predominant sales concept supplier (S3)	Production concept buyer (B2)	Share
A	Serial or batch production	JIT/JIS; make-to-forecast/make-to-stock	Serial or batch production	11.2%
B	Serial or batch production	VMI or delivery to buyer's warehouse (inventory management by supplier); make-to-forecast/make-to-stock	No production	9.2%
C	Serial or batch production	VMI or delivery to buyer's warehouse (inventory management by supplier); make-to-forecast/make-to-stock	Serial or batch production	12.2%
D	Serial or batch production	Delivery to buyer's warehouse (inventory management by buyer); make-to-customer order/make-to-forecast	No production	16.8%
E	Serial or batch production	Delivery to buyer's warehouse (inventory management by buyer); make-to-customer order/make-to-forecast	Single item production	7.1%
F	Serial or batch production	Delivery to buyer's warehouse (inventory management by buyer); make-to-customer order/make-to-forecast	Serial or batch production	30.1%
G	Mass production	Delivery to buyer's warehouse (inventory management by buyer) ; make-to-forecast/make-to-stock	Serial or batch production	8.2%
H	Process production	Delivery to buyer's warehouse (inventory management by buyer); make-to-forecast/make-to-stock	Serial or batch production	5.1%

[64] The supplier's distribution concept will not be further differentiated at this point, as it is – in comparison to the other concepts – expected to be of minor importance. This assumption is based on the assumption that distribution and transportation processes are usually aligned to either buyer's needs or the supplier's production capabilities and its sales concept applied.

[65] Based on Jursch and Schweicher (2006) and Meyr and Stadtler (2005) specific concepts for each category have been specified. Not all combinations occurred. Moreover, concepts with related characteristics were combined due to the limited sample size, such as serial- and batch production. A complete overview of these categorical variables is given in table 26 in the annex.

Relativization of interface performance values

BSRs of the same peer-group are assumed to face approximately homogeneous preconditions in terms of achievable and required interface performance. Consequently, it is assumed[66] that absolute performance measurement values (given in 'days' or 'ratios') are comparable, allowing evaluation of these absolute values vis-à-vis their relative performance, compared to other BSRs in the same group. In turn, BSRs of all groups can be summated again, as they are all now assessed in comparison to similar BSRs. As a result, relative performance values of all BSRs – independent of their actual peer-group – can be similarly treated in the statistical analysis.

To guarantee that conversion from absolute to relative performance was based on the same standards, the following procedure was equally applied for each of the eight groups. First, absolute performance values were standardized by z-transformation. Then, z-scores were recoded to a 5-point Likert scale. Z-values smaller than -1.5 were classified '1' on the Likert scale reflecting 'relatively poor performance', z-values larger than +1.5 accordingly 'relatively high performance'. This way, it was also possible catch outliers that might otherwise have a strong biasing impact. -0.5 and +0.5 were selected as limits. The whole proceeding was done for separately for each of the five performance variables. The limits of -1.5, -0.5, 0.5 and 1.5 were selected based on the percentiles of the standard normal distribution. For instance, z-values greater than +1.5, assigned to the top Likert-scale value of '5', are in the range where about 5% of cases usually ccur (representing the top 5% of BSRs), whereas the values between -0.5 and +0.5, assigned to the average Likert-scale value of '3', usually aggregate about 40% of all cases. An integrated overview of limits for recoding z-scores, including the actual number of occurred cases in the sample (for each of the five variables), can be found in table 30 in the annex. Finally, distributions of converted performance values

66 To further support this assumption, Kruskal-Wallis-test was applied for all of the five interface performance items to check whether medians between the eight groups significantly diverge from each other. A non-parametrical test was selected as normal distribution was not given within each group. Null hypothesis that the populations from which the samples originate have the same median was rejected with a significance of .01 or even smaller. This indicated the need for compensating group-specific differences by relativizing performance values.

were discussed again with several researchers from the field to double-check applicability of transformation and recoding processes.

7.4. Results of measurement and structural equation model

The two-step approach suggested by Anderson and Gerbing (1988) is followed for discussing the empirical model results. Accordingly, the measurement model is evaluated first (section 7.4.1), before the structural equation model is tested (section 7.4.2). The latter also includes discussion of the mediating role of dyadic performance control.

7.4.1. Measurement model

The measurement model is tested in three basic steps, building on each other. First, it is checked for uni-dimensionality before reliability and validity of the measurement model are assessed.

Uni-dimensionality

To test uni-dimensionality of the latent variables, an exploratory factor analysis is conducted including all items of the model. Using principal component extraction with varimax rotation, the six constructs of the hypothesized model were affirmed, with each showing an eigenvalue greater than one. The rotated component matrix is shown in table 31 in the annex.

Reliability

Scale reliability is tested on indicator and construct level. To measure the magnitude of the direct correlations between indicators and constructs, the squared multiple correlation coefficients R^2 are calculated (Bollen, 1989; Netemeyer et al., 2003). Usually a value of .40 or .50 is considered as an acceptable lower-bound. Two items, INT_2=.379 and IT_2=.357 fall below this threshold. However, because both indicators play a constituent role for their constructs, and for deletion would decrease content validity, both items will be kept as suggested by Homburg and Klarmann (2006) as appropriate items.

On construct level, three measures are used to assess the scales' internal consistency. Cronbach's alpha (alpha) (Cronbach, 1951), composite reliability (C.R.) (Werts et al., 1974) and average variance extracted (AVE) (Hildebrandt and Temme, 2006) are calculated. Alpha and C.R. of all latent variables are above the commonly accepted threshold of .70 except for IT showing a C.R. of .694. Regarding AVE, the two constructs IT and FLEX, are below the recommended limit of .50, mainly resulting from the two items INT_2 and IT_2, which were knowingly kept to guarantee content validity. As alpha and C.R. for both constructs are in an acceptable range, scale reliability is still assumed in both cases. Reliability measures are listed in table 19.

Table 19: Measurement models: Uni-dimensionality and scale reliability of constructs

Construct	Item	Stdz. loadings	*t*-values	R^2	Alpha	C.R.	AVE
Supply planning integration (INT)	INT_1	.916	*fixed*	.839	.726	.750	.609
	INT_2	.616	5.495***	.379			
IT-system support (IT)	IT_1	.676	*fixed*	.456	.700	.694	.432
	IT_2	.597	6.035***	.357			
	IT_3	.694	6.294***	.481			
Available (in-house) information (INFO)	$INFO_1$	.807	*fixed*	.651	.809	.807	.676
	$INFO_2$	.837	6.621***	.701			
Dyadic performance control (CONT)	$CONT_1$	.850	*fixed*	.722	.863	.891	.672
	$CONT_2$	.921	16.334***	.848			
	$CONT_3$	.719	11.583***	.517			
	$CONT_4$	.776	12.954***	.603			
Delivery flexibility (FLEX)	$FLEX_1$	.637	*fixed*	.409	.735	.737	.484
	$FLEX_2$	.714	7.012***	.510			
	$FLEX_3$	.733	7.045***	.537			
Delivery reliability (REL)	REL_1	.714	*fixed*	.510	.733	.738	.586
	REL_2	.814	5.794***	.663			
Criterion		**≥0.7**	**min ***	**≥.5, <.9**	**≥.7**	**≥.6**	**≥.5**

t-values significant at p-level: *** p<.001, ** p<.01, *p<.05

Validity

Several types of validity are tested in the following, namely content validity, convergent validity, discriminant validity and predictive validity.

As content validity is determined by the quality of theoretical considerations and the scientist's knowledge to evaluate these within the chosen theory (Garver and Mentzer, 1999), it is referred to the methodology applied for development of the hypothesized model (section 7.3). Scale development for the six constructs was based on a broad review of relevant contributions where almost all considered items originated. Moreover, scales were confirmed by other academics from the field, including practitioners. For the sake of content validity, INT_2 and IT_2 were kept, though both showed a relatively low scale reliability with an R^2 below .40. Consequently, content validity is assumed in the measurement model.

Convergent validity measures how much scale items correlate with the latent variable they refer to (Anderson and Gerbing, 1988); it can be checked by assessing uni-dimensionality of indicators relating to a construct (Henseler et al., 2009). This has already taken place in the first paragraph of this section. Accordingly, convergent validity of the measurement model is assumed as well.

To assure discriminant validity, Fornell-Larcker criterion (Fornell and Larcker, 1981) is checked to assure that constructs share more variance with their assigned indicators than with other constructs. Each construct is tested to see whether squared multiple correlation with any other latent variable is below the constructs AVE. As shown in table 20, Fornell-Larcker criterion is met in all cases.

Table 20: Discriminant validity – Fornell-Larcker criteria

Construct	**AVE**	**Squared multiple correlations**					
		INT	IT	INFO	CONT	FLEX	REL
INT	.61		.08	.16	.05	.00	.00
IT	.43	.08		.02	.18	.00	.01
INFO	.67	.16	.01		.13	.00	.01
CONT	.67	.01	.18	.13		.00	.07
FLEX	.48	.00	.00	.00	.00		.25
REL	.59	.00	.01	.01	.07	.25	

Finally, predictive validity is assessed by evaluating whether constructs correlate with the other latent variables that they are expected to predict (Dunn et al., 1994). Accordingly, the constructs of the theoretical model are proven to bear predictive validity if the proposed causal interdependencies are confirmed by significant and positive path coefficients in the structural equation model. As discussion of hypotheses is subject to the following section, predictive validity will be checked as well.

7.4.2. Structural equation model

This section presents and discusses results of the structural equation model by examining the estimated path coefficients between the latent variables. The model including standardized parameter estimates, t-values and significance is shown in figure 29.

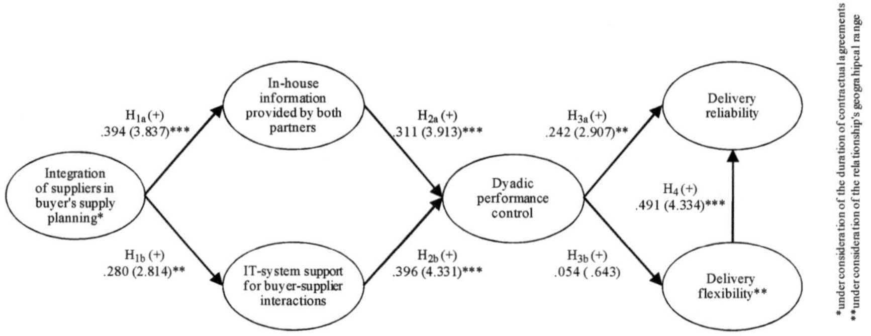

Figure 29: Structural equation model

The overall fit statistics indicate good fit for the complete model with a χ^2/df of 1.386 and a RMSEA of .044. This is in line with other commonly used fit indices such as CFI=.958, TLI=.949 and IFI=.958. Only NFI=.865 shows a value below .90. According to scholars like Marsh et al. (1996), NFI tends to be biased strongly if sample sizes are small, which is the case in this study. Moreover, as TFI (also non-normed fit index – NNFI) is defined much like NFI (Bentler and Bonnett, 1980) and has been proven to show greater robustness against varying sample sizes than NFI, (Anderson and Gerbing, 1988), a good model fit can still be assumed, as well as homogeneity of items and uni-dimensionality of constructs for the underlying measurement model. Table 21 gives an overview of fit indices including the commonly accepted ranges for these indices (e.g. Baumgartner and Homburg, 1996; Cudeck and Browne, 1983).

Table 21: Structural equation model – Model fit

Index	χ^2/df	CFI	TLI	IFI	NFI	RMSEA
Model fit	1.386	.958	.949	.958	.865	.044
Criterion	≤3	≥.90	≥.90	≥.90	≥.90	≤.06

Analyzing hypothesized relationships between control capabilities, the independent latent variable 'supply planning integration' has a significant positive effect on both, 'available information' (t=3.837, $p<.001$) and 'IT system support' (t=2.814, $p <.01$). Thus, H_{1a} and H_{1b} are supported. The same applies to H_{2a} and H_{2b}, as both dependent control capabilities also show a strong significant ($p<.001$) and positive effect on 'dyadic performance control'. The impact of 'dyadic performance control' on the two dimensions of interface performance is only tested significantly on 'delivery reliability' (t=2.907, $p< .01$). No significant effect on 'delivery flexibility' is revealed (t=.054, $p>.01$). In consequence, H_{3b} must be rejected and a moderating role of 'dyadic performance control' for 'delivery flexibility' cannot be assumed. The mediating impact on 'delivery reliability' as proposed in H_{3a} will be discussed separately in the next paragraph. The expected interdependency between 'delivery flexibility' and 'delivery reliability' turned out to be highly significant (t=4.334, $p<.001$) and H_4 is supported. An overview of model estimates and results of hypotheses testing are provided in table 22.

Table 22: Structural equation model – Parameter estimates and hypothesis testing

Hypothesis	Relationship	Stdz. ß-coefficient (t-value)	Result
H_{1a}	INT → (+) INFO	.394 (3.837)***	Supported
H_{1b}	INT → (+) IT	.280 (2.814)**	Supported
H_{2a}	INFO → (+) CONT	.311 (3.913)***	Supported
H_{2b}	IT → (+) CONT	.396 (3.331)***	Supported
H_{3a}	CONT → (+) EFF	.242 (2.907)**	Supported
H_{3b}	CONT → (+) FLEX	.054 (.634)	Not supported
H_4	FLEX → (+) EFF	.497 (4.428)***	Supported

Standardized parameter estimates (t-values) significant at p-level: *** p<.001, ** p<.01, *p<.05

As assumed, a systematic impact of both control variables is also confirmed as shown in table 23. The 'share of long-term agreements' indicates a highly significant effect on 'supply planning integration' (t=4.771, p<.001). 'Geographical magnitude of the relationship' significantly influences 'delivery flexibility' (t=3.052, p<.01).

Table 23: Standardized loadings and t-values of control variables

Variable	Description	Stdz. ß-coefficient (t-value)
$Control_1$	Share of customers (in terms of sales volume) with long-term contracts such as framework contracts and master agreements	.347 (4.771)***
$Control_2$	Geographical range of the markets: regional, national, international (neighboring countries), international (continent), global	.253 (3.052)**

Standardized parameter estimates (t-values) significant at p-level: *** p<.001, ** p<.01, *p<.05

The mediating effect of dyadic performance control

As indicated by the model results, H_{3b} cannot be supported and a mediating effect of 'dyadic performance control' is not confirmed. However, as H_{2a} and H_{2b} as well as H_{3a} are supported, a mediating role for 'delivery reliability' is indicated. To further analyze this mediating impact, two steps are taken. First, indirect effects of control capabilities on 'delivery reliability' are examined. As shown in table 24, an indirect effect of all of the three capabilities on 'delivery reliability' exists; 'IT systems support' seems to be of particular importance.

Table 24: Standardized total, direct and indirect effects

	IT	INFO	CONT	FLEX	REL
INT	0.280a	0.394	0.233	0.013	0.063
	0.280b	0.394	0.000	0.000	0.000
	0.000c	0.000	0.233	0.013	0.063
IT			0.396	0.021	0.106
			0.396	0.000	0.000
			0.000	0.021	0.106
INFO			0.311	0.017	0.083
			0.311	0.000	0.000
			0.000	0.017	0.083
CONT				0.054	0.268
				0.054	0.242
				0.000	0.026
FLEX					0.491
					0.491
					0.000

[a] Total effect
[b] Direct effect
[c] Indirect effects

Second, to statistically assess the mediation effect of 'dyadic performance control' on 'delivery reliability', two additional alternative models are estimated as suggested by Venkatraman (1989). First, the construct of 'dyadic performance control' was removed and only the direct effects of 'available information' and 'IT system support' on performance constructs were estimated. In this model, 'IT system support' has weak, but significant, direct effect on 'delivery reliability' ($t=2.145$, $p<.05$). The same applies to the direct effect of 'available information', significant only on a .10 level ($t=1.696$). Second, direct effects of both capabilities were added to the original model with 'dyadic performance control', now including direct effects on 'delivery reliability' as well as indirect effects, as mediated by 'dyadic performance control'. In this model, none of the direct effects of the control capabilities on 'delivery reliability' were significant at the .10 level. Thus, we conclude that the effects of both, 'available information' and 'IT system support' are mediated by control capabilities (Venkatraman, 1989).

7.5. Summary 3rd phase of analysis

As described in section 7.3.3, several pre-emptive measures have been taken to minimize biases in the investigation and ex ante tests were made to double-check their severity. However, this examination cannot be considered bias-free for several reasons discussed in the following paragraph.

In self-reporting and key-informant bias, perceptive performance items were avoided and absolute values were asked instead. As these absolute values needed to be recoded into comparable relative values based on peer-groups, relativization is presumed to be critical. It must be assumed that differences still exist, limiting comparability between BSRs of the same group. Moreover, the range of contingency variables, used to characterize the BSRs cannot be considered complete. Here, a larger number of peer-groups, based on a more detailed classification of BSR characteristics, would have been desirable to enhance quality of the transformation and recoding processes. This lack of precision might also be a reason why the expected mediating effect of dyadic control activities on delivery flexibility could not be confirmed. The same applies to key informant bias and non-response bias. Although neither influence is expected to be severe, one must assume some effect on the analysis. Another important issue is the limited sample size; 200 respondents cannot be considered representative for drawing universally valid conclusions. This limitation is also amplified by the geographical range as the survey was only conducted in Germany, Switzerland and Austria.

In conclusion, several methodological approach weaknesses exist; these must be considered when analyzing the analysis results, which is done in the subsequent section.

To increase the conceptual and empirical findings' value, conclusions for practice and science are drawn, limitations of the study are outlined and the need for further research is discussed.

Managerial implications

As results of the empirical analysis show, dyadic performance control plays an important mediating role for delivery reliability in BSRs. The analysis of about 200 BSRs confirmed that relationships with intensive control-related coordination activities showed significantly higher performance ratios than relationships where performance was not systematically controlled. This means that even if information is shared between partners, and both companies have a highly integrated IT basis, the usefulness of these shared resources is decided by how they are utilized to measure and evaluate performance and, based on this, how they eliminate deficiencies and improve processes. In other words, this study indicates that the value of information and cross-company IT integration for reliability performance can be decisively enhanced by application of systematic MCSs. This study addresses – in detail – the following dyadic control activities, commonly executed by buyer and supplier:

- Relevant performance indicators must be defined and responsibilities for measuring and processing performance data determined. Performance indicators' ability to comprehensively reflect BSR's interface performance must be regularly evaluated.
- Control of indicators has to be guaranteed, requiring a common understanding of performance. Also, subjective assessments should be avoided by focusing on absolute performance values.
- Performance values must be analyzed and evaluated regularly and resulting evaluations intensively analyzed to eliminate deficiencies and improve processes for cross-company material and information flows.
- Results need to be thoroughly and systematically discussed with the partnering company. This requires human resources from both sides, as well as an institutionalized cross-company task force.
- Clear standards have to be defined for each figure that indicate when corrective measures have to be executed. Ideally, agreements with suppliers exist that are connected to these figures (e.g. bonus malus systems).

- The task force requires authority, means and instruments to initiate corrective actions (i.e. top management attention in both companies is essential).
- Effectiveness of initiated countermeasures needs to be systematically tracked and, if necessary, additional action taken.

In addition to available information and IT integration within BSRs, integrating suppliers into buyers' supply planning activities is the major prerequisite; it defines the amount of available sensitive information and degree of IT integration between the partnering companies. Control capabilities can be created and dyadic performance control activities introduced only if long-term commitment between partners is assured. This can be achieved by systematically integrating the supplier in the buyer's middle- and long-term supply planning, e.g. as rolling demand planning, or regular meetings and long-term agreements.

In conclusion, involving suppliers in the buyer's supply planning activities by simultaneously sharing relevant sensitive in-house information and integrating IT systems to enhance automation of information exchange activities creates a sound basis for effective dyadic performance control.

Limitations and future research

However, no mediating effect of dyadic performance control on delivery flexibility could be confirmed. This result was also discussed with other researchers and possible reasons have been identified. Flexibility measures are also determined by upstream production and supply processes. Gunasekaran (2001) lists order entry time, order planning time, scheduling time, order sourcing, assembly and follow up time as well as finished goods delivery time. A causal relationship can principally be assumed, as confirmed by; e.g. Eng (2006); da Silveira and Arkader (2007); Narasimhan and Mahapatra (2004); Simatupang and Ramaswami, 2005; Varadarajan and Jayachandran, 1999). However, the impact of specific time components that can be addressed by dyadic control activities at the cross-company interface might be too weak to significantly influence overall response times, (i.e. average delivery time

($FLEX_1$) or response time to unplanned orders ($FLEX_2$)). To examine this issue, intermediate analysis of flexibility indicators actually determined by operational processes within the BSRs is required and should be addressed by future research activities.

Other possible aspects determining influence on delivery flexibility that cannot be directly addressed by dyadic performance control activities might result from soft factors such as commitment of the companies and trust between partners are not considered. Issues like the willingness of both partners to retain BSRs when difficulties occur and commitment to solving problems concerning cooperation together would shed more light on how to improve flexibility and interface performance in BSRs in general. Another commitment-related aspect with a direct influence on delivery flexibility could be the supplier's motivation to perform in an extraordinary manner: i.e. favoring buyers with established business relations during capacity bottlenecks or to ship short term or time-critical goods immediately, even if the buyers's official approval has not yet been confirmed. Future contributions should focus on these soft factors as well.

In conclusion, the assumption of dyadic performance control as a powerful tool in systematically enhancing performance in business relationships (Mahama, 2006) is basically supported by this study's findings. However, knowledge about the expected mediating role for flexibility performance, indicated in related investigation, still remains insufficient and underdeveloped. Thus, it would be advisable to further address this research to increase knowledge on systematically enhancing flexibility performance in BSRs. This need is also supported by the fact that delivery flexibility plays a highly significant role in delivery reliability, as indicated by the model results.

Furthermore, the relativization-approach, used to systematically convert absolute performance values to comparable relative values, should be refined to enhance quality and detail of results.

It is assumed that this contingency-based procedure can be used to further reduce self-reporting bias in general; it is expected to be basically adaptable to any other areas of performance management. Thus, the process of standardizing and recoding of performance, based on contingent performance-determining factors, should also be further developed.

PART III

Critical appraisal & future research

8. Conclusions, limitations and implications for future research

In the following section research results and key findings of the three analysis phases are presented (chapter 8.1) and implications from a managerial (chapter 8.2) and scientific (chapter 8.2) perspective are drawn. Based on the findings limitations are discussed (chapter 8.4) and recommendations for future research are given (chapter 8.5).

8.1. Basic research results and key findings

Basic research results and key findings of analysis phase I

In this phase, classification schemes for the different key elements of formal performance control in BSRs are developed (RQ_b RQ_c RQ_d). This includes relationship capability and contingency variables as well as variables for interface-performance and relational firm-performance. Moreover, a control process-oriented guideline is developed, helping managers to systematically identify and analyze the weak points of their cross-company control activities, and a conceptual model is provided to better understand conditions where formal managerial control is effective BSRs (RQ_a). These identified variables and the three control sub-processes are brought together in a causal model, reflecting expected interdependencies. Semi-structured interviews helped to test these propositions.

Key findings are as follows:

- Expected causal relationships between relationship capabilities and interface-performance, as well as contingencies and both types of performance could be confirmed by semi-structured interviews.
- The evaluation of perspective showed clear results. Several connections exhibited differences between buyers and suppliers; within those groups, however, the questions were answered homogeneously.

- The anticipated correlations about process-related propositions also appeared to be valid.
- No clear statements can be made about the causal relationship between capability variables and the effectiveness of corrective action.
- All interviewed firms conduct standardized performance measurements and comparisons regarding reference values. The assumption that almost no information about comparable BSRs of competitive supply chains exists was, however, confirmed.

Basic research results and key findings of analysis phase II

The second phase aims to improve assessment of performance in BSRs by identifying potential influence factors on comparability of interface-performance (RQ_b). This includes two types of factors: relationship-specific attributes, describing the way partners interact, as well as contingent environmental variables resulting from market- and production-specific conditions. Based on a large-scale survey, statistical methods were applied to quantify these biasing impacts and to analyze natural differences in performance between three specific relationship types: 'highly integrated', 'moderately connected' and 'loose' relationships. Analysis was done for eight selected interface-performance indicators.

Key findings are as follows:

- Analysis of impacts on *on-time delivery* reveals the significance of the BSR type. Demand fluctuations as well as competitiveness between suppliers seem to play an important role for suppliers in being able to fulfill reliability promises. No significant influence could be proven for geographic range of the markets where relational exchanges take place.
- As expected, transport distances, as well as intensity of demand fluctuations are significant to the *average delay* when goods are delivered late. However, neither systematic impact from the level of competiveness between suppliers nor from the BSR type is verifiable.

- As assumed, the BSR type is highly significant for *average delivery time* and *speed of compensation deliveries*. The two market-related contingencies included also showed strong effects on both flexibility items. The influence of standardization on the supplier's production processes cannot be statistically confirmed; only very low shares of variability can be traced back to this contingency.
- Examination of *average storage times in the suppliers' finished goods warehouse* statistically confirmed a systematic effect resulting from the group-specific difference in the way the companies interact. In addition, both expected performance-determining impacts from environmental variables turned out to be significant as well.
- Although the impact of relationship type is tested significant, no causalities between both of the contingent influence factors and *inventory efficiency on the buyer's side* of the dyad could be confirmed. Notably, the poor role of the buyer's production process standardization indicates that storage times are mainly determined by relationship-specific attributes. Comparable to on-time delivery, transportation distance does not seem to play a decisive role, indicating that even transportation over very long distances causes little trouble for scheduling.

Basic research results and key findings of analysis phase III

The third phase aims to empirically assess effectiveness of formal performance control in BSRs by identifying control capabilities and analyzing causalities between them, as well as determining the effect of control activities on performance of BSRs (RQ_e). Structural equation modeling was applied to empirically assess effectiveness of dyadic performance control on interface-performance (delivery flexibility and reliability) in BSRs. Due to the heterogeneity of relationships, a contingency-theoretical perspective on performance is taken to convert absolute performance values, gathered in a large-scaled survey, into relative values, reflecting actual performance.

Key findings are as follows:

- The expected causalities between control capabilities were statistically confirmed.
- Dyadic performance control has a significant mediation effect on delivery reliability in BSRs.
- No significant effect on delivery flexibility is revealed. A moderating role of dyadic performance control for delivery flexibility cannot be assumed.

8.2. Contributions to practice and managerial implications

The use of formal MCSs in BSRs in practice to enhance interface-performance is, in principle, recommendable, as relationships with intensive control-related coordination activities showed significantly higher performance ratios than relationships where performance was not systematically controlled.

However, in order to enable powerful and effective control activities, control-related capabilities must be provided in an adequate manner. This study showed that long-term commitment between partners is required, as relevant sensitive in-house information must be shared, for instance, by integrating suppliers into buyers' supply planning activities. Information must be prepared in an automated and standardized manner. This is promoted by an integrated IT basis.

The usefulness of these shared resources is decided by how they are utilized to measure and evaluate performance and, based on this, how they are used eliminate deficiencies and improve processes. To increase efficiency and effectiveness of control activities, it is recommended to implement systematic and standardized control processes. This covers aspects as the clear definition of responsibilities for measuring and processing performance data, a regular analysis and evaluation of performance values by thoroughly discussing the identified issues with the partnering company, as well as the definition of clear standards for each figure that indicate when corrective measures have to be executed. Effectiveness of initiated countermeasures needs to be systematically tracked and, if necessary, additional action taken.

Formal performance control can be done either on an intra-BSR level (reference values based on historical data or contractual agreements) or on an inter-BSR level (reference values based on actual performance values of related BSRs). The latter is preferable as it might reveal additional information about actual potential still remaining in the relationship. Especially in companies with a large number of suppliers (upstream) and/or customers (downstream), moving away from analyzing isolated business relationships to a more potential-oriented approach could reveal substantial additional possibility for improvement, i.e. by enabling effective BSR benchmarking. However, this kind of control requires putting special attention on the quality of reference values. BSRs cannot simply be compared to each other. The author suggests assessing comparability of different BSRs by analyzing the supplier's performance capabilities and the buyer's performance requirements. Following this approach, BSRs are to be considered 'similar' in case they show homogeneous characteristics regarding these two aspects. Moreover, supplementary effects that influence comparability need to be compensated to enable correct performance control. This avoids using erroneous comparison values when identifying optimization potentials

8.3. Contributions to research and scientific implications

Literature review revealed a general shortage of studies on the use of formal MCSs in SCM, while BSR-specific examinations seem to be neglected in management accounting. As a result, contributions, comprehensively addressing formal MCSs in BSRs, appear to be underrepresented in both areas. Thus, one of the main objectives of this doctoral thesis was it, to contribute to science by harmonizing existing knowledge from both disciplines and by putting forward the discussion about formal MCSs in BSRs as a whole. This was tried to be reached in several steps. Concretely, the following issues were addressed:

A lack of sophisticated approaches to analyzing formal MCSs in BSRs is assumed. Thus, a conceptual framework was developed, systematically connecting control processes (performance measurement, evaluation and implementation of corrective action) to the key elements of performance control in BSRs (performance variables, contingencies and capabilities). A major advantage of this framework is its ability to systematically connect contingency theory to control processes of formal MCSs by embedding the main control processes in an inter-organizational context. Due to the general acceptance of these interdependencies, the guideline for systematically identifying key aspects affecting formal control systems could be applied to other areas of management accounting by researchers as well.

Second, a systematic and comprehensive analysis of relevant influence factors on performance still seems to be missing. This study addressed this issue by developing classification schemes for the different key elements of formal performance control in BSRs; including indicator variables, capabilities contingencies for interface-performance as well capabilities for formal performance control processes in BSRs. Although these schemes cannot be considered exhaustive, they can be taken as a first try to structure the field and to give researches an overview of relevant variables and existing studies empirically analyzing them.

Third, analysis of BSRs in supply chains has mainly focused on performance of either the buying or the supplying company. In consequence, this research project tried to analyze interface-performance in BSRs from an unbiased point of view by equally considering both sides of the dyad. Even though the concept of designing two equally structured questionnaires to analyze such an interface-related phenomenon from both sides is not new, it might motivate scholars to make an increased use of this technique in future research activities.

Fourth, scientists claimed that examination of such BSRs must capture the context in which the BSRs are embedded. Following this appeal, activities in all three analysis phases tried to consider contextual influences. This was done by considering contingencies in the analysis framework (phase I), by providing an approach to classifying BSRs with comparable relationship settings (phase II) and – based on this classification – by developing a procedure for how absolute performance values can be relativized and thus made comparable to each other (phase III).

All of these findings can be seen as part of a comprehensive control approach, ranging from the identification of appropriate performance indicators to the selection and implementation of corrective action. This procedure, in principle, can be adapted to any other research areas related to formal performance control. Thus, it is the procedure itself which represents actual additional value for management control in dyadic business relationships. Additional potential areas of opportunity include product portfolio management, site assessment or evaluation of customer profitability, or other performance aspects. However, discussion of limitations in the next chapter shows that the above mentioned deliverables still leave room for improvement and that essential parts of such a comprehensive approach are still missing.

8.4. Limitations

The work at hand presents several concepts and approaches to support the design and use of formal MCSs in BSRs. These deliverables can be seen as an attempt to harmonize existing knowledge and to put forward the scientific discussion on this topic. However, discussions and conclusions of research activities in this thesis are limited. This particularly concerns limitations in terms of issues addressed and the level of detail as well as methods applied and the underlying empirical basis.

Limitations in terms of issues addressed and the level of detail

First of all, classification schemes for performance indicators, contingent influences and performance capabilities are not complete. So is the list of control capabilities whose influences on effectiveness of control activities were analyzed. Also the framework for analyzing formal MCSs in BSRs cannot be considered exhaustive, because of further possibilities to refine theoretical models. Relational firm-performance, for instance, is not included even though its causal relationships with interface-performance represent a contentious issue of current research on performance control in BSRs.

The same condition applies to the approach to classifying BSRs. Several aspects have been neglected here that are expected to influence either supplier's performance capabilities or buyer's performance requirements. For example, distribution structure and transportation means were not considered, so was the deployment of logistics service providers. Furthermore, it would have been desirable to go into more detail. To give an example: Relationship types actually considered in the empirical analysis remain on an abstract level. On the buy side, it would also have been desirable to differentiate between JIT/JIS. On the supply side, a more detailed analysis of sales concepts would have improved findings and managerial implications. Further, a more differentiated treatment of wholesaling and retailing companies (only performed on the buy side) would enhance the findings' value.

When assessing the effectiveness of formal MCSs, inventory efficiency on the buy and the supply side were not considered. The discussion of interface performance was thus limited to performance indicators that both parties such as delivery reliability and response times. Contribution to science and practice is further limited by the fact that the control system's mediation effect on delivery flexibility could not be confirmed. Having neglected soft factors such as commitment of the companies and trust between partners might be a reason for this. Possibly, issues like the willingness of both partners to retain BSRs when difficulties occur and commitment to solving problems concerning cooperation together would shed more light on how to improve flexibility and interface performance in BSRs in general.

Limitations in terms of methods applied and empirical basis

A structured literature review was conducted to identify key elements of formal performance control in BSRs and to develop classification schemes. Only eight journals have been reviewed. Including more journals might have led to additional findings. The list of capabilities, contingencies and performance variables (both types) should not be considered exhaustive.

This conclusion also applies to semi-structured interviews, as a sample size of six caused a strong heterogeneity in the findings. The empirical evidence needs to be strengthened to verify the framework and to assess applicability of the implementation guideline.

Statistical analysis (mean comparison, ANCOVA and SEM) cannot be considered bias-free for several reasons. As absolute values needed to be recoded into comparable relative values based on peer-groups, relativization is presumed to be critical. It must be assumed that differences still exist, limiting comparability between BSRs of the same group. A larger number of peer-groups, based on a more detailed classification of BSR characteristics, would have been desirable to enhance quality of the transformation and recoding processes. The same applies to key informant bias and non-response bias. Although neither influence is expected to be severe, one must assume some effect on the analysis. Another important issue is the limited sample size; 200 respondents cannot be considered representative for drawing universally valid conclusions. This limitation is also amplified by the geographical range as the survey was only conducted in Germany, Switzerland and Austria.

8.5. Recommendations for future research

Drawing from the stated limitations, future research is needed. One recommendation is to refine dyadic performance control in BSRs by conducting more detailed empirical studies. Especially in large companies with a large supplier (or customer) base, information would be available in the detail required; factors like distribution structure and transportation means could be considered in an adequate manner.

Knowledge about the expected mediating role for flexibility performance, indicated in related investigation, still remains insufficient and underdeveloped. Thus, it would be advisable to further address this research to increase knowledge on systematically enhancing flexibility performance in BSRs. This need is also supported by the fact that delivery flexibility plays a highly significant role in delivery reliability, as indicated by the model results.

It is important to gain further knowledge about how effectiveness of corrective actions, as part of cross-company control activities, can be improved. As an example, statistical analysis of causal relationships between performance and its capabilities can help to increase effectiveness of countermeasures to address performance issues.

Furthermore, the relativization-approach, used to systematically convert absolute performance values to comparable relative values, should be refined to enhance quality and detail of results. It is the author's conviction that this contingency-based procedure can be used to further reduce self-reporting bias in general; it is expected to be basically adaptable to any other areas of performance management. Thus, the process of standardizing and recoding of performance, based on contingent performance-determining factors, should also be further developed.

Furthermore, the overall control approach in which the developed concepts, procedures and approaches can be embedded, might be adapted to other performance management disciplines. Applications could also be useful in other areas of performance management.

References

Ahlert, D., Evanschitzky, H., 2003. Dienstleistungsnetzwerke: Management, Erfolgsfaktoren und Benchmarks im internationalen Vergleich. Springer, Berlin.

Amit, R., Schoemaker, P.J.H., 1993. Strategic assets and organizational rent. Strategic Management Journal 14, 33-46.

Anderson, J. C., Gerbing, D. W., 1988. Structural Equation Modeling in Practice: A Review and Recommended Two-Step Approach. Psychological Bulletin 103, 411-423.

Anderson, J.C., 1995. Relationships in Business Markets: Exchange Episodes, Value Creation, and their Empirical Assessment. Journal of the Academy of Marketing Science 23, 346-350.

Anderson, J.C., Narus, J.A., 1990. A model of the distributor firm and manufacturer firm working partnerships. Journal of Marketing 54, 42–58.

Ansari, S.L., 1977. An integrated approach to control system design. Accounting, Organizations and Society 2, 101-112.

Armstrong, J. S., Overton, T. S., 1977. Estimating Non-response Bias in Mail Surveys. Journal of Marketing Research 14, 396-402.

Arndt, J., 1979. Toward a Concept of Domesticated Markets. Journal of Marketing 43, 69-75.

Arshinder, K., Deshmukh, S.G., 2007. Coordination in supply chains: an evaluation using fuzzy logic. Production Planning and Control 18, 420-435.

Artz, K.W., 1999. Buyer-Supplier Performance - The Role of Asset Specificity, Reciprocal Investmeuts and Relational Exchange. British Journal of Management 10, 113-126.

Åström, K.J., Murray, R.M., 2009. Feedback Systems: An Introduction for Scientists and Engineers. Princeton Universitiy Press, Princeton.

Autry, C.W., Golicic, S.L., 2009. Evaluating buyer-supplier relationship-performance spirals: a longitudinal study. Journal of Operations Management 28, 87-100.

Backhaus, K., Erichson, B., Plinke, W., Weiber, R., 2011. Multivariate Analysemethoden: Eine anwendungsorientierte Einführung. 13th edition. Springer, Berlin.

Baiman, S., Rajan, M.V., 2002. Incentive issues in inter-firm relationships. Accounting, Organizations and Society 27, 213-238.

Ballou, R.H., Gilbert, S.M., Mukherjee, A., 2000. New managerial challenges from supply chain opportunities. Industrial Marketing Management 29, 7-18.

Barratt, M., Oliveira, A., 2001. Exploring the experiences of collaborative planning initiatives. International Journal of Physical Distribution and Logistics Management 31, 266-289.

Baumgartner, H., Homburg, C., 1996. Applications of structural equation modeling in marketing and consumer research: A review. International Journal of Research in Marketing 13, 139-161.

Beamon, B.M., 1999. Measuring supply chain performance. International Journal of Operations and Production Management 19, 275-292.

Beged-dov, A.G., Klein, T.A., 1970. Research Methodology in the Management Sciences: Formalism or Empiricism. Operational Research Quarterly 21, 311-326.

Behr, M., Semlinger, K., 2004. Internationalisierung kleiner und mittlerer Unternehmen: Neue Entwicklungen bei Arbeitsorganisationen und Wissensmanagement. Campus, Frankfurt/New York.

Bensaou, M., Anderson, E., 1999. Buyer-supplier relations in industrial markets: when do buyers risk making idiosyncratic investments?. Organization Science 10, 460-81.

Bentler, P.M., Bonett, D.G., 1980. Significance tests and goodness of fit in the analysis of covariance structures. Psychological Bulletin 88, 588-606.

Beugelsdijk, S., Koen, C., Noorderhaven, N., 2009. A dyadic approach to the impact of differences in organizational culture on relationship-performance. Industrial Marketing Management 38, 312-323.

Bharadwaj, A.S., 2000. A resource-based perspective on information technology capability and firm-performance: An empirical investigation. MIS Quarterly 24, 169-196.

Blanche, T.M., Durrheim, K., Painter, D., 2006. Research in Practice: Applied Methods for the Social Sciences. University of Capetown Press, Capetown.

Bock, R.D., 1975. Multivariate statistical methods in behavioral research. McGraw-Hill, New York.

Bollen, K.A., 1989. A new incremental fit index for general structural equation models. Sociological Methods and Research 17, 303-316.

Bortz, J., 2005. Statistik für Human- und Sozialwissenschaftler. 6th edition. Springer, Heidelberg.

Bower, J.L., Hout, T.M., 1988. Fast cycle capability for competitive power. Harvard Business Review, 110-18.

Bowersox, D.J., Closs, D.J., Stank, T.P., 2000. Ten mega-trends that will revolutionize supply chain logistics. Journal of Business Logistics 21, 1-15.

Brown, D.A., 2005. Management control systems as a coupled package: an analytical framework and empirically grounded implications. Ph.D. Thesis. University of Technology, Sydney.

Bucklin, L.P., Sengupta, S., 1993. Organizing successful co-marketing alliances. Journal of Marketing 57, 32-46.

Burgess, K., Singh, P.J., Koroglu, R., 2006. Supply chain management: a structured literature review and implications for future research. International Journal of Operations and Production Management 26, 703-729.

Burrell, G., Morgan, G., 1979. Sociological Paradigms and Organizational Analysis: Elements of the Sociology of Corporate Life. Ashgate Publishing Ltd., Hants.

Buttermann, G., Germain, R., Iyer, K.N.S., 2008. Contingency theory "fit" as gestalt - An application to supply chain management. Transportation Research Part E 44, 955-969.

Byrne, B.M., 2010. Structural equation modeling with AMOS: basic concepts, applications and programming. Routledge, New York, NY.

Caglio, A., Ditillo, A., 2008. A review and discussion of management control in inter-firm relationships: Achievements and future directions. Accounting, Organizations and Society 33, 865-898.

Carter, C.R., Ellram, L.M., 2003. Thirty Years of The Journal of Supply Chain Management: Where Have We Been and Where are We Going?. Journal of Supply Chain Management 39, 27-39.

Chase, R.B., 1980. A Classification and Evaluation of Research in Operations Management. Journal of Operations Management 1, 9-14.

Chen, C.C., Chen, X.P., Meindl, J.R., 1998. How can Cooperation Be Fostered? The Cultural Effects of Individualism and Collectivism. Academy of Management Review 23, 285-304.

Chenhall, R.H., 2005. Integrative strategic performance measurement systems, strategic alignment of manufacturing, learning and strategic outcomes - an exploratory study. Accounting, Organizations and Society 30, 395-422.

Chenhall, R.H., 2007. Theorizing Contingencies in Management Control Systems Research. In: Chapman, C.S., Hopwood, A.G., Shields, M.D. (eds.), Handbook of Management Accounting Research, vol. 1. Elsevier, Oxford, UK, 163-205.

Cherryholmes, C.C., 1992. Notes on pragmatism and scientific realism. Educational Researcher 21, 13-17.

Cho, E., Lee, M., 2005. An exploratory study on contingency factors affecting R&D performance measurement. International Journal of Manpower 26, 502-512.

Chopra, S., Meindl, P., 2004. Supply Chain Management: Strategy, Planning and Operation, 2nd edition, Prentice Hall International, New Jersey.

Christensen, W.J., Germain, R., Birou, L., 2005. Build-to-order and just-in-time as predictors of applied supply chain knowledge and market performance. Journal of Operations Management 23, 470-481.

Christopher, M., 1992. Logistics and Supply Chain Management. Pitman Publishing, London.

Christopher, M., 2000. The Agile Supply Chain: Competing in Volatile Markets. Industrial Marketing Management 29, 37-44.

Christopher, M., 2005. Logistics and Supply Chain Management: Creating Value-Adding Networks. Pearson Publishers, Harlow.

Churchill, G. A., Surprenant, C. 1982. An Investigation into the Determinants of Customer Satisfaction. Journal of Marketing Research 19, 491-504.

Claycomb, C., Dröge, C., Germain, R., 1999. The Effect of Just-in-time with Customers on Organizational Design and Performance. International Journal of Logistics Management 10, 37-58.

Coletti, A.L., Sedatole, K.L., Towry, K.L., 2005. The effect of control systems on trust and cooperation in collaborative environments. The Accounting Review 80, 477-500.

Collis, D.J., 1994. Research note: How valuable are organizational capabilities?. Strategic Management Journal 15, 143- 152.

Cooper, M.C., Lambert, D.M. ,Pagh, J.D., 1997. Supply Chain Management: More than a new name for Logistics. The International Journal of Logistics Management 8, 1-14.

Cooper, R., Slagmulder, R., 2004. Interorganizational cost management and relational context. Accounting, Organizations and Society 29, 1-26.

Cousins, P.D., Lawson, B., Squire, B., 2008. Performance measurement in strategic buyer-supplier relationships: The mediating role of socialization mechanisms. International Journal of Operations and Production Management 28, 238-258.

Cudeck, R., Browne, M.W., 1983. Cross-validation of covariance-structures. Multivariate Behavioral Research 18, 147-168.

Curcovic, S., Vickery, S., Dröge, C., 2000. Quality-related Action Programs: The Impact on Quality and Firm Performance. Decision Sciences 31, 885-905.

da-Silveira, G.J.C., Arkader, R., 2007. The direct and mediated relationships between supply chain coordination investments and delivery performance. International Journal of Operations and Production Management 27, 140-158.

Daugherty, P.J., Richey, R.G., Hudgens, B.J., Autry, C.W., 2003. Reverse Logistics in the Automobile Aftermarket Industry. International Journal of Logistics Management 14, 49-62.

Day, G.S., 2000. Managing market relationships. Journal of the Academy of Marketing Science 28, 28-30.

Defee, C.C., Stank, T.P., 2005. Applying the strategy-structure performance paradigm to the supply chain environment. The International Journal of Logistics Management 16, 28-50.

Dehning, B., Richardson, V.J., Zmud, R.W., 2007. The financial performance effects of IT-based supply chain management systems in manufacturing firms. Journal of Operations Management 25, 806-824.

Dekker, H.C., 2003. Value chain analysis in inter-firm relationships: a field study. Management Accounting Research 14, 1-23.

Dekker, H.C., 2004. Control of inter-organizational relationships: evidence on appropriation concerns and coordination requirements. Accounting, Organizations and Society 29, 27-49.

Delery, J.E., Doty, H.D., 1996. Modes of Theorizing in Strategic Human Resource Management - Tests of Universalistic, Contingency, and Configurational Performance Predictions. Academy of Management Journal 39, 802-835.

Dillman, D.A. 2007. Mail and Internet Surveys: The Tailored Design Method. John Wiley and Sons, Hoboken, NJ.

Donaldson, L., Whetten, D., 2001. The Contingency Theory of Organizations. Sage, Thousand Oaks, CA.

Drazin, R., Van de Ven, A.H., 1985. Alternative Forms of Fit in Contingency Theory. Administrative Science Quarterly 30, 514-539.

Dretzke, B.J., Levin, J.R., Serlin, R.C. 1982. Testing for regression homogeneity under variance heterogeneity. Psychological Bulletin 91, 376-383.

Droge, C., Jayaram, J., Vickery, S.K., 2004. The effects of internal versus external integration practices on time-based performance and overall firm-performance. Journal of Operations Management 22, 557-573.

Dunn, S.C., Seaker, R.F., Waller, M.A., 1994. Latent variables in business logistics research: Scale development and validation. Journal of Business Logistics 15, 145-172.

Dwyer, F.R., Schurr, P.H., Oh, S., 1987. Developing Buyer-Seller Relationships. Journal of Marketing 51, 11-27.

Dyer, J.H., 1996. Specialized supplier networks as a source of competitive advantage: evidence from the auto industry. Strategic Management Journal 17, 271-291.

Easterby-Smith, M., Thorpe, R., Lowe, A., 2002. Management research: An introduction. Sage, Thousand Oaks, CA.

Eisenhardt, K.M., 1985. Control: Organizational and economic approaches. Management Science 31, 134-149.

Eng, T.-Y., 2006. An investigation into the mediating role of cross-functional coordination on the linkage between organizational norms and SCM performance. Industrial Marketing Management 35, 762-773.

Eschweiler, M., Evanschitzky, H., Woisetschläger, D., 2007. Ein Leitfaden zur Anwendung varianzanalytisch ausgerichteter Laborexperimente. Wirtschafts-wissenschaftliches Studium 36, 546-554.

Evans, J.R., Laskin, R.L., 1994. The Relatioship Marketing Process: A Conceptualization and Application. Industrial Marketing Management 23, 439-452.

Ferreira, A., Otley, D., 2009. The design and use of performance management systems: An extended framework for analysis. Management Accounting Research 20, 263-282.

Field, J.M., Meile, L.C., 2008. Supplier relations and supply chain performance in financial services processes. International Journal of Operations and Production Management 28, 185-206.

Fine, C.H., 1998. Clockspeed: Winning Industry Control in the Age of Temporary Advantage. Perseus, reading.

Fisher, J., 1995. Contingency-Based Research On Management Control Systems: Categorization By Level Of Complexity. Journal of Accounting Literature 14, 24-53.

Fisher, J.G., 1998. Contingency theory, management control systems and firm outcomes: past results and future directions. Behavioral Research in Accounting 10, 47-64.

Fisher, M.L., 1997. What is the right supply chain for your product? Harvard Business Review 75, 105-116.

Flynn, B.B., Huo, B., Zhao, X., 2009. The impact of supply chain integration on performance: A contingency and configuration approach. Journal of Operations Management 28, 58-71.

Foggin J.H., Mentzer J.T., 2004. A supply chain diagnostic tool. International Journal of Physical Distribution and Logistics Management 34, 827-855.

Fornell, C., Larcker, D. F., 1981. Evaluating Structural Equation Models with Unobservable Variables and Measurement Error. Journal of Marketing Research 18, 39-50.

Frances, J., Garnsey, E., 1996. Supermarkets and suppliers in the United Kingdom: system integration, information and control. Accounting, Organization and Society 21, 591-610.

Free, C., 2008. Walking the talk? Supply chain accounting and trust among UK supermarkets and suppliers. Accounting, Organization and Society 33, 629-62.

Fynes, B., Voss, C., de Búrca, S., 2005. The impact of supply chain relationship dynamics on manufacturing performance. International Journal of Operations and Production Management 25, 6-19.

Ganesan, S., 1994. Determinants of long-term orientation in buyer-seller relationships. Journal of Marketing 58, 1.

Garver, M.S., Mentzer, J.T., 1999. Logistics research methods: Employing structural equation modeling to test for construct validity. Journal of Business Logistics 20, 33-57.

Gaski, J.F., Nevin, J.R., 1985. The Differential Effects of Exercised and Unexercised Power Sources in a Marketing Channel. Journal of Marketing Research 22, 130-142.

Germain, R., Claycomb, C., Dröge C., 2008. Supply chain variability, organizational structure, and performance: The moderating effect of demand unpredictability. Journal of Operations Management 26, 557-570.

Giannakis, M., 2007. Performance measurement of supplier relationships. Supply Chain Management: An International Journal 12, 400-411.

Giglioni, G.B., Bedeian, A.G., 1974. A Conspectus of Management Control Theory: 1900-1972. Academy of Management Journal 17, 292-305.

Gimenez, C., Ventura, E., 2005. Logistics-production, logistics-marketing and external integration: Their impact on performance. International Journal of Operations and Production Management 25, 20-38.

Giunipero L.C., Hooker, R.E., Joseph-Matthews, S., Yoon, T.E., Brudivig, S., 2008. A decade of SCM literature Past, present and future implications. Journal of Supply Chain Management 44, 66-86.

Glaser, W.R.; 1978. Varianzanalyse. Fischer, Stuttgart.

Glass, G.V., Peckham, P.D., Sanders, J.R., 1972. Consequences of failure to meet assumptions underlying the fixed effects analysis of variance and covariance. Review of educational research 42, 237-288.

Govindarajan, V., Fisher, J., 1990. Strategy, Control Systems, and Resource Sharing: Effects on Business-Unit Performance. Academy of Management Journal 33, 259-285.

Green, S.G., Welsh, M.A., 1988. Cybernetics and Dependence: Reframing the Control Concept. Academy of Management Review 13, 287-301.

Gunasekaran, A., Patel, C., McGaugheyc, R.E., 2004. A framework for supply chain performance measurement. International Journal of Production Economics 87, 333-347

Gunasekaran, A., Patel, C., Tirtiroglu, E., 2001. Performance measures and metrics in a supply chain environment. International Journal of Operations and Production Management 21, 71-87.

Hair, J.F., Black, W.C., Babin, B.J., Anderson, R.E., Tatham, R.L., 2006. Multivariate Data Analysis. Pearson Education, Upper Saddle River, NJ.

Håkansson, H., Lind, J., 2004. Accounting and network coordination. Accounting, Organizations and Society 29, 51-72.

Håkansson, H., Lind, J., 2007. Acconting in an Interorganizational Setting. In: Chapman, C.S., Hopwood, A.G., Shields, M.D. (eds.), Handbook of Management Accounting Research, vol. 2. Elsevier, Oxford, UK, 885-902.

Halldórsson, A., Arlbjorn, J.S., 2005. Research Methodologies in Supply chain Management - What Do We Know?. In: Kotzab, H., Seuring, S., Müller, M., Reiner, G. (eds.), Research Methodologies in Supply Chain Management. Physica, Heidelberg, 107-122.

Halldórsson, A., Kotzab, H., Mikkola, J.H., Skjøtt-Larsen, T., 2007. Complementary theories to supply chain management. Supply Chain Management: An International Journal 4, 284–296.

Hamilton, B.L., 1977. An empirical investigation of the effects of heterogeneous regression slopes in analysis of covariance. Educational and Psychological Measurement 37, 701-712.

Hardy, M.A., Bryman, A., 2004. Handbook of data analysis. Sage, London/Thousand Oaks.

Harland, C.M., 1996. Supply chain management: Relationships, chains and networks. British Journal of Management 7, 63-80.

Harland, C.M., Lamming, R.C., Zheng, J., Johnsen, T.E., 2001. A taxonomy of supply networks. International Journal of Operations and Production Management 37, 21-27.

Herrmann, A., Seilheimer, C., 2000. Varianz- und Kovarianzanalyse. in: Herrmann, A., Homburg, C. (eds.), Marktforschung - Methoden, Anwendungen, Praxisbeispiele, 2nd edition. Wiesbaden, 267-294.

Herrmann, A., Seilheimer, C., 2000. Varianz- und Kovarianzanalyse. In: Herrmann, A., Homburg, C. (eds.), Marktforschung - Methoden, Anwendungen, Praxisbeispiele, 2nd edition. Wiesbaden, 267-294.

Hildebrandt, L., Temme, D., 2006. Probleme der Validierung mit Strukturgleichungs-modellen. Die Betriebswirtschaft 66, 618-639.

Hill, W., Ulrich, P., 1979. Wissenschaftliche Aspekte ausgewählter betriebswirtschaftlicher Konzeptionen. In: Raffée, H., Abel, B. (eds.), Wissenschaftstheoretische Grundlagen der Wirtschaftswissenschaften. München, 161-190.

Hofmann, E., 2004. Strategisches Synergie- und Dyssynergiemanagement. Bergisch Gladbach.

Homburg, C., Klarmann, M., 2006. Die Kausalanalyse in der empirischen betriebswirtschaftlichen Forschung: Problemfelder und Anwendungsempfehlungen. Die Betriebswirtschaft 66, 717-748.

Hopwood, A.G., 1974. Leadership Climate and the Use of Accounting Data in Performance Evaluation. Accounting Review 49, 485-495.

Hsu, C.-C., Kannan, V.R., Tan, K.-C., Leong, G.K., 2008. Information sharing, buyer-supplier relationships, and firm-performance - A multi-region analysis. International Journal of Physical Distribution and Logistics Management 38, 296-310.

Hsu, L.-L., 2005. SCM system effects on performance for interaction between suppliers and buyers. Industrial Management and Data Systems 105, 857-875.

Huber, G.P., Power, D.J., 1985. Retrospective Reports of Strategic-level Managers: Guidelines for Increasing their Accuracy. Strategic Management Journal 6, 171-180.

Hult, G.T., Ketchen, D.J., Chabowski, B.R., 2007. Leadership, the buying center, and supply chain performance: A study of linked users, buyers, and suppliers. Industrial Marketing Management 36, 393-403.

Humphreys, P.K., Wong, Y.K., Chan, F.T.S., 2003. Integrating environmental criteria into the supplier selection process. Journal of Materials Processing Technology 138, 349-356.

Hunt, S.D., 1983. General Theories and the Fundamental Explanada of Marketing. Journal of Marketing 47, 9-17.

Iyer, K.N., Germain, R., Frankwick, G.L., 2004. Supply chain B2B e-commerce and time-based delivery performance. International Journal of Physical Distribution and Logistics Management 34, 645-661.

Jarillo, J.C., 1988. On strategic networks. Strategic Management Journal 9, 31-41.

Joseph, W.B., Gardner, J.T., Thach, S., Vernon, F., 1995. How industrial distributors view distributor-supplier partnership arrangements. Industrial Marketing Management 24, 27-36.

Kalwani, M.U., Narayandas, N., 1995. Long-Term Manufacturer-Supplier Relationships: Do They Pay off for Supplier Firms?. Journal of Marketing 59, 1-16.

Kaplan, R.S., 1998. Innovation action research: Creating new management theory and practice. Journal of Management Accounting Research 10, 89-118.

Karrer, M., 2006. Explorative empirische Untersuchung zum Supply Chain Performance Management in der Unternehmenspraxis. Wiesbaden.

Kathawala, Y.K., Abdou, K., 2003. Supply chain evaluation in the service industry: A framework development compared to manufacturing. Managerial Auditing Journal 18, 140-149.

Kaynak, H., Hartley, J.L., 2008. A replication and extension of quality management into the supply chain. Journal of Operations Management 26, 468-489.

Ketchen, D., Hult, G.T., 2007. Bridging organization theory and supply chain management: The case of best value supply chains. Journal of Operations Management 25, 573-580.

Kim, S.W., 2006. The effect of supply chain integration on the alignment between corporate competitive capability and supply chain operational capability. International Journal of Operations and Production Management 26, 1084-1107.

Kingshott, R.P.J., 2006. The impact of psychological contracts upon trust and commitment within buyer-supplier relationships: A social exchange view. Industrial Marketing Management 35, 724–739.

Kirk, D.E., 1998. Optimal Control Theory: An Introduction. Mineola.

Kirsch, W., 1990. Unternehmenspolitik und strategische Unternehmensführung. München.

Klein, R., Rai, A., Straub, D.W., 2007. Competitive and Cooperative Positioning in Supply Chain Logistics Relationships. Decision Sciences 38, 611-646.

Kotler, P., Levy, S.J., 1969. Broadening the Concept of Marketing. Journal of Marketing 33, 10-15.

Kouvelis, P., Chester, C., Wang, H., 2006. Supply Chain Management Research and Production and Operations Management. Production and Operations Management 15, 449-469.

Krause, D.R., 1999. The antecedents of buying firms' effort to improve suppliers. Journal of Operations Management 17, 205-224.

Kumar, N., Stern, L.W., Achrol, R.S., 1992. Assessing Reseller Performance From the Perspective of the Supplier. Journal of Marketing Research 29, 238-253.

Kumar, N., Stern, L.W., Anderson, J.C. 1993. Conducting interorganizational research using key informants. Academy of Management Journal 36, 1633-1651.

LaBahn, D.W., Harich, K.R., 1997. Sensitivity to National Business Culture: Effects on U.S.-Mexican Channel Relationship Performance. Journal of International Marketing 5, 29-51.

Lambert, D.M., Cooper, M.C., 2000. Issues in Supply Chain Management. Industrial Marketing Management 29, 65-83.

Lambert, D.M., Cooper, M.C., Pagh, J.D., 1998. Supply Chain Management: Implementation Issues and Research Opportunities. International Journal of Logistics Management 9, 1-20.

Lambert, D.M., Pohlen, T.L., 2001. Supply Chain Metrics. International Journal of Logistics Management 12, 1-19.

Langfield-Smith, K., 2007. A review of quantitative research in management control systems and strategy. In: Chapman, C.S., Hopwood, A.G., Shields, M.D. (eds.), Handbook of Management Accounting Research, vol. 2. Elsevier, Oxford, UK, 753-784.

Lee, H.L., 2004. The triple-A supply chain. Harvard Business Review 82, 102-112.

Lejeune, M.A., Yakova, N., 2005. On characterizing the 4 C's in supply chain management. Journal of Operations Management 23, 81-100.

Li, S., Ragu-Nathan, b., Regu-Nathan, T.S., Rao, S.S., 2004. The impact of supply chain management practices on competitive advantage and organizational performance. Omega 34, 107-124.

Li, T., Calantone, R.J., 1998. The Impact of Market Knowledge Competence on New Product Advantage: Conceptualization and Empirical Examination. Journal of Marketing 62, 13-29.

Luck D.J., 1969. Marketing Notes And Communications. Broadening the Concept of Marketing-Too Far. Journal of Marketing 33, 53-63.

Luthans, F., Stewart, T., 1977. A General Contingency Theory of Management. Academy of Management Review 2, 181-195.

Macneil, I.R., 1980. Power, Contract, and the Economic Model. Journal of Economic Issues 14, 909-923.

Mahama, H., 2006. Management control systems, cooperation and performance in strategic supply relationships: a survey in the mines. Management Accounting Research 17, 315-339.

Malmi, T., Brown, D.A., 2008. Management control systems as a package: Opportunities, challenges and research directions. Management Accounting Research 19, 287-300.

McCutcheon, D.M., Meredith, J.R., 1993. Conducting case study research in operations management. Journal of Operations Management 11, 239-256.

McCutcheon, D.M., Stuart, F.I., 2000. Issues in the choice of supplier alliance partners. Journal of Operations Management 18, 279-301.

McNeilly, K.M., Russ, F.A., 1992. Co-ordination in the marketing channel. In: Frazier, G.L. (ed.), Advances in Distribution Channel Research, vol. 1. JAI Press, London, 161-186.

Meira, J., Kartalis, N.D., Tsamenyi, M., Cullen, J., 2010. Management controls and inter-firm relationships: a review. Journal of Accounting and Organizational Change 6, 149-169.

Menachof, D., Gibson, B.J., Hanna, J.B., 2009. An analysis of the value of supply chain management periodicals. International Journal of Physical Distribution and Logistics Management 39, 145-166.

Mentzer, J.T., DeWitt, W., Keebler, J.S., Min, S., W. Nix, N.W., Carlo D. Smith, C.D., 2001. Defining Supply Chain Management. Journal of Business Logistics 22, 11-17.

Mentzer, J.T., Kahn, K.B., 1995. A framework of logistics research. Journal of Business Logistics 16, 231-250.

Meredith, J., 1993. Theory Building through Conceptual Methods. International Journal of Operations and Production Management 13, 3-11.

Meredith, J., Raturi, A., Amoako-Gyampah, K., Kaplan, B., 1989. Alternative research paradigms in operations. Journal of Operations Management 8, 297-326.

Meyr, H., Stadtler, H., 2005. Types of Supply Chains. In: Stadtler, H; Kilger, C. (eds.). Supply Chain Management and Advanced Planning: Concepts, Models, Software and Case Studies, 3rd Edition. Springer, Berlin, 65-80.

Miller, D.C., Salkind, N.J., 2002. Handbook of research design and social measurement. Sage Publications, London, UK.

Mitroff, I.I., Mason, R.O., 1984. Business Policy and Metaphysics: Some Philosophical Considerations. Unpublished manuscript, University of Southern California.

Mohr, J.J., Fisher, R.J., Nevin, J.R., 1996. Collaborative Communication in Interfirm Relationships: Moderating Effects of Integration and Control. Journal of Marketing 60, 103-115.

Morgan, G., 1979. Cybernetics and organization theory: Epistemology or technique? Unpublished manuscript.

Morgan, G., Smircich, L., 1980. The Case for Qualitative Research. Academy of Management Review 5, 491-500.

Morgan, R.M., Hunt, S.D.: 1994. The Commitment-Trust Theory of Relationship Marketing. Journal of Marketing 58, 20-38.

Morris, M., Carter, C.R., 2005. Relationship Marketing and Supplier Logistics Performance: An Extension of the Key Mediating Variables Model. Journal of Supply Chain Management 41, 32-43.

Mouritsen, J., Hansen, A., 2006. Management accounting, operations, and network relations: debating the lateral dimension. In: Bhimani, A. (ed.), Contemporary Issues in Management Accounting, Oxford University Press, New York, NY.

Mouritsen, J., Hansen, A., Hansen, C.Ø., 2001. Inter-organizational control and organizational competencies: episodes around target cos management/functional analysis and open book accounting. Management Accounting Research 12, 221-244.

Nakano, M., 2009. Collaborative forecasting and planning in supply chains: The impact on performance in Japanese manufacturers. International Journal of Physical Distribution and Logistics Management 39, 84-105.

Narasimhan, R., Mahapatra, S., 2004. Decision models in global supply chain management. Industrial Marketing Management 33, 21-27.

Netemeyer, R.G., Bearden, W.O., Sharma, S., 2003. Scaling procedures. Issues and applications. Sage, Thousand Oaks.

Nyaga, G.N., Whipple, J.M., Lynch, D.F., 2010. Examining supply chain relationships: Do buyer and supplier perspectives on collaborative relationships differ?. Journal of Operations Management 28, 101-114.

O'Toole, T., Donaldson, B., 2002. Relationship-performance dimensions of buyer-supplier exchanges. European Journal of Purchasing and Supply Management 8, 197-207.

Odekerken-Schroder, G., De Wulf, K., Schumacher, P., 2003. Strengthening outcomes of retailer-consumer relationships: The dual impact of relationship marketing tactics and consumer personality. Journal of Business Research 56, 177-190.

Ordanini, A., Rubera, G., 2008. Strategic capabilities and internet resources in procurement. International Journal of Operations and Production Management 28, 27-52.

Otley, D.T., 1980. The contingency theory of management accounting: achievement and prognosis. Accounting, Organizations and Society 5, 413-428.

Otley, D.T., 1999. Performance management: a framework for management control systems research. Management Accounting Research 10, 363-382.

Otley, D.T., Berry, A.J., 1980. Control, Organisation And Accounting. Accounting, Organizations and Society 5, 231-244.

Otto, A., 2002. Managment und Controlling von Supply Chains: Ein Modell auf Basis der Netzwerktheorie. Wiesbaden.

Paulin, W.L., Coffey, R.E., Spaulding, M.E., 1982. Entrepreneurship Research: Methods and Directions. In: Kent., C.A., Sexton., D.L., Vesper, K.H. (eds.), Encyclopedia of Entrepreneurship. Prentice-Hall, Englewood Cliffs, NJ, 352-369.

Paulraj, A., Chen, I.J., 2007. Environmental Uncertainty and Strategic Supply Management: A Resource Dependence Perspective and Performance Implications. Journal of Supply Chain Management 43, 29-42.

Paulraj, A., Lado, A., Chen, I., 2008. Inter-organizational communication as a relational competency: Antecedents and performance outcomes in collaborative buyer-supplier relationships. Journal of Operations Management 26, 45-64.

Perea, E., Grossmann, I., Ydstie, E., Tahmassebi, T., 2000. Dynamic modeling and classical control theory for supply chain management. Computers and Chemical Engineering 24, 1143-1149.

Ploetner, O, Ehret, M., 2006. From relationships to partnerships - new forms of cooperations between buyer and seller. Industrial Marketing Management 35, 4-9.

Podsakoff, P.M., Mackenzie, S.B., Jeong-Yeon, L., Podsakoff, N.P., 2003. Common Method Biases in Behavioral Research: A Critical Review of the Literature and Recommended Remedies. Journal of Applied Psychology 88, 879-903.

Podsakoff, P.M., Organ, D.W., 1986. Self-Reports in Organizational Research: Problems and Prospects. Journal of Management 12, 531-544.

Presutti, W.D. Jr., Mawhinney, J.R., 2007. The supply chain finance link. Supply Chain Management Review, September 2007, 32-38.

Ramaswani, S., Srivastava, R., 2009. Market-based capabilities and financial performance of firms: Insights into marketing's contribution to firm value. Journal of the Academy of Marketing Science 37, 97-116.

Reason, P., 2006. Choice and quality in action research practice. Journal of Management Inquiry 15, 187-203.

Remenyi, D., Williams, B., Money, A., Swartz, E., 1998. Doing research in business and management: An introduction to process and method. London.

Rogosa, D., 1980. Comparing nonparallel regression lines. Psychological Bulletin 88, 307-321.

Roslender, R., Hart, S.J., 2003. In search of strategic management accounting: Theoretical and field study perspectives. Management Accounting Research 14, 255-279.

Ross, A.D., Buffa, F.P., Droge, C., Carrington, D., 2009. Using Buyer-Supplier Performance Frontiers to Manage Relationship Performance. Decision Sciences 40, 37-64.

Sachan, A., Datta, S., 2005. Review of SCM and logistics research. International Journal of Physical Distribution and Logistics Management 35, 664-705.

Sanders, N.R., 2005. IT Alignment in Supply Chain Relationships: A Study of Supplier Benefits. Journal of Supply Chain Management 41, 4-13.

Sanders, N.R., 2007. An empirical study of the impact of e-business technologies on organizational collaboration and performance. Journal of Operations Management 25, 1332-1347.

Sanders, N.R., 2008. Pattern of information technology use: The impact on buyer-suppler coordination and performance. Journal of Operations Management 26, 349-367.

Schanz, G., 1990. Die Betriebswirtschaftslehre als Gegenstand kritisch-konstruktiver Betrachtungen. Stuttgart.

Scherer, A.G., 1999. Kritik der Organisation oder Organisation der Kritik? Wissenschaftstheoretische Bemerkungen zum kritischen Umgang mit Organisationstheorien. In: Kieser, A. (ed.), Organisationstheorien. 3rd edition. Stuttgart, 1-37.

Schweicher, B., Jursch, S., 2006. SCM-Navigator: Unterstützung der Priorisierung und Auswahl von SCM-Konzepten. FIR-Zeitschrift für Betriebsorganisation und Unternehmensentwicklung 36, 47-51.

Seal, W.B., Berry, A., Cullen, J., 2004. Disembedding the supply chain: institutionalized reflexivity and inter-firm accounting. Accounting, Organizations and Society 29, 73-92.

Seal, W.B., Cullen, J., Dunlop, A., Berry, T., Ahmed, M., 1999. Enacting a European supply chain: the role of management accounting. Management Accounting Research 10, 303-322.

Seidler, J., 1974. On using informants: A technique for collecting quantitative data and controlling for measurement error in organizational analysis. American Sociological Review 39, 816-831.

Sengupta K., Heiser D.R., Cook L.S., 2006. Manufacturing and Service Supply Chain Performance: A Comparative Analysis. Journal of Supply Chain Management 42, 4-15.

Sheu, C., Yen, H.R., Chae, B., 2006. Determinants of supplier-retailer collaboration: Evidence from an international study. International Journal of Operations and Production Management 26, 24-49.

Shook, C.L., Ketchen Jr., D.J., Hult, G.T.M., Kacmar, K.M., 2004. An assessment of the use of structural equation modeling in strategic management research. Strategic Management Journal 25, 397-404.

Shook, C.L., Ketchen, D.J., Hult, G.T.M., Kacmar, K.M., 2004. An assessment of the use of structural equation modeling in strategic management research. Strategic Management Journal 25, 397-404.

Simatupang, T.M., Ramaswami, S., 2005. The collaboration index: a measure for supply chain collaboration. International Journal of Physical Distribution and Logistics Management 35, 44-62.

Simchi-Levi, D., Kaminsky, P., Simchi-Levi, E., 2003. Designing and managing the supply chain: Concepts, Strategies and Case Studies, 2nd edition. McGraw-Hill, New York, NJ, 347.

Simons, R., 1995. Levers of Control: How Managers Use Innovative Control Systems to Drive Strategic Renewal. Harvard Business School Press, Boston, MA.

Sousa, R., Voss C.A., 2008. Contingency research in operations management practices. Journal of Operations Management 26, 697-713.

Spekman, R.E., 1988. Strategic Supplier Selection: Understanding Long-Term Buyer Relationships. Business Horizons 31, 75-81.

Squire, B., Cousins, P.D., Lawson, B., Brown, S., 2009. The effect of supplier manufacturing capabilities on buyer responsiveness: The role of collaboration. International Journal of Operations and Production Management 29, 766-788.

Stevens, J.P., 1990. Intermediate statistics: A modern approach. Lawrence Erlbaum, New Jersey.

Stevenson, M., Spring, M., 2009. Supply chain flexibility: An inter-firm empirical study. International Journal of Operations and Production Management 29, 946-971.

Stölzle, W., 1999. Industrial Relationships. Oldenburg, München.

Stölzle, W., 2002. Supply Chain Controlling und Performance Management: Konzeptionelle Herausforderungen für das Supply Chain Management. Logistik Management 4, 10-21.

Straub, D.W., Rai, A., Klein, R., 2004. Measuring firm-performance at the network level: 'A nomology for the impact of digital supply networks. Journal of Management Information Systems 21, 83-114.

Swink, M., Narasimhan, R., Wang, C., 2007. Managing beyond the factory walls: Effects of four types of strategic integration on manufacturing plant performance. Journal of Operations Management 25, 148-164.

Tan, K.C., 2001. A framework of supply chain management literature. European Journal of Purchasing and Supply Management 7, 39-48.

Teece, D.J., Pisano, G., Shuen, A., 1997. Dynamic Capabilities And Strategc Management. Strategic Management Journal 18, 509-533.

Terpend, R., Tyler, B.B., Krause, D.R., Handfield, R.B., 2008. Buyer-Supplier Relationships: Derived Value Over Two Decades. Journal of Supply Chain Management, 44, 28-55.

Tomkins, C., 2001. Interdependencies, trust and information in relationships, alliances and networks. Accounting, Organizations and Society 26, 161-191.

Towill, D.R., 1997. The seamless supply chain: The predator's strategic advantage. International Journal of Technology Management 14, 37-55.

Tracey, M., 2004. Transportation Effectiveness and Manufacturing Firm Performance. International Journal of Logistics Management 15, 31-50.

Varadarajan, P. R., Jayachandran, S., 1999. Marketing strategy: An assessment of the state of the field and outlook. Journal of the Academy of Marketing Science 27, 120-143.

Venkatraman, N., 1989. The Concept of Fit in Strategy Research: Toward Verbal and Statistical Correspondence. Academy of Management Review 14, 423-444.

Vereecke, A., Muylle, S., 2006. Performance improvement through supply chain collaboration in Europe. International Journal of Operations and Production Management 26, 1176-1198.

Vickery, S.K., Jayaram, J., Droge, C., Calantone, R., 2003. The effects of an integrative supply chain strategy on customer service and financial performance: an analysis of direct versus indirect relationships. Journal of Operations Management 21, 523-539.

Vonderembse, M.A., Uppal, M., Huang, S.H., Dismukes, J.P., 2006. Designing supply chains: Towards theory development. International Journal of Production Economics 100, 223-238.

Wang, Y., Lalwani, C.S., 2007. Using e-business to enable customized logistics sustainability. The International Journal of Logistics Management 18.

Weber, J., Schäfer, U., 2000. Balanced Scorecard und Controlling, 3rd edition. Gabler, Wiesbaden.

Werts, C.E., Linn, R.L., Jöreskog, K.G.. 1974. Intraclass reliability estimates: Testing structural assumptions. Educational and Psychological Measurement 34, 25-33.

Westhaus, M., 2007. Supply Chain Controlling: Definition, Forschungsstand, Konzeption. Wiesbaden.

Williamson, O.E., 1991. Comparative economic organization: The analysis of discrete structural alternatives. Administrative Science Quarterly 36, 269-296.

Williamson, O.E., 1996. The Mechanisms of Governance. Oxford University Press, Oxford.

Wood, D.J., Gray, B., 1991. Towards a comprehensive theory of collaboration. Journal of Applied Behavioral Science 27, 139-162.

Wu, F., Yeniyort, S., Kim, D., Cavusgil, S.T., 2006. The impact of information technology on supply chain capabilities and firm-performance: A resource-based view. Industrial Marketing Management 35, 493-504.

Xu, L., Beamon, B.M., 2006. Supply chain coordination and cooperative mechanisms: An attribute-based approach. Journal of Supply Chain Management 42, 4-12.

Zenger, T.R., Hesterly, W.S., 1997. The disaggregation of corporations: Selective intervention, high-powered incentives, and molecular units. Organization Science 8, 209-222.

References (structured literature review)

[1] **Autry, C.W., Golicic, S.L., 2009.** Evaluating buyer-supplier relationship-performance spirals: a longitudinal study. Journal of Operations Management 28, 87-100.

[2] **Bagchi, P.K., Ha, B.C., Skjoett-Larsen, T., Soerensen, L.B., 2005.** Supply chain integration: a European survey. International Journal of Logistics Management 16, 275-294.

[3] **Benton, W.C., Maloni, M., 2005.** The influence of power driven buyer/seller relationships on supply chain satisfaction. Journal of Operations Management 23, 1-22.

[4] **Cai, S., Jun, M., Yang, Z., 2006.** The Impact of Interorganizational Internet Communication on Purchasing Performance: A Study of Chinese Manufacturing Firms. Journal of Supply Chain Management 42, 16-29.

[5] **Cai, S,, Yang, Z., 2008.** Development of cooperative norms in the buyer-supplier relationship: The Chinese experience. Journal of Supply Chain Management 44, 55-70.

[6] **Carr, A.S., Kaynak, H., 2007.** Communication methods, information sharing, supplier development and performance. International Journal of Operations and Production Management 27, 346-370.

[7] **Carr, A.S., Kaynak, H., 2008.** Supplier dependence: impact on supplier's participation and performance. International Journal of Operations and Production Management 28, 899-916.

[8] **Carter, C.R,, Kaufmann, L., 2007.** The Impact of Electronic Reverse Auctions on Supplier Performance: The Mediating Role of Relationship Variables. Journal of Supply Chain Management 43, 16-26.

[9] **Carter, C.R., 2005.** Purchasing social responsibility and firm-performance - The key mediating roles of organizational learning and supplier performance. International Journal of Physical Distribution and Logistics Management 35, 177-194.

[10] **Chen, I.J., Paulraj, A., Lado, A.A., 2004.** Strategic purchasing, supply management, and firm-performance. Journal of Operations Management 22, 505-523.

[11] **Christensen, W.J., Germain, R., Birou, L., 2005.** Build-to-order and just-in-time as predictors of applied supply chain knowledge and market performance. Journal of Operations Management 23, 470-481.

[12] **Claro, D.P., Hagelaar, G., Omta, O., 2003.** The Determinants of Relational Governance and Performance: How to Manage Business Relationships?. Industrial Marketing Management 32, 703-716.

[13] **Closs, D.J., Mollenkopf, D.A., 2004.** A global supply chain framework. Industrial Marketing Management 33, 37-44.

[14] **Corsten, D., Felde, J., 2005.** Exploring the performance effects of key-supplier collaboration - An empirical investigation into Swiss buyer-supplier relationships. International Journal of Physical Distribution and Logistics Management 35, 445-461.

[15] **Cousins, P.D., Lawson, B., Squire, B., 2008.** Performance measurement in strategic buyer-supplier relationships - The mediating role of socialization mechanisms. International Journal of Operations and Production Management 28, 238-258.

[16] **Cousins, P.D., Lawson, B., Squire, B., 2006.** An empirical taxonomy of purchasing functions. International Journal of Operations and Production Management 26, 775-794.

[17] **Curkovic, S., Vickery, S., Droge, C., 2000.** Quality-related Action Programs: The Impact on Quality and Firm Performance. Decision Sciences, 31, 885-905.

[18] **Das, A., Narasimhan, R., Talluri, S., 2006.** Supplier integration--Finding an optimal configuration. Journal of Operations Management 24, 563-582.

[19] **da-Silveira, G.J.C., Arkader, R., 2007.** The direct and mediated relationships between supply chain coordination investments and delivery performance. International Journal of Operations and Production Management 27, 140-158.

[20] **Daugherty, P.J., Richey, R.G., Hudgens, B.J., Autry, C.W., 2003.** Reverse Logistics in the Automobile Aftermarket Industry. International Journal of Logistics Management 14, 49-62.

[21] **Dehning, B., Richardson, V.J., Zmud, R.W., 2007.** The financial performance effects of IT-based supply chain management systems in manufacturing firms. Journal of Operations Management 25, 806-824.

[22] **Droge, C., Germain, R., 2000.** The relationship of electronic data interchange with inventory and financial performance. Journal of Business Logistics 21, 209-230.

[23] **Droge, C., Jayaram, J., Vickery, S.K., 2004.** The effects of internal versus external integration practices on time-based performance and overall firm-performance. Journal of Operations Management 22, 557-573.

[24] **Eltantawy, R.A., Giunipero, L., Fox, G.L., 2009.** A strategic skill based model of supplier integration and its effect on supply management performance. Industrial Marketing Management 38, 925-936.

[25] **Eng, T.-Y., 2006.** An investigation into the mediating role of cross-functional coordination on the linkage between organizational norms and SCM performance. Industrial Marketing Management 35, 762-773.

[26] **Flynn, B.B., Huo, B., Zhao, X., 2001.** The impact of supply chain integration on performance: A contingency and configuration approach. Journal of Operations Management 28, 58-71.

[27] **Forslund, H., 2006.** Performance gaps in the dyadic order fulfillment process. International Journal of Physical Distribution and Logistics Management 36, 580-595.

[28] **Frohlich, M.T., 2002.** e-integration in the supply chain: Barriers and performance. Decision Sciences 33, 537-556.

[29] **Frohlich, M.T., Westbrook, R., 2001.** Arcs of integration: an international study of supply chain strategies. Journal of Operations Management 19, 185-200.

[30] **Fynes, B., Voss, C., de Búrca, S., 2005.** The impact of supply chain relationship dynamics on manufacturing performance. International Journal of Operations and Production Management 25, 6-19.

[31] **Fynes, B., Voss, C., 2002.** The moderating effect of buyer-supplier relationships on quality practices and performance. International Journal of Operations and Production Management 22, 589-613.

[32] **Germain, R., Claycomb, C., Dröge C., 2008.** Supply chain variability, organizational structure, and performance: The moderating effect of demand unpredictability. Journal of Operations Management 26, 557-570.

[33] **Giménez, C., Ventura, E., 2005.** Logistics-production, logistics-marketing and external integration: Their impact on performance. International Journal of Operations and Production Management 25, 20-38.

[34] **Grawe, S.J., Chen, H., Daugherty, P.J., 2009.** The relationship between strategic orientation, service innovation, and performance. International Journal of Physical Distribution and Logistics Management 39, 282-300.

[35] **Gunasekaran, A., Patel, C., Tirtiroglu, E., 2001.** Performance measures and metrics in a supply chain environment. International Journal of Operations and Production Management 21, 71-87.

[36] **Handfield, R., Petersen, K., Cousins, P., Lawson, B., 2009.** An organizational entrepreneurship model of supply management integration and performance outcomes. International Journal of Operations and Production Management 29, 100-126.

[37] **Handfield, R.B., Bechtel, C., 2002.** The role of trust and relationship structure in improving supply chain responsiveness. Industrial Marketing Management 31, 367-382.

[38] **Hsu, C.-C., Kannan, V.R., Tan, K.-C., Leong, G.K., 2008.** Information sharing, buyer-supplier relationships, and firm-performance - A multi-region analysis. International Journal of Physical Distribution and Logistics Management 38, 296-310.

[39] **Hult, G.T., Ketchen, D.J., Cavusgil, S.T., Calantone, R.J., 2006.** Knowledge as a strategic resource in supply chains. Journal of Operations Management 24, 458-475.

[40] **Iyer, K.N., Germain, R., Frankwick, G.L., 2004.** Supply chain B2B e-commerce and time-based delivery performance. International Journal of Physical Distribution and Logistics Management 34, 645-661.

[41] **Jayaram, J., Vickery, S.K., Droge, C., 2000.** The effects of information system infrastructure and process improvements on supply-chain time performance. International Journal of Physical Distribution and Logistics Management 30, 314-330.

[42] **Johnston, D.A, McCutcheon, D.M, Stuart, F.I., Kerwood, H., 2004.** Effects of supplier trust on performance of cooperative supplier relationships. Journal of Operations Management 22, 23-38.

[43] **Kannan, V.R, Tan, K.C., 2002**. Supplier selection and assessment: Their impact on business performance. Journal of Supply Chain Management 38, 11-21.

[44] **Kannan, V.R., Tan, K.C., 2006.** Buyer-supplier relationships. International Journal of Physical Distribution and Logistics Management 36, 755-775.

[45] **Kaufmann, L., Carter, C.R., 2006.** International supply relationships and non-financial performance-A comparison of U.S. and German practices. Journal of Operations Management 24, 653-675.

[46] **Kaynak, H., Hartley, J.L., 2008.** A replication and extension of quality management into the supply chain. Journal of Operations Management 26, 468-489.

[47] **Kim, S.W., 2006.** The effect of supply chain integration on the alignment between corporate competitive capability and supply chain operational capability. International Journal of Operations and Production Management 26, 1084-1107.

[48] **Koufteros, X., Vonderembse, M., Jayaram, J., 2005.** Internal and External Integration for Product Development: The Contingency Effects of Uncertainty, Equivocality, and Platform Strategy. Decision Sciences 36, 97-133.

[49] **Krause, D.R., Scannell, T.V, Calantone, R.J., 2000.** A structural analysis of the effectiveness of buying firms' strategies to improve supplier performance. Decision Sciences 31, 33-55.

[50] **Krause, D.R., Handfield, R.B., Tyler, B.B., 2007.** The relationships between supplier development, commitment, social capital accumulation and performance improvement. Journal of Operations Management 25, 528-545.

[51] **Krause, D.R., Pagell, M., Curkovic, S., 2001.** Toward a measure of competitive priorities for purchasing. Journal of Operations Management (JOM) 19, 497-512.

[52] **Large, R.O., 2005.** Communication capability and attitudes toward external communication of purchasing managers in Germany. International Journal of Physical Distribution and Logistics Management 35, 426-444.

[53] **Larson, P.D., Kulchitsky, J.D, 2000.** The use and impact of communication media in purchasing and supply management. Journal of Supply Chain Management 36, 29-39.

[54] **Lawson, B., Tyler, B.B., Cousinsl P.D. 2008.** Antecedents and consequences of social capital on buyer performance improvement. Journal of Operations Management 26, 446-460.

[55] **Martin, J.H., Grbac, B., 2003.** Using supply chain management to leverage a firm's market orientation. Industrial Marketing Management 32, 25-38.

[56] **Mesquita, L.F., Lazzarini, S.G., Cronin, P., 2007.** Determinants of firm competitiveness in Latin American emerging economies. International Journal of Operations and Production Management 27, 501-523.

[57] **Moberg, C.R., Whipple, T.W., Cutler, B.D., Speh, T.W., 2004.** Do the Management Components of Supply Chain Management Affect Logistics Performance?. International Journal of Logistics Management 15, 15-30.

[58] **Modi, S.B., Mabert, V.A., 2007.** Supplier development: Improving supplier performance through knowledge transfer. Journal of Operations Management 25, 42-64.

[59] **Morris, M., Carter, C.R., 2005.** Relationship Marketing and Supplier Logistics Performance: An Extension of the Key Mediating Variables Model. Journal of Supply Chain Management 41, 32-43.

[60] **Nahm, A.Y., Vonderembs, M.A., Koufteros, X.A., 2004.** The Impact of Organizational Culture on Time-Based Manufacturing and Performance. Decision Sciences 35, 579-607.

[61] **Nakano, M., 2009.** Collaborative forecasting and planning in supply chains: The impact on performance in Japanese manufacturers. International Journal of Physical Distribution and Logistics Management 39, 84-105.

[62] **Nyaga, G.N., Whipple, J.M., Lynch, D.F., 2010.** Examining supply chain relationships: Do buyer and supplier perspectives on collaborative relationships differ?. Journal of Operations Management 28, 101-114.

[63] **Ordanini, A., Rubera, G., 2008.** Strategic capabilities and internet resources in procurement. International Journal of Operations and Production Management 28, 27-52.

[64] **Pagano, A., 2009.** The role of relational capabilities in the organization of international sourcing activities: A literature review. Industrial Marketing Management 38, 903-913.

[65] **Parker, D.B., Zsidisin, G.A., Ragatz, G.L., 2008.** Timing and extent of supplier integration in new product development: A contingency approach. Journal of Supply Chain Management 44, 71-83.

[66] **Paulraj, A., Lado, A.A., Chen, I.J., 2008.** Inter-organizational communication as a relational competency: Antecedents and performance outcomes in collaborative buyer-supplier relationships. Journal of Operations Management 26, 45-64.

[67] **Paulraj, A., Chen, I.J., 2007.** Environmental Uncertainty and Strategic Supply Management: A Resource Dependence Perspective and Performance Implications. Journal of Supply Chain Management 43, 29-42.

[68] **Paulraj, A., Chen, I.J., 2007.** Strategic Buyer-Supplier Relationships, Information Technology and External Logistics Integration. Journal of Supply Chain Management 43, 2-14.

[69] **Paulraj, A., Chen, I.J., 2005.** Strategic Supply Management and Dyadic Quality Performance: A Path Analytical Model. Journal of Supply Chain Management 41, 4-18.

[70] **Petersen, K.J., Ragatz, G.L., Monczka, R.M., 2005.** An Examination of Collaborative Planning Effectiveness and Supply Chain Performance. Journal of Supply Chain Management 41, 14-25.

[71] **Pohlen, T.L., Goldsby, T.J., 2003.** VMI and SMI programs: How economic value added can help sell the change. International Journal of Physical Distribution and Logistics Management 33, 565-581.

[72] **Prahinski, C., Benton, W.C., 2004.** Supplier evaluations: strategies to improve supplier performance. Journal of Operations Management 22, 39-62.

[73] **Prahinski, C., Fan, Y., 2007.** Supplier Evaluations: The Role of Communication Quality. Journal of Supply Chain Management 43, 16-28.

[74] **Qi, Y., Boyer, K.K., Zhao, X., 2009.** Supply Chain Strategy, Product Characteristics, and Performance Impact: Evidence from Chinese Manufacturers. Decision Sciences 40, 667.

[75] **Richey, G., Tokman, M., Wheeler, A.R., 2006.** A supply chain manager selection methodology: Empirical test and suggested application. Journal of Business Logistics 27, 163-191.

[76] **Richey, G., Daugherty, P.J., Roath, A.S., 2007.** Firm technological readiness and complementarity: Capabilities impacting logistics service competency an performance. Journal of Business Logistics 28, 195-229

[77] **Rodrigues, A.M., Stank, T.P., Lynch, D.F. 2004.** Linking strategy, structure, process, and performance in integrated logistics. Journal of Business Logistics 25, 65-94.

[78] **Rosenzweig, E.D., Roth, A.V., Dean Jr., J.W., 2003.** The influence of an integration strategy on competitive capabilities and business performance: An exploratory study of consumer products manufacturers. Journal of Operations Management 21, 437-456.

[79] **Ryu, S., Eyuboglu, N., 2007.** The environment and its impact on satisfaction with supplier performance: An investigation of the mediating effects of control

mechanisms from the perspective of the manufacturer in the U.S.A.. Industrial Marketing Management 36, 458-469.

[80] **Saeed, K.A., Malhotra, M.K., Grover, V., 2005.** Examining the Impact of Interorganizational Systems on Process Efficiency and Sourcing Leverage in Buyer-Supplier Dyads. Decision Sciences 36, 365-396.

[81] **Salvador, F., Forza, C., Rungtusanatham, M., Choi, T.Y., 2001.** Supply chain interactions and time-related performances An operations management perspective. International Journal of Operations and Production Management 21, 561-475.

[82] **Sánchez, A.M., Pérez, M.P., 2005.** Supply chain flexibility and firm-performance - A conceptual model and empirical study in the automotive industry. International Journal of Operations and Production Management 25, 681-700.

[83] **Sanders, N.R., Premus, R., 2002.** IT applications in supply chain organizations: A link between competitive priorities and organizational benefits. Journal of Business Logistics 23, 65-83.

[84] **Sanders, N.R., Premus, R., 2005.** Modeling the relationship between firm it capability, collaboration, and performance. Journal of Business Logistics 26, 1-23.

[85] **Sanders, N.R., 2005.** IT Alignment in Supply Chain Relationships: A Study of Supplier Benefits. Journal of Supply Chain Management 41, 4-13.

[86] **Sanders, N.R., 2007.** An empirical study of the impact of e-business technologies on organizational collaboration and performance. Journal of Operations Management 25, 1332-1347.

[87] **Sanders, N.R., 2008.** Pattern of information technology use: The impact on buyer-suppler coordination and performance. Journal of Operations Management 26, 349-367.

[88] **Sharland, A., Eltantawy, R.A., Giunipero, L.C., 2003.** The impact of cycle time on supplier selection and subsequent performance outcomes. Journal of Supply Chain Management 39, 4-12.

[89] **Shin, H., Collier, D.A., Wilson, D.D., 2000.** Supply management orientation and supplier/buyer performance. Journal of Operations Management 18, 317-333.

[90] **Simatupang, T.M., Ramaswami, S., 2005.** The collaboration index: a measure for supply chain collaboration. International Journal of Physical Distribution and Logistics Management 35, 44-62.

[91] **Simpson, D., Power, D., Samson, D., 2007.** Greening the automotive supply chain: a relationship perspective. International Journal of Operations and Production Management 27, 28-48.

[92] **Squire, B., Cousins, P.D., Lawson, B., Brown, S., 2009.** The effect of supplier manufacturing capabilities on buyer responsiveness: The role of collaboration. International Journal of Operations and Production Management 29, 766-788.

[93] **Stank, T.P., Keller, S.B., Daugherty, P.J., 2001.** Supply chain collaboration and logistical service performance. Journal of Business Logistics 22, 29-48.

[94] **Stanley, L.L, Wisner, J.D., 2001.** Service quality along the supply chain: Implications for purchasing. Journal of Operations Management 19, 287-306.

[95] **Stevenson, M., Spring, M., 2009.** Supply chain flexibility: an inter-firm empirical study. International Journal of Operations and Production Management 29, 946-971.

[96] **Sum, C.-C., Teo, C.-B., Ng, K.-K., 2001.** Strategic logistics management in Singapore. International Journal of Operations and Production Management 21, 1239-1260.

[97] **Swink, M., Narasimhan, R., Wang, C., 2007.** Managing beyond the factory walls: Effects of four types of strategic integration on manufacturing plant performance. Journal of Operations Management 25, 148-164.

[98] **Tracey, M., 2004.** Transportation Effectiveness and Manufacturing Firm Performance. International Journal of Logistics Management 15, 31-50.

[99] **Vaidyanathan, G., Devaraj, S., 2008.** The role of quality in e-procurement performance: An empirical analysis. Journal of Operations Management 26, 407-425.

[100] **Vanpoucke Evelyne, Boyer Kenneth K., Vereecke Ann, 2009.** Supply chain information flow strategies: an empirical taxonomy. International Journal of Operations and Production Management 29, 1213-1241

[101] **Vereecke, A., Muylle, S., 2006.** Performance improvement through supply chain collaboration in Europe. International Journal of Operations and Production Management 26, 1176-1198.

[102] **Vickery, S.K., Jayaram, J., Droge, C., Calantone, R., 2003**. The effects of an integrative supply chain strategy on customer service and financial performance: an analysis of direct versus indirect relationships. Journal of Operations Management 21, 523-539.

[103] **Wagner, S.M., Bode, C., 2008.** An empirical examination of supply chain performance along several dimensions of risk. Journal of Business Logistics 29, 307-326.

[104] **Whipple, J.M., Frankel, R., 2000.** Strategic alliance success factors. Journal of Supply Chain Management 36, 21-28.

[105] **Whipple, J.M., Voss, M.D., Closs, D.J., 2009.** Supply chain security practices in the food industry. International Journal of Physical Distribution and Logistics Management 39, 574-594.

[106] **Wisner, J.D., 2003.** A structural equation model of supply chain management strategies and firm-performance. Journal of Business Logistics 24, 1-26.

[107] **Wu, F., Yeniyurt, S., Kim, D., Cavusgil, S.T., 2006.** The impact of information technology on supply chain capabilities and firm-performance: A resource-based view. Industrial Marketing Management 35, 493-504.

[108] **Wu, Y.C., 2003.** Lean manufacturing: a perspective of lean suppliers. International Journal of Operations and Production Management 23, 1349-1376.

[109] **Zacharia, Z.G., Nix, N.W., Lusch, R.F., 2009.** An analysis of supply chain collaboration and their effect on performance outcomes. Journal of Business Logistics 30, 101-124.

Appendix

Table 25: Items for interface-performance

Performance dimension	Item	Description (Supplier's perspective)	Description (Buyer's perspective)	Scale
Delivery flexibility	$FLEX_1$	How long does your company averagely take (in days) to handle and complete normal orders concerning this commodity group (time from incoming order to delivery at the incoming goods department)?	How long do your suppliers take on average (in days) to handle and complete normal orders concerning this commodity group (time from incoming order to delivery at the incoming goods department)?	Continuous (days)
	$FLEX_2$	Regarding the cases where deliveries were so deficient that compensation delivery had to be effected (e.g. transport damage): How long did the compensation delivery usually take (in days)?	Regarding the cases where deliveries were so deficient that compensation delivery had to be effected (e.g. transport damage): How long did the compensation delivery usually take (in days)?	
	$FLEX_3$	Regarding the cases exceeding of the delivery date: How long was the delay usually (in days)?	Regarding the cases exceeding the delivery date: How long was the delay usually (in days)?	
Delivery reliability	REL_1	On Time Delivery: Which percentage of delivered goods was delivered on time by your company?	On Time Delivery: Which percentage of delivered goods was delivered on time by your suppliers?	Continuous (percentage)
	REL_2	Perfect Order Fulfillment: Which percentage of delivered goods were delivered without any faults by your company (correct amount at the right time in the right quality and at the right place)?	Perfect Order Fulfillment: Which percentage of delivered goods were delivered without any faults by your suppliers (correct amount at the right time in the right quality and at the right place)?	
Inventory efficiency	INV_{S1} / INV_{B1}	Average Storage Time: How long is the average dwelling time of this commodity group in the finished goods store before it is shipped to your buyers (in days)?	Average Storage Time: How long is the average dwelling time of this commodity group in the incoming goods warehouse before processing in production (in days)?"	Continuous (days)
	INV_{S1} / INV_{B1}	Average Inventory Level: How high was your average inventory level (total value of goods in your finished goods store) of this commodity group?	Average Inventory Level: How high was your average inventory level (total value of goods in your incoming goods warehouse) of this commodity group?	Continuous (values)

Table 26: Items for attributes of BSRs

Item	Description (Supplier's perspective)	Description (Buyer's perspective)	Scale
Sales concept (supplier)	On what contractual basis (order type) do you work together with your customers? *Make/Manufacture tostock* *Make/Manufacture to forecast* *Make/Manufacture to customer order* *Engineer to order*	On what contractual basis (order type) do you work together with your suppliers? *Make/Manufacture tostock* *Make/Manufacture to forecast* *Make/Manufacture to customer order* *Engineer to order*	Categorical
Distribution concept (supplier)	Distribution in your company: Which logistics concepts does your company use for the distribution of this commodity group? *Direct delivery* *Cross-Docking* *Single-level storage concept* *Multi-level storage concept (e.g. central storage with regional storages)*	Supplier Distribution: Which logistics concepts do your suppliers use during distribution of this commodity group? *Direct delivery* *Cross-Docking* *Single-level storage concept* *Multi-level storage concept (e.g. central storage with regional storages)*	Categorical
Procurement concept (buyer)	Procurement at your buyers: Which delivery and storage concepts characterize your buyers' procurement logistics for this commodity group? *Goods are delivered to the buyer's warehouse and stored* *Vendor Managed Inventory* *Just in Time / Just in Sequence*	Procurement within your company: Which delivery and storage concepts characterize the procurement logistics of your company for this commodity group? *Goods are delivered to your warehouse and stored* *Vendor Managed Inventory* *Just in Time / Just in Sequence*	Categorical

Table 27: Items for environmental market- and production-specific contingencies

Item	Description (Supplier's perspective)	Description (Buyer's perspective)	Scale
Stability of demand (MAR_1)	How intense is the competition between your company and other suppliers in this class of goods?	How intense is the competition between suppliers in this class of goods?	Likert scale *1=very low* *7=very high*
Geographic magnitude (MAR_2)	On which markets do you distribute this commodity group? *Regional* *National* *International (neighboring countries)* *International (continent)* *Global (worldwide)*	On which markets do you procure this commodity group? *Regional* *National* *International (neighboring countries)* *International (continent)* *Global (worldwide)*	Index*
Competitiveness between suppliers (MAR_3)	How intense is the competition between your company and other suppliers in this class of goods?	How intense is the competition between suppliers in this class of goods?	Likert scale *1=very low* *7=very high*

*Index reflecting the geographical magnitude, ranging from 1=regional' to 5='global', treated as quasi-metric scale

Table 19 (part 2): Items for environmental market- and production-specific contingencies

Item	Description (Supplier's perspective)	Description (Buyer's perspective)	Scale
Standardization of supplier's production processe ($PROD_1$)	*Production at your company: How are the goods you sell manufactured (production type)?*	*Supplier production: How does the supplier manufacture the goods you purchase (production type)?*	Index*
	Single item production	Single item production	
	Serial production / Continuous batch production	Serial production / Continuous batch production	
	Process production	Process production	
	Mass production	Mass production	
	No production (e.g. if your customer is a wholesaler)	No production (e.g. if your customer is a wholesaler)	
Standardization of buyer's production processes ($PROD_2$)	*Further processing at your buyers: How are the purchased goods further processed during your suppliers' production process (production type)?*	*Further processing in your company: How are the purchased goods further processed during production within your company (production type)?*	Index*
	Single item production	Single item production	
	Serial production / Continuous batch production	Serial production / Continuous batch production	
	Process production	Process production	
	Mass production	Mass production	
	No production (e.g. if your customer is a wholesaler)	No production (e.g. if your customer is a wholesaler)	

* Index reflecting the degree of standardization, ranging from 1='single item production' (very low degree of standardization) to 5='no production' (very high degree of standardization), treated as quasi-metric scale

Table 28: Items for control capabilities, dyadic performance control and interface-performance

Construct	Item	Description (Supplier's perspective)	Description (Buyer's perspective)	Scale
Supply planning integration		*Please indicate if the following statements about demand planning apply to your buyers.*	*Please indicate if the following statements about demand planning apply to your company*	*Likert scale* 1=does not apply 7=fully applies
	INT_1	Middle and long term demand planning is intensively coordinated with your company (e.g. in form of rolling demand planning or regular meetings).	Middle and long term demand planning is intensively coordinated with suppliers (e.g. in form of rolling demand planning or regular meetings).	
	INT_2	In case of unpredictable demand fluctuations, your company is informed as soon as possible (e.g. through terminated orders, large new orders or singular marketing campaigns).	In case of unpredictable demand fluctuations your suppliers are informed as soon as possible (e.g. through terminated orders, large new orders or singular marketing campaigns).	
IT-system support		*Please indicate the extent of IT-system support for the following activities, i.e. to what degree modern technology for the standardization and automation of the respective processes (including interconnectivity with buyers) is implemented.*	*Please indicate the extent of IT-system support for the following activities, i.e. to what degree modern technology for the standardization and automation of the respective processes (including interconnectivity with suppliers) is implemented.*	*Likert scale* 1=Manual processing 7=Very high degree of standardization and automatization
	IT_1	Supplier assessment, -monitoring und -change	Assessment, monitoring and switching of suppliers	
	IT_2	Requests from buyers (e.g price requests)	Requests for suppliers (e.g price requests)	
	IT_3	Orders from buyers (e.g. concrete orders of material)	Orders for suppliers (e.g. concrete orders of material)	
Dyadic performance control		*Please indicate to what extent the following statements regarding inter-company management of procurement and purchasing activites apply to your company.*	*Please indicate to what extent the following statements regarding inter-company management of procurement and purchasing activities apply to your company.*	*Likert scale* 1=does not apply 7=fully applies
	$CONT_1$	Coefficients are evaluated and analyzed regularly.	Coefficients are evaluated and analyzed regularly.	
	$CONT_2$	The evaluation's results are intensively used to eliminate deficiencies and improve processes.	The evaluation's results are intensively used to eliminate deficiencies and improve processes.	
	$CONT_3$	The results are standardly discussed with buyers	The results are standardly discussed with suppliers.	
	$CONT_4$	Clear standards exist for each figure that indicate from which degree of deviation from the nominal value corrective measures have to be initiated.	Clear standards exist for each figure that indicate from which degree of deviation from the nominal value corrective measures have to be initiated.	

Table 28 (part 2): Items for control capabilities, dyadic performance control and interface-performance

Construct	Item	Description (Supplier's perspective)	Description (Buyer's perspective)	Scale
Available in-house information		Which of the following in-house information of your company can your buyers access? Which of the following information from your buyers can your company access?	Which of the following information of your supplier can your company access? Which of the following in-house information of your company can your suppliers access?	Index*
	$INFO_1$	*The buyers can access information about...* *...the current status of their orders.* *...your company's current delivery capability (e.g. current inventory level and expected capacity utilization).* *...your company's business situation (e.g. overall order situation and financial figures).* *...your company's current and future product developments (product portfolio planning).* *...your company's strategic planning activities.*	*Your company can access information about...* *...the current status of your orders.* *...the supplier's current delivery capability (e.g. current inventory level and expected capacity utilization).* *...the supplier's business situation (e.g. overall order situation and financial figures)* *...the supplier's current and future product developments (product portfolio planning).* *...the supplier's strategic planning activities.*	
	$INFO_2$	*My company can access information about...* *...your buyer's expected short-term demand for this commodity group (e.g. your current inventory level and your production plan etc.).* *...your buyer's expected long-term demand for this commodity group (e.g. a planned increase in production capacity due to a large order)..* *...your buyer's business situation (e.g. overall order situation and financial figures).* *...your buyer's current and future product developments (product portfolio planning).* *...your buyer's strategic planning activities.*	*My suppliers can access information about...* *...your company's expected short-term demand for this commodity group (e.g. your current inventory level and your production plan etc.).* *...your company's expected long-term demand for this commodity group (e.g. a planned increase in production capacity due to a large order).* *...your company's business situation (e.g. overall order situation and financial figures).* *...your company's current and future product developments (product portfolio planning).* *...your company's strategic planning activities.*	

Index reflecting the amount of shared information, ranging from 1='no information' to 5= Very high access to partners in-house information, treated as quasi- treated as quasi-metric scale

Table 28 (part 3): Items for control capabilities, dyadic performance control and interface-performance

Construct	Item	Description (Supplier's perspective)	Description (Buyer's perspective)	Scale
Delivery flexibility	$FLEX_1$	How long does your company averagely take (in days) to handle and complete normal orders concerning this commodity group (time from incoming order to delivery at the incoming goods department)?	How long do your suppliers take on average (in days) to handle and complete normal orders concerning this commodity group (time from incoming order to delivery at the incoming goods department)?	Continuous (days)*
	$FLEX_2$	Regarding the cases where deliveries were so deficient that compensation delivery had to be effected (e.g. transport damage): How long did the compensation delivery usually take (in days)?	Regarding the cases where deliveries were so deficient that compensation delivery had to be effected (e.g. transport damage): How long did the compensation delivery usually take (in days)?	
	$FLEX_3$	Regarding the cases exceeding of the delivery date: How long was the delay usually (in days)?	Regarding the cases exceeding the delivery date: How long was the delay usually (in days)?	
Delivery reliability	REL_1	On Time Delivery: Which percentage of delivered goods was delivered on time by your company?	On Time Delivery: Which percentage of delivered goods was delivered on time by your suppliers?	Continuous (percentage)*
	REL_2	Perfect Order Fulfillment: Which percentage of delivered goods were delivered without any faults by your company (correct amount at the right time in the right quality and at the right place)?	Perfect Order Fulfillment: Which percentage of delivered goods were delivered without any faults by your suppliers (correct amount at the right time in the right quality and at the right place)?	

*Transformed to 5-point Liker scale ranging from 1='Comparably very poor performance' to 5='Comparably high performance'

Table 29: Items for attributes of the BSRs

Item	Description (Supplier's perspective)	Description (Buyer's perspective)	Scale
Production concept (supplier)	*Production at your company: How are the goods you sell manufactured (production type)?*	*Supplier production: How does the supplier manufacture the goods you purchase (production type)?*	Categorical
	Single item production	Single item production	
	Serial production	Serial production	
	Continuous batch production	Continuous batch production	
	Process production	Process production	
	Mass production	Mass production	
	No production (e.g. if you are a wholesaler)	No production (e.g. if your supplier is a wholesaler)	
Sales concept (supplier)	*On what contractual basis (order type) do you work together with your customers?*	*On what contractual basis (order type) do you work together with your suppliers?*	Categorical
	Make/Manufacture to stock	Make/Manufacture to stock	
	Make/Manufacture to forecast	Make/Manufacture to forecast	
	Make/Manufacture to customer order	Make/Manufacture to customer order	
	Engineer to order	Engineer to order	
Procurement concept (buyer)	*Procurement at your buyers: Which delivery and storage concepts characterize your buyers' procurement logistics for this commodity group?*	*Procurement within your company: Which delivery and storage concepts characterize the procurement logistics of your company for this commodity group?*	Categorical
	Goods are delivered to the buyer's warehouse and stored	Goods are delivered to your warehouse and stored	
	Vendor Managed Inventory	Vendor Managed Inventory	
	Just in Time/Just in Sequence	Just in Time/Just in Sequence	
Production concept (buyer)	*Further processing at your buyers: How are the purchased goods further processed during your suppliers' production process (production type)?*	*Further processing in your company: How are the purchased goods further processed during production within your company (production type)?*	Categorical
	Single item production	Single item production	
	Serial production / Continuous batch production	Serial production / Continuous batch production	
	Process production	Process production	
	Mass production	Mass production	
	No production (e.g. if your customer is a wholesaler)	No production (e.g. if your company is a wholesaler)	

Table 30: Recoding of z-scores to 5-point Likert scales – Overview

z-score	Assigned Likert-scale value	Description	Expected share of cases*	Number of actually occurred cases				
				$FLEX_1$	$FLEX_2$	$FLEX_3$	REL_1	REL_2
z < -1.5	1	'Comparably very poor performance'	6.6%	17	16	17	16	15
-1.5 <= z < -0.5	2	'Comparably poor performance'	24.2%	28	16	24	27	26
-0.5 <= z <= +0.5	3	'Comparably average performance'	38.4%	75	100	91	94	84
+0.5 < z <= +1.5	4	'Comparably good performance'	24.2%	81	69	69	61	76
> +1.5	5	'Comparably very good performance'	6.6%	0	0	0	3	0

* Percentage of cases that occur in this corridor of z-values in case of a standard normal deviation

Table 31: Rotated component matrix

Item	Component					
	1	**2**	**3**	**4**	**5**	**6**
$Cont_2$	.896					
$Cont_1$	.848					
$Cont_4$	.814					
$Cont_3$	.801					
$Flex_3$		.834				
$Flex_1$		.789				
$Flex_2$		.735				
$Info_1$			.893			
$Info_2$			.852			
REL_1				.850		
REL_2				.823		
IT_3					.796	
IT_1					.739	
IT_2					.561	
Int_2						.892
Int_1						.824

*Extraction Method: Principal Component Analysis. Rotation Method: Varimax with Kaiser Normalization. Rotation converged in 6 iterations.